Come and Read

Interpreting Johannine Literature

Series Editors: Sherri Brown, Creighton University and
Lindsey S. Jodrey, Princeton Theological Seminary

Series Advisory Board
Jaime Clark-Soles, Perkins School of Theology, Southern Methodist University
Alicia D. Myers, Campbell University Divinity School

The Interpreting Johannine Literature series is born from the desire of a group of Johannine scholars to bring rigorous study and explicit methodology into the teaching of these New Testament texts and their contexts. This series explores critical and perspectival approaches to the Gospel and Epistles of John. Historical- and literary-critical concerns are often augmented by current interpretive questions. Therefore, both a variety of approaches and critical self-awareness characterize titles in the series. Hermeneutical diversity and precision will continue to shed new light on the multifaceted content and discourse of the Johannine Literature.

Titles in the series
Come and Read: Interpretive Approaches to the Gospel of John
Alicia D. Myers and Lindsey S. Jodrey, eds.

Forthcoming
What John Knew and What John Wrote: A Study in John and the Synoptics
Wendy E. S. North
The Benefits of Discipleship in the Gospel of John
Mark B. Zhakevich
Apostles to the Apostles: The Role of Women in the Gospel of John
Sherri Brown

Come and Read

Interpretive Approaches to the Gospel of John

Edited by
Alicia D. Myers and Lindsey S. Jodrey

FORTRESS ACADEMIC
Lanham • Boulder • New York • London

Published by Fortress Academic
An imprint of The Rowman & Littlefield Publishing Group, Inc.
4501 Forbes Boulevard, Suite 200, Lanham, Maryland 20706
www.rowman.com

6 Tinworth Street, London SE11 5AL, United Kingdom

Copyright © 2020 The Rowman & Littlefield Publishing Group, Inc.

All rights reserved. No part of this book may be reproduced in any form or by any electronic or mechanical means, including information storage and retrieval systems, without written permission from the publisher, except by a reviewer who may quote passages in a review.

British Library Cataloguing in Publication Information Available

Library of Congress Cataloging-in-Publication Data Available

ISBN 978-1-9787-0747-4 (cloth)
ISBN 978-1-9787-0748-1 (electronic)

*To our colleagues, students, friends, and family who have beckoned us and joined together in the call to "come and read":
The sight of their eyes has brought light to our own.*

Contents

Acknowledgments   ix

Abbreviations   xi

Come and Read: Hermeneutics and Interpretive Perspectives
in the Gospel of John   1
Alicia D. Myers and Lindsey S. Jodrey

PART 1: JOHN 1:1–18: NARRATIVE, SOCIOCULTURAL, INTERTEXTUAL, AND RHETORICAL READINGS   27

1. Beginnings: Introducing the Narrative of the Word through the Prologue of John's Gospel   29
   Sherri Brown

2. John 1 Beyond the Binary   43
   Lindsey S. Jodrey

3. Revealing the Fuller Word   53
   Craig S. Keener

4. Ambiguity as a Rhetorical Strategy in the Prologue to John's Gospel   65
   Jo-Ann A. Brant

PART 2: JOHN 10: NARRATIVE, SOCIOCULTURAL, INTERTEXTUAL, AND RHETORICAL READINGS   79

5. The Parable of the Sheepfold: A Narrative Reading of John 10   81
   Dorothy A. Lee

6	Jesus the Good Shepherd: John 10 as Political Rhetoric *Warren Carter*	97
7	Persuasion through Allusion: Evocations of "Shepherd(s)" and Their Rhetorical Impact in John 10 *Catrin H. Williams*	111
8	Discerning Characters: *Parrēsia*, *Paroimia*, and Jesus's Rhetoric in John 10:1–21 *Alicia D. Myers*	125

PART 3: JOHN 20: NARRATIVE, SOCIOCULTURAL, INTERTEXTUAL, AND RHETORICAL READINGS — 139

9	Narrative-Critical Interpretation of John 20 *Craig R. Koester*	141
10	Reading Mary Magdalene with Stacey Abrams: Developing an Inclusive National Consciousness *Angela N. Parker*	155
11	Recognition and "Those Who Have Not Seen": John's Reception of Synoptic Resurrection Narratives *Helen K. Bond*	171
12	Rhetorical Vividness in John 20: Making Jesus Present before the Eyes *Kasper Bro Larsen*	185

Suggested Readings	201
Bibliography	203
Index	225
About the Contributors	229

Acknowledgments

This project sprang from a Johannine Literature Section program session at the 2017 Society of Biblical Literature Annual Meeting in Boston, where four invited panelists reflected together on various persuasive, or rhetorical, elements in John 10. These presenters include two who have revised and expanded their work in chapters for this volume: Warren Carter and Catrin H. Williams. The other two were George Parsenios and Christopher W. Skinner. The session prompted wonderful discussion due to the focused nature of the conversation on John 10 alone and the diverse ways in which this passage was interpreted and heard not only by our presenters, but by the audience of scholars listening and commenting on their works. The success of this session ultimately led us to collaborate to create this volume: a collection of essays with focused sections that display the diverse, complementary, contrasting, but nevertheless mutually beneficial ways that different interpretive strategies enrich the study of John's Gospel.

As with the creation of any volume, there are a number of people to thank, not least of these being all our contributors who entrusted us with their work. I (Alicia) especially thank Lindsey for sharing in the vision and creation of not only this collection, but the panel that inspired it. Even though Lindsey is now at Princeton, I'm thankful that we can remain close in our study of the Gospel of John and as friends in life. I also thank the members of the Johannine Literature Section steering committee for their encouragement of this collection as well as all those who participated in the 2017 session, whether as presenters or as conversation partners in the room. Thanks to my colleagues at Campbell University in the Divinity School and the Christian Studies Department for their support of this work, and to Marie Berry at Campbell University Library, who was instrumental for the production of this book with her tireless acquisition of needed volumes through interlibrary loan.

Finally, thanks must go to my family and friends who helped me continue working on this project even though the messiness of a hectic move and the daily messiness of life with two young boys. Thank you Scott, Keaton, and Gavin for your patience and your joy that reminds me to take a break and laugh.

I (Lindsey) would like to thank Alicia, with whom I gladly shared a year of graduate study at Baylor University and a year as colleagues on the same hallway at Campbell University. I still remember the office conversation about an SBL panel where we would feature different approaches to the same Johannine text. This book grew out of Alicia's work facilitating that panel, and its publication was completed due to her willingness to carry the lion's share of the editorial work. I would also like to offer a special thanks to Heidi Biermann, a friend and gifted biblical scholar in her own right, for her generosity in giving her time to editing and her thoughtfulness in commenting on drafts of this manuscript. My gratitude also goes out to the members of the Johannine Literature Section of SBL, whose lively conversations continue to inspire new questions and generate innovative approaches. I am also grateful to my new colleagues at Princeton Theological Seminary, whose invitation to teach Queer Hermeneutics has fueled this new research interest. Finally, I offer sincere gratitude to my partner, Deborah, who—by the time this goes to print—will be my spouse. Thank you, Deborah, for consistently challenging the questions I ask and encouraging me to bring my whole self to my studies and to every facet of my life.

Alicia D. Myers and Lindsey S. Jodrey

Abbreviations

Abbreviations listed below include ancient Greek and Latin texts along with writings from the Deuterocanonical Books (Apocrypha), Pseudepigrapha, Dead Sea Scrolls, Rabbinic writings, and other early Christian literature. Abbreviations for secondary materials include only those not in *The Society of Biblical Literature Handbook of Style*, 2d. ed. (Atlanta: SBL Press, 2014).

PRIMARY SOURCES

Adul. amic.	Plutarch, *How to Tell a Flatterer from a Friend*
Aen.	Virgil, *Aeneid*
Ag.	Aeschylus, *Agamemnon*
Ag. Ap.	Josephus, *Against Apion*
Agr.	Tacitus, *Agricola*
Alex.	Plutarch, *Life of Alexander*
Alleg. Interp.	Philo, *Allegorical Interpretation*
Ant.	Josephus, *Antiquities*
Art.	Plutarch, *Artaxerxes*
b. Ber.	Babylonian Talmud Berakhot
Bar.	Baruch
CD	Covenant of Damascus
Congr.	Philo, *On the Preliminary Studies*
Creation	Philo, *On the Creation of the World*
Cyr.	Xenophon, *The Education of Cyrus*
Demon.	Lucian, *Demonax*
De or.	Cicero, *On Oratory*
Dial.	Justin, *Dialogue with Trypho*

Diatr.	Epictetus, *Diatribes*
Disc.	*Discourses*
Dom.	Suetonius, *Life of Domitian*
1–3 En.	*1–3 Enoch*
Ep.	Seneca, *Epistles*
Eth. nic.	Aristotle, *Nicomachean Ethics*
Frag.	Fragment
Gen. Rab.	Genesis Rabbah
Glor. Ath.	Plutarch, *De gloria Atheniensium*
Hist.	*Histories*
Il.	Homer, *Iliad*
Inst.	Quintilian, *Institutes of Oratory*
Is. Or.	Plutarch, *On Isis and Osiris*
Joseph	Philo, *On the Life of Joseph*
Jub.	Book of Jubilees
J.W.	Josephus, *Jewish Wars*
LAB	Pseudo-Philo, *Biblical Antiquities*
Legat.	Philo, *On the Embassy to Gaius*
LXX	Septuagint (Greek translation of the OT)
Lys.	*Lysias*
1–4 Macc.	1–4 Maccabees
m. Avot	Mishnah Avot
m. Sanh.	Mishnah Sanhedrin
Meg.	Megillah
Mek.	Mekilta
Mem.	Xenophon, *Memorabilia*
Midr. Ps.	Midrash on the Psalms
Migr.	Philo, *On the Migration of Abraham*
Mor.	Plutarch, *Moralia*
Mos.	Philo, *On the Life of Moses*
Names	Philo, *On the Change of Names*
NT	New Testament
Od.	Homer, *Odyssey*
Off.	Cicero, *On Duties*
Op.	Hesiod, *Works and Days*
Or.	*Orations*
OT	Old Testament
Part. or.	Cicero, *Parts of Oratory*
Planc.	Cicero, *Pro Plancio*
Post.	Philo, *On the Posterity of Cain*
Prog.	*Progymnasmata*

Prot.	Plato, *Protagoras*
Pss. Sol.	Psalms of Solomon
Red. pop.	Cicero, *To the Citizens after His Return*
QG	Philo, *Questions and Answers on Genesis*
1QM	War Scroll
1QS	Rule of the Community
4Q402	Songs of the Sabbath Sacrifice
4Q415	Instruction
4Q422	Paraphrase of Genesis and Exodus
Rep.	Plato, *Republic*
Rhet.	Aristotle, *Rhetoric*
Rhet. Her.	*Rhetorica ad Herennium*
Sib. Or.	*Sibylline Oracles*
Sipre Deut.	Sipre Deuteronomy
Sipre Num.	Sipre Numbers
Sir.	Sirach/Ecclesiasticus
Spec. Laws	Philo, *On the Special Laws*
t. B. Qam.	Tosefta Bava Qamma
t. Sanh.	Tosefta Sanhedrin
Tg. Isa.	Targum Isaiah
Tib.	Suetonius, *Life of Tiberius*
Vesp.	Suetonius, *Life of Vespasian*
Wis.	Wisdom of Solomon

SECONDARY SOURCES

ABG	Arbeiten zur Bibel und ihrer Geschichte
CI	*Critical Inquiry*
CNNTE	Contexts and Norms of New Testament Ethics
CommQ	*Communication Quarterly*
EPS	European Perspectives Series
ETC ETC:	*A Review of General Semantics*
HeyM	Heythrop Monographs
JPSP	*Journal of Personality and Social Psychology*
POTTS	Pittsburgh Original Texts and Translations Series
SANt	Studia Aarhusiana Neotestamentica
SHR	Studies in the History of Religions
SRR	Studies in Rhetoric and Religion
THL	Theory and History of Literature
YCR	*Yale Classical Review*

Come and Read

Hermeneutics and Interpretive Perspectives in the Gospel of John

Alicia D. Myers and Lindsey S. Jodrey

It is perhaps an obvious truth that we all read things differently. After all, we also all experience the world differently, and we interpret those experiences differently, depending on our own contexts, likes, dislikes, and so on. Any glance at contemporary American society—with its persistent "like" and "unlike," "swipe right" or "swipe left" culture—demonstrates this fact. Yet, while we may willingly acknowledge such diversity on social media, the interpretation of news events (and coverage), or social issues, we may overlook the fact that this truth remains even when we are interpreting what, for many, is sacred text: the Bible, including the subject of our focus here, the Gospel of John.

When we approach "Scripture," many of us have an expectation—either expressed or not—of stability. We desire *one truth* that, whether by means of divine inspiration or deep exegetical inquiry, we can uncover and present to the acclaim and acceptance of all. A single class period in a biblical studies course, or among any group of people reading Scripture (regardless of canon or text), quickly reveals the elusiveness and even impossibility of such stability. Indeed, we discover, when a single interpretation claims dogmatic dominance, it is often ripe for deconstruction and adjustment.[1] Such a reality should not discourage us from scriptural interpretation, however, no matter how daunting it can now seem. Rather, the diversity of possibilities for reading should invite us to enter in more deeply, to explore alternative paths, and in so doing, to experience and learn from these writings things we would never have discovered on our own and left to our own "like" or "unlike" buttons.

This book, therefore, offers a glimpse of the diversity of possible ways to read the Gospel of John, demonstrating not only *how* these interpretive methods are employed, but also their interaction with and interdependence on one another, and the variety of payoffs that each renders. Although space constraints require we limit the number of interpretive (or hermeneutical) approaches showcased here to four (narrative, intertextual, sociocultural, and rhetorical), we have been intentionally broad in defining them, and we have taken care that no one method dominates the others. Rather than ranking these methods, therefore, we place them side by side, in deliberate conversation, so that you, our readers, can learn how to interact with, employ, and benefit from all of them—and so that you will be open to even more ways to "come and read" John's eternally perplexing and provocative story.

SETTING THE STAGE: COMING TO READ

One of our favorite activities to do with students in the classroom is to read biblical texts closely (and slowly) together. Breaking up the classroom first individually and then into small groups, we regularly have students conduct what Michael J. Gorman calls a "survey" of the biblical text: metaphorically mapping its topography by working verse by verse through a passage, making observations, asking questions, and putting forth inferences.[2] After students have explored the passage alone and then in a small group, we record results together on the white board. What inevitably results is a great diversity of interpretations. In small groups, students bubble over with new observations and questions they have never before asked, or they are surprised at another's different reading, "Could John possibly mean *that*?" they wonder together. *How*, exactly, can we ever answer the one question we all so eagerly desire: "What does this story mean?"

Rather than asking what the story means and expecting just one answer, we push our students (and ourselves) to realize that a single story can have multiple possible, and equally legitimate, meaning*s*. Even if we come to privilege *one* reading above the others, we should at least know that there are other ways of reading and respect the benefits diversity offers. Indeed, a flat text serves few well. For Scripture to continue its relevance, it needs to have some flexibility; the meanings we privilege one day need not be the same we privilege the next, much less ten years from now.

Looking briefly at one particularly challenging passage from the Gospel of John illustrates this point: John 7:37–39. This is a challenging passage because it is ambiguous. It naturally opens itself up to a variety of interpretations. After teaching in Jerusalem in 7:14–30, Jesus has stirred up the crowd gathered for the celebration of the Feast of Tabernacles or *Sukkot* (see Exod. 23:14–19; Deut. 16:13–17; Lev. 23:33–43; Num. 29:12–40), causing enough of a disturbance to warrant a reaction from the religious leaders. In John 7:31–36, we learn of a number of reactions to Jesus: many from the crowd believed while the Pharisees and high priests, alarmed at the crowd's "grumbling," sent temple police to arrest Jesus. Jesus then warns everyone—and confuses them further—by predicting his coming departure, concluding, "You will seek me but you will not find me" (vv. 34, 36). It is to this confused gathering—a crowd, Pharisees, high priests, and temple police—that Jesus offers another confounding teaching in 7:37–39:

> On the last day of the festival, the great day, while Jesus was standing there, he cried out saying, "Let anyone who thirsts come to me and drink. The one who believes in me, just as it has been written, 'Rivers of living water will flow out of his belly.'" Now he said this concerning the spirit which the ones who believe in him were about to receive, for as of yet, there was no spirit, because Jesus was not yet glorified.[3]

A number of things make these verses challenging, particularly when we read the Greek, and not just English translations that are forced to offer clearer interpretations. First, what Scripture is Jesus quoting here? No passage from the Hebrew Bible (OT) matches the quotation as it is given here. Second, out of whose belly will the "rivers of living water flow"—the believer's (as translated in the NRSV, NAS, T/NIV, and NKJV) or Jesus's (as left ambiguous in the NLT, NET, and CEB)? Of course, we have heard of Jesus offering "living water" in John 4, could he possibly here suggest believers will be able to offer such a "drink" in the future as well? And how can it come from someone's "belly"? Or, should it really be translated "womb" (*koilia*)?! And third, what is the role of the "spirit" in all of this? John repeatedly associates spirit and water, sometimes in complementary ways (as here, perhaps, and John 4), but also as a contrast (as in John the Baptist's description of his baptism versus Jesus's in 1:29–34, or in Jesus's conversation of new-birth/birth-from-above with Nicodemus in John 3). How we resolve these questions depends, in large part, upon what hermeneutical tools we use—even if we do not have language to define what those tools are called just yet.

Working on our own or in groups, our observations might center on "intertextual" elements: the context of the festival and the reference to Scripture. We could interpret more in light of "intratextual," or narrative elements—the ways that this passage recalls John 4, the hindsight perspective in the narrator's comment, the significant theme of the Spirit in John's Gospel, or the place of this episode in the overall plot. We might consider the relationship of this episode to the miraculous feeding in the chapter before or Jesus's claim to be the light of the world in the next chapter. We may look more toward sociocultural elements: How does the lack of access to clean water and the sociopolitical realities of Jewish Palestine in the first century impact this passage? What were the realities of the temple location—religious, political, geographical, and otherwise—for this claim in navigating power dynamics, and how does the Johannine Jesus stand in relation to those power structures? We may have more rhetorical questions about the persuasive techniques and effects of this passage. What impact could this story have had on its early readers or what power did it have to speak to their specific situations? What persuasive power does it have today? As each of us focused on certain observations and took up certain questions, we would emerge with a beautifully diverse array of answers.

What does this story mean, then?

- *A Narrative Answer*: As one episode within a complex story, this passage develops the theme of "living water" to contribute to a narrative that powerfully presents Jesus, God incarnate, offering life to those who radically accept him.
- *A Sociocultural Answer:* Inhabiting a space associated with power and yet during a festival that served as a reminder of human dependency on God, Jesus shouts out an image of abundance, a potent counter-message to those playing the "power-game" in the contentious context of first-century, Roman-ruled Palestine and to those who continue to navigate systems of power today.
- *An Intertextual Answer*: At a feast of Jewish remembrance, Jesus's words move the reader's mind back to the Hebrew Scriptures, weaving echoes of various texts together to root John's Christological claims in the story of Israel and the message of the prophets.
- *A Rhetorical Answer*: Addressing a Jesus-following community wrestling with their own identity and place of belonging, the Fourth Evangelist presents the significant resources available to his readers that surpassed even the resources available to those who followed Jesus in his earthly life—persuading them to accept his claims about Jesus and to take up Jesus's mission in their own context.

Rather than just choosing *one* of these answers, perhaps we can see that each of these responses contributes to a complex and meaningful reading of this passage. Each one "speaks" in different ways, to different and yet intimately related realities, and when we listen to these voices in concert we learn more than if we rely on one in isolation.

THE GOALS AND STRATEGY OF THIS BOOK

This book presents some examples of what happens when we read with certain questions in mind and particular methods in tow.[4] *Come and Read* has two goals: (1) to introduce hermeneutical approaches to biblical literature and (2) to demonstrate these approaches in action by featuring essays from top scholars in the field. This book outlines four broad hermeneutical approaches to the Bible and applies each of them to three passages from John's Gospel. We have chosen the Gospel of John in part because it is a favorite Gospel for the two of us who are editing this book—and for good reason! John's Gospel provides many well-loved stories that recount Jesus's life and some of the most beloved pieces of biblical literature. The familiarity of John's Gospel story provides a good starting point as we venture into the complexity of biblical interpretation.

While providing a familiar foundation, the Fourth Gospel also includes diverse literary forms, so exploring within John's Gospel offers both variety in literary form and continuity in source material. Our three focus passages—John 1:1–18, John 10, and John 20—represent three major subgenres featured in the Gospel. As these three texts move us through the Gospel story, they also expose us to poetic literature (or at least elevated prose) in John 1:1–18, discourse in John 10, and narrative prose in John 20. Although there is value to seeing different methods of biblical interpretation applied to a variety of biblical texts, we have chosen to maintain consistency in the source material so that the reader can more easily focus on the diversity in the hermeneutical approaches that frame interpretation.[5]

Each section of the book will include readings of the focus passage from the four different hermeneutical approaches mentioned above: narrative readings, sociocultural readings, intertextual readings, and rhetorical readings. These four umbrella approaches are intentionally broadly conceived so that a variety of particular methods are surveyed in the collection. By laying out these categories, we are able to see how different methods work within each category and how these methods relate to one another. Setting the four hermeneutical approaches to each text side by side, this book illustrates the value of using a variety of approaches for interpreting the text, and demonstrates how the hermeneutical approach taken affects interpretation.

INTRODUCING OUR HERMENEUTICAL APPROACHES

Many introductions to biblical interpretation are organized according to where the interpreter might go looking for meaning. Noticing the three major foci of background, text, and reader, authors and editors often form categories for interpretive methods based on meaning pursued in (1) the world behind the text ("background"); (2) the world within the text ("text"); and (3) the world beyond the text ("reader").[6] For example, in *Searching for Meaning*, Paula Gooder draws upon these divisions, separating her categories as stops along a journey from event to reader. "From event to text" includes interpretive methods that focus on the development of tradition that led to the text and the relationship between the text and its historical context (e.g., social science or redaction criticism). The second grouping, "Text," includes methods that focus on the final form of the text itself rather than the situation or event behind it (e.g., narrative criticism). The third grouping, "From text to reader," examines interpretation from the perspective of the relationship between the text and the reader and acknowledges the reader's role in meaning-making (e.g., feminist or postcolonial criticism).

This third section does not so much feature specific *tools* for interpreting the text (like redaction criticism or narrative criticism in the first two groupings); rather, it features hermeneutical "standpoints," which use a variety of interpretive methods (including those from her other groupings) all the while self-consciously reading "in front of the text," often from a particular perspective.[7] The valuable contribution of "standpoint" criticisms is that they remind us to be self-conscious readers, since all interpretation is affected by the reader, and all readers come to the text from a particular perspective. So-called standpoint criticisms demonstrate the power of intentional perspective-taking for disrupting the perception that any reading is neutral or should be considered normative.

In the discussion of "hermeneutics" we pay focused attention to the contemporary reader, intentionally reflecting on what factors contribute to a reading (or a reader's interpretation). Sometimes "hermeneutics" refers to the broad philosophical reflection on the interpretive process, or various ways that readers engage the text—factors at work, for example, in the divisions of methods described above. But we can also speak of particular hermeneutical approaches, not as competing strategies, but rather *as ways to focus on particular sets of questions to see what interpretive conclusions result*. Recognizing that all of these "locations"—background, text, and reader—contribute valuable information for interpretation, we have invited each of our authors to explore their passage guided not by a singular method or focal point for meaning but by a broad hermeneutical approach that extends beyond the bounds of these traditional delineations. We are interested in what happens when these texts are read with certain questions in mind.

This collection, therefore, is not so much a book defining methods of interpretation as it is a book displaying broad hermeneutical approaches and exploring the types of readings that arise from them.[8] The hermeneutical approaches we have outlined for this book each provide an intentional focus area, or perspective, from which a scholar may engage interpretation of the text. By featuring scholars who each take up a common text from different hermeneutical vantage points, we will be able to see what difference the hermeneutical approach makes for interpretation. This is not to determine which approach is best or "the right" approach—quite the opposite. We hope, instead, that this collection will demonstrate the value of multiple hermeneutical approaches for interpretation of our multifaceted text. In defining our four hermeneutical approaches, our aim is to be heuristic, not conclusive. The lines for these categories could be drawn in many different ways—they overlap a good deal, and no categorization is definitive. These connections will become apparent as we describe each hermeneutical approach in more detail below.

Narrative Readings: Focusing on the Internal Features of John's Story

Narrative Readings in Theory

John may not begin his Gospel with "once upon a time," but it is nonetheless clear that when we turn the pages of the Fourth Gospel, we are reading a story. Following the poetic introduction, we are transported to a rocky, reed-filled spot beside the Jordan River, where we meet the first characters: John who is baptizing, the Jews and Pharisees sent from Jerusalem, the first disciples, and Jesus. When we recognize the Gospel as a story, we might say we are taking a narrative approach. Narrative readings focus on the internal features of a story and utilize tools from literary criticism to explore possible meanings that may emerge from these combinations of features.[9] Narrative readings of John focus on the Gospel as a unified story, analyzing its literary and narrative features such as the narrator, setting, characters, conflict, plot, implied author and audience, or point of view.[10] A narrative approach examines literary devices like foreshadowing, repetition, framing, or the use of metaphor, symbolism, or irony and attends to significant themes throughout the Gospel or to the role a certain episode plays in the overall storyline.[11]

Narrative readings not only seek to identify these features, they use literary criticism in order to discern meaning. Narrative approaches offer a strong connection to the internal world of the text, which shifts attention slightly away from the mind of the historical author (e.g., considering what meaning the author may have intended to communicate) and onto the communicative power of the literary features themselves as they appear and function within the story. They ask what internal literary and narrative features are present in the text and how those features might communicate meaning to the implied reader.

Narrative readings use the tools of narrative criticism, literary criticism, comparative literary methods, structuralism and semiotics, post-structural criticism, and more.[12] If the significant value of the narrative approach is its intentional focus on the internal features of the text itself, this value also has a downside of ascribing agency to a text, without due attention to the role of the actual readers (or authors) in creating meaning. Some more recent narrative approaches, however, *do* consider elements outside of the text. These narrative readings extend beyond the story level into the "discourse level," where literary analysis contributes to an investigation of "the dynamic process of communication between the author and audience."[13]

When they venture into discourse analysis, narrative approaches take on multiple interests that overlap with the other three approaches outlined in this book. For example, in analyzing how the story might *persuade* the audience to believe or act in a certain way, narrative readings overlap with rhetorical readings, which attend to the communicative exchange between the author and the audience that is created by the story. Narrative approaches that utilize post-structural criticism and consider *other texts or material culture* that inform the reading of the story overlap with the intertextual approach. Narrative approaches that emphasize the *role of the reader or audience*, especially when viewed through the lens of postmodern philosophy, venture into the sphere sociocultural analysis.[14] Where these approaches utilize other fields of study (like ancient and modern rhetorical theory, postcolonial theory, or Marxist theory) to evaluate the discourse, narrative approaches predominately draw on categories from literary theory.[15]

Narrative Readings in Action

This volume features three chapters that foreground narrative elements and questions, one chapter in each section. Sherri Brown offers a narrative approach to John's Prologue (John 1:1–18) demonstrating the crucial role of these first eighteen verses for the telling of the remainder of the narrative. Equipping readers and audiences with information other characters do not have, Brown argues that the rest of the Gospel "*shows* what the Prologue *tells*" about God's covenant faithfulness in the world, especially through the revelatory incarnation of Jesus "the Christ and Son of God." Dorothy A. Lee utilizes a narrative approach to reading John 10, focusing on how form contributes to, and indeed creates, the theological meaning of the passage. Lee outlines three steps in her reading, exploring the passage's context and employment of literary devices before moving on to outline theological meaning, and showing how the "polemical nature of the story" of John 10 "intensifies" the revelation it offers about Jesus as both gate and shepherd. Craig R. Koester's work on John 20 rounds out the narrative analyses in this collection. Koester highlights the consistent theme of sight and belief in John 20, arguing that this chapter "is a dramatic narrative that demonstrates how seeing does not guarantee believing." Beginning with helpful definitions of key components of his narrative analysis, Koester proceeds through the passage, showing how John 20 repeatedly sets sight and belief in relief before

Jesus's climactic blessing in verse 29: "Blessed are the ones who have not seen and yet have come to believe."

Sociocultural Readings: Exposing the Dynamics of Making Meaning from John's Story

Sociocultural Readings in Theory

In contrast to narrative readings, sociocultural readings intentionally focus on the role of *actual readers* (in contrast to "implied readers" [see Koester]) who engage with biblical texts. Whether or not we are aware of it, we each view the world through a set of lenses made up of our own unique background, identity, assumptions, traditions, and desires. It is through this set of lenses that we make sense of our experiences, understand our place in the world, and find meaning in the messages we encounter. This is, perhaps, especially the case when we read a text that we hold as sacred. Many of us implicitly assume that the way we see the world is neutral, objective, or straightforward—it's just the way things are. And, unfortunately, this myth has made its way into the history of NT interpretation as well, with some interpreters assuming that "mainstream" NT interpretations are neutral, that interpreters can and should approach the text objectively to uncover a stable meaning *in* the text. As the collective authors of *The Postmodern Bible* observe, "biblical scholars have been slow to awaken . . . to the realization that our representations of and discourse about what the text meant and how it means are inseparable from what we *want* it to mean, from how we *will* it to mean."[16]

Modern biblical interpreters have often made the mistake of supposing that traditional readings in the history of interpretation were neutral or objective when in reality, the majority of these readings were performed by a homogeneous group (white, heterosexual, cis[17] men, usually of high socioeconomic status and from the context of the industrialized West) whose shared perspective yielded a shared meaning. Interpretations by readers outside of this group who self-consciously read from their unique perspectives stood out among "mainstream" interpretations. Many of these readings have been grouped under the heading "Ideological Criticism," which considers how power dynamics affect meaning as readers encounter texts from the perspective of their own lived experiences and social locations.[18] So-called ideological approaches, also called "standpoint" criticisms, are often viewed as peripheral and secondary to "mainstream" or traditional interpretations.[19] They may be dismissed by those who maintain stable conceptions of meaning as well as by those who do not recognize the power dynamics that these readings observe. However, selecting only certain readings under the heading "ideological" is problematic, since "there is no innocent reading of the Bible, no reading that is not already ideological."[20]

So-called ideological or standpoint criticisms recognize the subjectivity of readers and elevate readings that offer a counterbalance to the perspectives that have guided traditional readings or readings that have been deemed normative.[21] "Standpoint" readings flow from postmodern approaches to interpretation and attend to the power dynamics at work among these categories, noticing that the readings deemed "normal" have most often been performed by those in positions of power.[22] Recognizing this, *The Postmodern Bible* issues a harsh critique:

> To read the Bible in the traditional scholarly manner has all too often meant reading it, whether deliberately or not, in ways that reify and ratify the status quo—providing warrant for the subjugation of women . . . justifying colonialism and enslavement, rationalizing homophobia, or otherwise legitimizing the power of the hegemonic classes of people.[23]

Thus, "standpoint" criticisms promote a *"transformed"* and *"transforming"* biblical criticism that pushes against notions of objective recovery of meaning and challenges interpretations that claim preeminence over others, insisting on self-conscious reading that recognizes "the contingent and constructed character of meaning" and considers the practical social implications of interpretation.[24] Such approaches emerged out of deconstructive strategies within critical literary studies in the context of poststructuralism, evolving to pay necessary attention not only to the internal workings of texts but to the relationships between that text and other social and cultural realities (i.e., gender, sexuality, race and ethnicity, and colonialism and postcolonialism).[25] In some cases, such readings may be performed by a reader who self-consciously identifies with a category outside of those listed above, often a person who has been minoritized in some way. In all cases, such readings resist notions of stable meaning and insist that all readers bring with them perspectives and agendas that shape their reading.

Because the term "standpoint" criticism participates in some of the assumptions of modernity, we prefer the term "sociocultural" to describe approaches that intentionally read with these issues in mind or from a particular location—often defined along lines of class, gender, ethnicity, or race—and usually paying special attention to the power dynamics and structures emerging from those categories. For example, feminist criticism embraces what Elisabeth Schüssler Fiorenza calls a "hermeneutic of suspicion" which, recognizing the lack of women's perspectives in the shaping of the Bible, its content, and its interpretation, promotes readings that call out oppressive, male-dominated messages and the systems they perpetuate.[26] Such readings often seek to counterbalance or critique other readings. As Kathy Ehrensperger explains, they do not perceive themselves as "additional method(s)" of interpretation; rather, these readings constitute a "paradigm shift which assumes that all interpretations are contextual, that is, shaped by their social location (gender, race, class, sexual orientation, age, etc.)."[27] Furthermore, a sociocultural approach foregrounds "both its potential and actual impact on the lives of [people] in the church and society," recognizing the necessity of hermeneutical self-awareness and the ethical obligation to check any reading that perpetuates oppressive systems or advances the perspective of an "in-power" group as normative.[28]

Readings within this approach are quite diverse, and they often critique one another. For example, womanist and *mujerista* readings offer a necessary critique to earlier white feminist approaches that assumed a shared female experience regardless of race and other social, cultural, or economic factors. Queer readings counterbalance readings that may attend to power dynamics determined by other categories while disregarding the oppressiveness assumed by heteronormativity or binary constructions of gender. More and more sociocultural approaches are paying attention to intersectionality, recognizing that the various categories with which we identify combine together in complex ways. Intersectionality recognizes that people often find themselves identifying with one category that brings them privilege (e.g., being cis, white, male) while also identifying with a category that is underprivileged, oppressed, or minoritized (e.g., female, nonbinary, and queer).

Other sociocultural readings may be more theoretically or philosophically driven, drawing on "the rich resources of contemporary thought on language, epistemology, method, rhetoric, power, [and] reading" by engaging interdisciplinary critical theory.[29] These readings suggest that critical theory can play a valuable role in exposing the "interestedness of both texts and their readings."[30] For example, much of the current work in queer criticism utilizes post-structuralist or postmodern philosophy (especially from Michel Foucault and Jacques Derrida) to analyze "the intersections of the production of meaning, power and the formation of modern Christianity," particularly in terms of how certain readings of the Bible promote heterosexuality and binary gender constructions as normative and contribute to a theological system that leads to oppression of those who do not fit the constructed norms.[31] Other readings that fit under the sociocultural approach include liberation criticism and sociopolitical criticism, which build on liberation theology, utilizing Marxist analysis and other socio-historical tools and methods to examine power and emphasize the perspective of the poor and oppressed.[32] These two modes of criticism are very similar; however, liberation criticism usually arises directly out of communities facing poverty and oppression, while sociopolitical criticism most often arises in industrialized countries in Europe or the United

States.[33] Similarly, postcolonial criticism attends to the broad power dynamics at work in and because of colonization, analyzing how those dynamics appear in the Bible and in the history of biblical interpretation. Those who read from the vantage point of postcolonial criticism observe how a certain text or author engages the empire as well as how the text or author constructs the "other." Postcolonial readings recognize the lack of attention to the powerless in these texts and maintain that the Bible should be a "contested" book.[34] What some might call the "limitations" of a sociocultural approach are at the same time what make it so valuable. Sociocultural approaches remind us to read responsibly, recognizing power dynamics at work in the text and its interpretation and considering the practical and ethical implications of our reading. At the same time, however, sociocultural readings that focus on deconstruction alone can leave readers without much meaning with which to move forward, regardless of their contexts.

As we have seen, readings falling within the sociocultural approach are diverse, as are the methods and disciplines they employ for biblical interpretation. Examples include postcolonial approaches such as imperial-critical readings as well as liberation and sociopolitical criticism, African American, womanist, *mujerista*, feminist, and queer readings, or readings informed by disability studies. These diverse readings share a concern "about systems of power—institutional, ecclesiastical, cultural—that authorize or block what can be said or written about the Bible" and for the real ethical consequences to certain readings.[35]

Sociocultural Readings in Action

The examples featured in this volume demonstrate the diversity in the methods employed by those who read along the lines of a sociocultural approach. In the first section of this book, I (Lindsey S. Jodrey) utilize queer theory as a critical method for discerning the rhetorical function of the famous dualistic language in John, particularly as it is set up in the Prologue. Rather than remaining in the subfield of Christian theology, where commentary from a queer perspective contributes to theological discussions or appears as theological reflection by, for, or about LGBTQIA[36] people, the chapter puts queer theory to work in the context of biblical interpretation and extends its reach beyond where the biblical text deals explicitly with gender and sexuality, exploring new possibilities for understanding the biblical text and proposing new answers to existing questions regarding the interpretation of these texts. Utilizing the categories of transgression and resistance to binaries from queer theory, I argue that rather than reinforcing or affirming dualistic categories (as is so often the case in other literature that includes dualistic motifs), these motifs actually work against a purely binary worldview. The "good news" according to John, therefore, is that boundaries between two binaries are not fixed; rather, the binary is subverted as the boundaries are broken by the queer forces of incarnation, revelation, love, and resurrection.

Warren Carter utilizes the tools of imperial criticism to cut against a history of scholarship that has spiritualized interpretation of Jesus's good shepherd discourse in John 10 and limited its relevance to the realm of religious rhetoric.[37] Considering the rhetorical features of its literary context, reexamining the commonly cited intertexts, and adding new intertexts that frame meaning, he argues that the discourse challenges the power dynamics and social structures of life in the Roman Empire. Rather than reading along an axis of "religious identity," Carter pushes us to "read along an axis of power and societal structures rather than an axis of religious identity."[38] Carter shows that the conflict surrounding John 10 is not so much about calling for proper articulation of Jesus's identity but about calling out an elite group for improper participation in an oppressive power system.

Focusing on John 20, Angela N. Parker uses a womanist hermeneutic to read the story of Mary Magdalene in conversation with Stacey Y. Abrams, a 2018 gubernatorial candidate in Georgia, who also delivered the official Democratic response to the State of the Union address in February 2019. Noting the traditional down-playing of Mary Magdalene's apostolic role and office, Parker sets her alongside Abrams, who likewise operates at a juncture of various systems, trying to deliver messages that are similarly down-played—even by those would appear to be "allies," such as Bernie Sanders who delivered his own response to Trump after Abrams's "official" speech. Using the work of Franz Fanon and Anne McClintock, Parker engages in a womanist postcolonial reading of John 20 to suggest that Mary Magdalene can act as a "symbol of national consciousness" with implications for how "the United States of America must reimagine African American women as symbols of inclusive consciousness through the work of Stacey Abrams."

Intertextual Readings: Conversing with the Allusive Features of John's Story

Intertextual Readings in Theory

Our third approach in this collection is intertextual. Although we may not use the term, all of us read intertextually. This means that we read things in light of our contexts (as outlined above), and these contexts contain a number of "texts"—be they actual, literary texts (e.g., novels, the Bible, and histories), or more informal texts (e.g., twitter hashtags, songs, or cultural idioms), and images, as well as material culture (e.g., art, artifacts, and architecture). It is in conversation with these various "texts" that we, as readers create (or, if you prefer, decipher) meanings. In addition to reading, we all write intertextually: that is, we make use of well-known references to help clarify and vivify our thoughts. We write with analogies, allusions, quotations, metaphors, and similes that we hope help others to make sense of our own thoughts. When in the hands of readers, though, our writings also resonate with texts that we may not even recognize at the time, or may not even know, due to the various contexts of our readers. Despite our assumptions to the contrary, no author is in complete control of interpretation. Instead, meanings are produced by readers, interpreters, as they engage with any number of texts (culture) depending on their own contexts. As Stefan Alkier explains, "Texts *have* no meaning but rather enable the production of meaning in the act of reading."[39] This, in the broadest sense of the term, is the phenomenon of "intertextuality."

The theory of intertextuality traces its roots to French philosopher Julia Kristeva (b. 1941). Kristeva's work developed the literary theory of Mikhail Bakhtin, who emphasized the ways Dostoevsky's novels simultaneously promoted multiple value systems through his characters, never bringing them together in a single "truth."[40] Rather than focusing on novels, Kristeva broadened Bakhtin's concept, arguing that all communication systems are "dialogical" and that "texts" are not simply literary products, but are all sign systems or "culture." As a result, meaning is not controlled by authors (or by "experts") who alone have the tools to deduce the singular *truth* of individual texts), but it is created by any and all readers who understand texts on the basis of their own (intertextual) contexts. As Kristeva explains, "any text is constructed as a mosaic of quotations; any text is the absorption and transformation of another. The notion of *intertextuality* replaces that of intersubjectivity, and poetic language is read as at least *double*."[41] No text, author, or reader exists in a vacuum; and none limits possible meanings.

Kristeva's work was subsequently picked up by literary theorists and others, some of whom tried to establish a methodology, something Kristeva herself was very uninterested in doing since it would, by definition, put limitations on meaning.[42] Biblical scholars have likewise appealed to "intertextuality" in their interpretations, although they may or may not articulate precisely what they mean by the term.[43] Of course, such openness was one of the aims of Kristeva's project, but it is one that makes the use of intertextuality difficult, since the term itself is slippery as are related concepts such as "text" and "sign." Various biblical scholars have attempted to resolve this issue, but in the present volume I (Alicia D. Myers) will rely on Alkier's model, which is well grounded in the history of intertextual theory and achieves some methodological underpinning without sacrificing the crucial plurality of meanings at the core of intertextual and post-structuralist theories.

Alkier first separates "intertextual" from what he describes as "intratextual" and "extratextual" based on his definition of texts as "linguistic signs that, when organized, become texts and are received in this expectation."⁴⁴ In other words, for biblical scholars, texts are written verbal signs rather than simply *any* sign. *Intratextual analysis* focuses on "text-immanent exploration" within a particular text (e.g., how does John's characterization of the disciples' questioning Jesus reverberate within the Gospel?). *Extratextual analysis* focuses on exploration of meanings that are created between a text and a variety of external signs, be they texts or not (e.g., how does John's presentation of Jesus as "savior" resonate with monuments to emperors in the Roman world?). *Intertextual analysis*, however, differs from both these by exploring the meanings created between two (or more) specified texts (e.g., how does the Gospel of John use the book of Isaiah?).⁴⁵

Even within intertextuality, however, Alkier cautions that there are at least three different approaches: (1) the production-oriented perspective, which focuses on texts available in the historical context of a given text; (2) the reception-oriented perspective, which explores the ways a given text could or has been received outside of a single, limited time frame; and (3) the experimental perspective, which could encompass reading a text in conversation with *any* other texts. For Alkier, these definitions and models serve to at once enable dialogue about intertextual meanings with a usable set of terms, while also enabling multiplicity of meanings since no one approach is meant to be "set off against the others" as superior or more valuable.⁴⁶ Like the present project, these ways of reading should be set side by side.

Intertextual Readings in Action

Perhaps the most apparent way of reading any NT work "intertextually" is by exploring quotations and allusions to OT books. Indeed, this has been the most prolific use of intertextual readings among NT scholars, including those who study the Gospel of John.⁴⁷ In Alkier's terminology, most of these studies focus on production-oriented and reception-oriented perspectives, and are often indebted to the criteria for intertextuality established by Richard B. Hays's *Echoes of Scripture in the Letters of Paul*.⁴⁸

In this collection, we have several chapters that likewise emphasize these perspectives but not to the exclusion of some additional, extratextual and intratextual analyses. In the first section, Craig S. Keener's reading of the Prologue of John focuses on intertextual connections between John and various Logos ("Word") traditions from Second Temple Judaism. Keener notes how many scholars have explored John's characterization of the Logos in light of Wisdom traditions from this period, and while he agrees with many of these observations, he also adds one more twist. The Logos is not simply Wisdom now incarnate as Jesus, but rather, the Logos is the Torah and indeed, is God's very glory (Greek: *doxa*; Hebrew: *shekinah*) made flesh. Focusing in particular on Exodus 33–34, Keener argues that John understands Jesus to be the only way one can encounter God's glory and live (Exod. 33:20; John 1:17–18).

In the second section, Catrin H. Williams also focuses on OT intertexts to interpret Jesus's use of shepherd imagery in John 10. Looking especially to pervasive connections between John 10 and Ezekiel 34, Williams acknowledges the extensive use of this imagery in the wider ancient Mediterranean world. Incorporating insights from ancient rhetorical handbooks, Williams examines the persuasive impact of the scriptural allusions and motifs in this speech as it aims to convince the audience of its own particularly Johannine interpretation of Jesus as "the good shepherd."

The final intertextual chapter in this collection, however, takes things in a different direction. Rather than focusing on OT allusions in John 20, Helen K. Bond centers her attention on connections to the Synoptics, especially the Gospel of Mark. John's opening resurrection scene resonates with Mark's Gospel with the reference to time of day, and the appearance of Mary Magdalene at the tomb, as well as the initial confusion over the removal of the stone, Jesus's missing body, and an angelic intervention offering guidance (see John 20:1–18; Mark 16:1–8). Bond explores these connections, along with similarities to Luke and Matthew, suggesting that John's composition might not have existed in isolation, just as the interpretation of his story has not.

Although these three chapters are the only ones labelled "intertextual," we should not overlook the pervasiveness of intertextuality, particularly in its broadest conceptions, throughout this collection (and, indeed, all of biblical interpretation). Each of the other approaches identified in this collection makes use of intertextuality since, as Kristeva has noted, "Any text is constructed as a mosaic of quotations; any text is the absorption and transformation of another." Since we cannot read a text in isolation, any more than a text is composed in isolation, we will read intertextually, crafting meaning in light of our own contexts and, hopefully, in conversation with others across time and space, to discover new ways of reading and new meanings thus making the message of John's Gospel relevant 2,000 years beyond its composition.

Rhetorical Readings: Acknowledging the Persuasive Elements of John's Story

Rhetorical Readings in Theory

We have termed the final approach outlined in this collection as "rhetorical." Like the other approaches explored above, rhetorical readings are varied and broad. When approaching the Gospel of John from a rhetorical angle, however, interpreters actively acknowledge and analyze the persuasive elements and methods of this writing. Rhetorical analyses emphasize that the Gospel of John is not just a collection of facts, but it is a story meant to *persuade* its audience to action, whether that action is new or continued. John 20:30–31 is the often-suggested "thesis statement" of the Gospel, and it makes this rhetorical, or persuasive, intention quite plain: "Jesus, therefore, did many other signs before his disciples, which have not been written in this book. But these have been written *so that you all should believe that Jesus is the Christ, the Son of God, and so that believing, you all should have life in his name.*" A similar refrain appears in John 21:24–25, the portion of the Gospel long-considered an addendum to the narrative proper: "This one is the disciple witnessing concerning these things and who wrote these things, and we know that his witness is true. And Jesus did many other things, which if each were written down, I suppose the world itself could not make room for the books being written." The emphasis on the superlative number of signs Jesus performed, compounded with the focus on truthfulness here and elsewhere in the Gospel (see especially 19:35), reinforce the persuasive intent of the work. John's Gospel is not, nor does it ever pretend to be, a simple recording of "the bare facts." Instead, it is a book that is meant to persuade; it is a piece of rhetoric.

Rhetorical analyses of the Gospel, and the NT writings more broadly, explore *how* a writing persuades: what methods are used and what the effects of those methods could be, both among ancient audiences and contemporary ones. As Ruth Sheridan notes, scholars regularly make a distinction between two major types of rhetorical studies: (1) Those that focus on ancient, or classical, models of rhetoric based on rhetorical handbooks and professional rhetorical pieces from the Greco-Roman world;[49] and (2) Those that employ methods from the what she describes as "the so-called New Rhetoric," which focuses on the psychological impact of all written material as argumentation, and the ways in "which language functions symbolically to 'induce cooperation' in readers."[50]

The quotation in the midst of Sheridan's definition above is from Kenneth Burke who, along with Chaim Perelman and Lucie Olbrechts-Tyteca, is credited with beginning studies in "New Rhetoric" and especially the resurgence in exploring the ethical implications of argumentation.[51] For practitioners of New Rhetoric, rhetoric is acknowledged to be everywhere rather than just in formalized speeches or literature that are explicitly deliberative or forensic in form. Instead, all people use rhetoric to persuade others, and they do so often in implicit ways, ways not always known even by the authors and speakers themselves. Instead, emotions, gestures, intertextual references, and even figures of speech tap in to shared social identities in order to create collaboration

(Perelman and Olbrechts-Tyteca) or acquire agreement (Burke) that is at the core of social groups.[52]

Writing shortly after World War II, Perelman and Olbrechts-Tyteca argued that understandings of reason codified in rigid rhetorical proofs and narrowly defined systems of "logic" limited acknowledged use of "rhetoric" to those in power. As a result, it truncated awareness of human communication and freedom, ignoring much more broad uses of rhetoric, or "argumentation," that all people employ. Perelman and Olbrechts-Tyteca, therefore, worked to "rehabilitate forms of reasoning believed to be 'extraneous to the purely formal' study of logic," and, in this way, they formulated a more expansive understanding of reason, one that was not opposed to emotion, and one that recognized the ethical element of persuasion.[53] Rather than engaging in argumentation as "violence," the New Rhetoric saw one's interlocutor as a subject complete with "free judgment" rather than as an "object" requiring domination.[54] As John T. Gage summarizes, "Only a rhetoric that justifies, rather than compels, puts human freedom and responsibility on the line" is an ethical rhetoric. No longer should the goal of rhetoric be to *win*, but rather, it should be to *reason* and to "search for truth."[55]

Nevertheless, as Sheridan also notes, while classical rhetoric and New Rhetoric are often set at odds, in reality, they have much in common.[56] Richard Graff and Wendy Winn note that, "[f]or Burke and Perelman, the impulse toward the development of 'new' rhetoric does not entail a radical break with the 'old' but gives prominence to certain ideas that were not or could not be clearly articulated in rhetorical theories of the past."[57] Thus, for Burke, fresh ground is broken by exploring the role of rhetorical figures in all genres of communication to see how they acquire assent from audiences, regardless of their content. Perelman and Olbrechts-Tyteca, in contrast, emphasize the content of arguments, suggesting that references to shared experiences, lauded voices and texts, and common mores enable rhetoric (especially epideictic rhetoric) to persuade by creating "communion" between individual people.[58]

What all three theorists agree upon, however, is the deeply embedded nature of all persons. Resonating with notions of "intertextuality" that were later defined and developed by Julia Kristeva, these theorists of New Rhetoric argue that every individual is a collection of group values just as Kristeva argues that every text is an amalgamation of previous texts. We are products of our cultures as much as, or more than, we are creators of them. Thus, rhetorical analysis should not be limited to figures of argumentation alone, but rather should expand into uncovering the shared values that make them effective—and seeing if those values are positive or negative. In other words, we should ask, "What are the *ethics* of communication?"[59]

It should be noted, however, that classical rhetoricians are also ultimately concerned with ethics.[60] Moreover, they are acutely aware of the need to discover and utilize shared mores in order to be persuasive, and they regularly advise the use of emotions to help make a reasoned argument. What they are less able to do, and what New Rhetoric offers, is the perspective to deconstruct what mores and implicit aspects of communication are also present in argumentation. For example, rather than seeing classical rhetoricians as exclusively prescriptive in their discussion of *how to argue*, most scholars now see that these authors are descriptive of *possibilities* for argumentation, offering their models (which were based on their interpretations and incorporations of previous ones) in a competitive atmosphere. These rhetoricians (and their students) were not the only ones persuading in the ancient Mediterranean world. If they were, there would be no need to argue for one's own rhetorical methods! Keeping these elements in mind, therefore, we see how ancient rhetorical practices *and* theories of New Rhetoric can work hand in hand to describe methods of argumentation in the Gospel of John, beyond just explicit rhetorical figures, and provide ways to explore the ethical potential and limitations of such argumentation.[61]

Rhetorical Readings in Action

In this collection, therefore, we have left our definition of "rhetorical" open to both classical and new approaches, as well as for those who mix these two horizons. While all three of the chapters that deal with rhetorical readings make use of classical models and authors, they also reach beyond rigid descriptions to offer thoughts on what the possible affects of the Gospel's rhetoric could be on readers ancient and contemporary. Jo-Ann A. Brant's rhetorical exploration of the Gospel Prologue notes not only this section's narrative importance, but its persuasive power with its intentional and strategic use of ambiguity. The multiple meanings that flow throughout the passage give these opening verses charm and eloquence, while they also "inspire trust" from the Gospel audience "so that they become engaged in the play of meanings and awaken to a new or a renewed appreciation of the divine gifts they have received." Brant's reading gains insights from ancient rhetoricians, while also incorporating the work of current scholars of rhetoric who note the power of ambiguous communication.

In the second portion of the book, my (Alicia D. Myers's) chapter focuses on rhetoric in John 10, especially the first twenty-one verses of the chapter, which continue Jesus's comments to the Pharisees "with him" in 9:39–41. It is these same religious leaders who are the target of Jesus's metaphor, or *paroimia*, in John 10:1–6, as well as his later expansions on it in the remainder of the chapter. Using elements of classical rhetoric, I explore the different types of speech Jesus uses in this chapter—*paroimia* (figurative language) and *parrēsia* (bold or frank speech)—comparing the surprising overlaps between them. I also take cues from New Rhetoric to examine the ethics of Jesus's communication not only toward the Pharisees in the Gospel, but also toward the Gospel's primary audiences, both ancient and contemporary.

Kasper Bro Larsen's chapter on John 20 rounds out the rhetorical readings in this collection, as well as the collection itself. In his chapter, Larsen focuses on the rhetorical impact of the vivid description, or *ekphrasis*, used throughout the chapter. Larsen notes the importance of vivid language for ancient rhetoric, as well as its effectiveness in contemporary storytelling. The persuasive power and reassurance of visual imagery in narrative is crucial to the Gospel of John largely due to the absence of Jesus's physical presence among the community any longer. With this insight at its center, Larsen's chapter explores how John's *ekphrastic* language enables it to communicate Jesus's "vivid presence" in spite of his physical absence.

FINAL THOUGHTS

Now that you have been introduced to the four hermeneutical approaches, we invite you to encounter these approaches in action. In the following chapters you will find chapters from biblical scholars applying each of the four approaches to common passages in John. We advise you to read over each passage from John first, if not the whole Gospel, so that it is in the forefront of your mind. As you read through each chapter, watch for how each scholar, guided by their interpretive approach, emerges with unique insights about the text. By exploring these approaches side by side, we hope you will see the value of multiple approaches and witness firsthand the significant ways our hermeneutical starting points affect how we make meaning of John's story.

NOTES

1. For example, one might consider the overwhelming influence of J. Louis Martyn's theory concerning the history of the Johannine community first published in 1968 (*The History and Theology of the Fourth Gospel*, 3rd ed., NTL [Louisville: Westminster John Knox, 2003]). Martyn's work was the dominate approach of much of Johannine scholarship, particularly in North America, through at least the beginning of the twenty-first century. Nevertheless, serious challenges have also come from Adele Reinhartz, *Befriending the Beloved Disciple: A Jewish Reading of the Gospel of John* (London: Continuum, 2001), Richard Bauckham, ed., *The Gospels for All Christians: Rethinking the Gospel Audiences* (Grand Rapids: Eerdmans, 1998), and from Udo Schnelle, *Antidocetic Christology in the Gospel of John: An Investigation of the Place of the Fourth Gospel in the Johannine School*, trans. Linda M. Maloney

(Minneapolis: Fortress, 1992). Robert Kysar offers his own journey from wholeheartedly agreeing with Martyn, to now being entirely skeptical of historical-critical methodologies in *John: The Maverick Gospel*, 3rd ed. (Louisville: Westminster John Knox, 2007).

2. Michael J. Gorman, *Elements of Biblical Exegesis: A Basic Guide for Students and Ministers*, rev. and expanded ed. (Peabody, MA: Hendrickson, 2009), 63–68.

3. Unless otherwise noted, all translations of the NT are the authors'.

4. This is similar to the goals of Douglas Estes and Ruth Sheridan, eds., *How John Works: Storytelling in the Fourth Gospel*, RBS 86 (Atlanta: SBL Press, 2016) and Christopher W. Skinner, ed., *Characters and Characterization in the Gospel of John*, LNTS 461 (London: Bloomsbury/T&T Clark, 2013), although each of these is more narrowly focused.

5. Some books that introduce interpretive methods have opted instead to cover a range of texts. For example, Paula Gooder, *Searching for Meaning: An Introduction to Interpreting the New Testament* (Louisville: SPCK, 2009), xvii–xviii; Steven L. McKenzie and Stephen R. Haynes, eds., *To Each Its Own Meaning: An Introduction to Biblical Criticisms and Their Applications*, rev. ed. (Louisville: Westminster John Knox, 1999), 11. Neither of these collections, however, feature full-fledged examples of the interpretive work in action.

6. Gooder, *Searching for Meaning*; Joel B. Green, ed., *Hearing the New Testament: Strategies for Interpretation*, 2nd ed. (Grand Rapids: Eerdmans, 2010); Jaime Clark-Soles, *Engaging the Word: The New Testament and the Christian Believer* (Louisville: Westminster John Knox, 2010), 16–26.

7. Gooder, *Searching for Meaning*, xviii–xxi. Also see Green, *Hearing the New Testament*, 10–14. McKenzie and Haynes (*To Each Its Own Meaning*) notice that these distinctions do breakdown, and they opt for categories that represent the development of biblical interpretation as a discipline.

8. For books that focus on particular interpretive methods, see McKenzie and Haynes, *To Each Its Own Meaning*; Green, *Hearing the New Testament*; Gooder, *Searching for Meaning*; Elizabeth A. Castelli et al., eds., *The Postmodern Bible: The Bible and Culture Collective* (New Haven: Yale University Press, 1995).

9. Gooder, *Searching for Meaning*, 87; Mark Allan Powell, "Narrative Criticism," in Green, *Hearing the New Testament*, 240.

10. David M. Rhoads, Joanna Dewey, and Donald Michie, *Mark as Story: An Introduction to the Narrative of a Gospel*, 3rd ed. (Minneapolis: Fortress, 2012).

11. Powell, "Narrative Criticism," 241–49.

12. For further reading, see Gooder, *Searching for Meaning*, 88–104; Daniel Patte, *The Religious Dimensions of Biblical Texts: Greimas's Structural Semiotics and Biblical Exegesis*, SemSt 19 (Atlanta: Scholars Press, 1990); Castelli, et al., *The Postmodern Bible*, 70–148; Umberto Eco, *A Theory of Semiotics, Advances in Semiotics* (Bloomington, IN: Indiana University Press, 1979); Gérard Genette, *Narrative Discourse: An Essay in Method*, trans. Jane E. Lewin (Ithaca, NY: Cornell University Press, 1980); Roland Barthes, *S/Z: An Essay*, trans. Richard Miller (New York: Hill and Wang, 1974); Barthes, *The Semiotic Challenge*, trans. Richard Miller (New York: Hill and Wang, 1988); Jacques Derrida, *A Derrida Reader: Between the Blinds*, ed.

Peggy Kamuf (New York: Columbia University Press, 1991); Michel Foucault, *The Foucault Reader*, ed. Paul Rabinow (New York: Pantheon Books, 1984); Stephen D. Moore, *Mark and Luke in Poststructuralist Perspectives: Jesus Begins to Write* (New Haven: Yale University Press, 1992); Gary A. Phillips, ed., "Poststructural Criticism and the Bible: Text/History/Discourse," *Sem* 51 (1990): 1–240; David Jobling and Stephen D. Moore, eds., "Poststructuralism as Exegesis," *Sem* 54 (1991): 1–255.

13. Gooder, *Searching for Meaning*, 82; Joel B. Green, "Discourse Analysis and New Testament Interpretation," in Green, *Hearing the New Testament*, 218–39. Scholars often use technical terms like "implied author" and "implied audience" as a way of recognizing the lack of access to the actual people who created and received these texts. Literary critics thus speak of the "implied author" as a construct of the author that emerges as a reader makes inferences about the author based on observations concerning features of text and knowledge concerning the context. Some use the term "implied audience" to refer to a hypothetical audience who would possess the requisite knowledge and interpretive skills to understand the text (James Phelan, *Narrative as Rhetoric: Technique, Audiences, Ethics, Ideology* [Columbus: Ohio State University Press, 1996], 28 n1). The term "authorial audience" is sometimes used when this group is viewed as a construct in the mind of the author, but the two terms are often used synonymously (e.g., Martin M. Culy, *Echoes of Friendship in the Gospel of John*, NTM 30 [Sheffield: Sheffield Phoenix, 2010], 15). Alicia D. Myers (*Characterizing Jesus: A Rhetorical Analysis on the Fourth Gospel's Use of Scripture in Its Presentation of Jesus*, LNTS 458 [London: Bloomsbury/T&T Clark, 2012], 17–20) explains that the "authorial audience," much the same as the "implied reader," is a construction that pairs data concerning the historical and cultural context with observations from the analysis of the text itself. See also Peter J. Rabinowitz, "Truth in Fiction: A Reexamination of Audiences," *CI* 4 (1977): 126–29; Charles H. Talbert, *Reading Luke-Acts in Its Mediterranean Milieu*, NovTSup 107 (Leiden: Brill, 2003), 16–17; Kirsten Marie Hartvigsen, *Prepare the Way of the Lord: Towards a Cognitive Poetic Analysis of Audience Involvement with Characters and Events in the Markan World*, BZNW 180 (Berlin: De Gruyter, 2012), 13–14; Michael R. Whitenton, *Hearing Kyriotic Sonship: A Cognitive and Rhetorical Approach to the Characterization of Mark's Jesus*, BibS 148 (Leiden: Brill, 2017), 26–29; Lindsey M. Trozzo, *Exploring Johannine Ethics: A Rhetorical Approach to Moral Efficacy in the Fourth Gospel Narrative*, WUNT 2/449 (Tübingen: Mohr Siebeck, 2017), 21–23.

14. See the works in n. 13 as well as Wolfgang Iser, *The Implied Reader: Patterns of Communication in Prose Fiction from Bunyan to Beckett* (Baltimore: Johns Hopkins University Press, 1978); Iser, *The Act of Reading: A Theory of Aesthetic Response* (Baltimore: Johns Hopkins University Press, 1994); Stanley E. Fish, *Is There a Text in This Class?: The Authority of Interpretive Communities* (Cambridge, MA: Harvard University Press, 1980); Kathy Reiko Maxwell, *Hearing Between the Lines: The Audience as Fellow-Workers in Luke-Acts and Its Literary Milieu*, LNTS 425 (New York: T&T Clark, 2010).

15. See also David M. Gunn, "Narrative Criticism," in McKenzie and Haynes, *To Each Its Own Meaning*, 201–29; Edgar V. McKnight, "Reader-Response Criticism," in McKenzie and Haynes, *To Each Its Own Meaning*, 230–52; William A. Beardslee,

"Poststructuralist Criticism," in McKenzie and Haynes, *To Each Its Own Meaning*, 253–67; Gooder, *Searching for Meaning*.

16. Castelli et al., *The Postmodern Bible*, 14.

17. "*Cis*" is a Latin prefix meaning "on the (same) side of." When used in the context of discussing gender, "cisgender" describes a person who identifies with the gender they were assigned at birth. Thus, a "cis man" is a person who was assigned male gender at birth and identifies as male.

18. Castelli et al., *The Postmodern Bible*, 272.

19. Gooder, *Searching for Meaning*, 107–9.

20. Castelli et al., *The Postmodern Bible*, 4.

21. Gooder, *Searching for Meaning*, 108.

22. Postmodernism "arises from but critiques modernism and its concern for objectivity, rationalism and certainty. . . . [It] is consciously subjective . . . prefers plurality to a single meaning . . . and believes that meaning can be found as much outside of the text as in it" (Gooder, *Searching for Meaning*, 148). See Castelli et al., *The Postmodern Bible*, 1–19.

23. Castelli et al., *The Postmodern Bible*, 4.

24. Castelli et al., *The Postmodern Bible*, 2–3.

25. Stephen D. Moore, "Are There Impurities in the Living Water That the Johannine Jesus Dispenses? Deconstruction, Feminism, and the Samaritan Woman," *BibInt* 1 (1993): 207.

26. Gooder, *Searching for Meaning*, 135–36. Elisabeth Schüssler Fiorenza, *Bread Not Stone: The Challenge of Feminist Biblical Interpretation* (Boston: Beacon, 1984).

27. Ehrensperger is speaking specifically of feminist criticism. Gooder, *Searching for Meaning*, 136.

28. Gooder, *Searching for Meaning*, 136–37.

29. Castelli et al., *The Postmodern Bible*, 2.

30. Castelli et al., *The Postmodern Bible*, 225.

31. Gooder, *Searching for Meaning*, 146.

32. Gooder, *Searching for Meaning*, 152–66.

33. Gooder, *Searching for Meaning*, 163.

34. Gooder, *Searching for Meaning*, 177.

35. Castelli et al., *The Postmodern Bible*, 15.

36. LGBTQIA is an acronym that names several identities claimed by those within the queer, non-heteronormative community: lesbian, gay, bisexual, transgender, queer, intersex, and asexual. Many of these individual terms are umbrella terms under which a number of particular identities (e.g., nonbinary or genderqueer) might fit. This form of the acronym is the one currently used by the majority of queer scholars in the field of Biblical Studies, and so it is adopted in this book. Many iterations of the acronym have existed, and the acronym will likely grow and change to be more inclusive in scope. Because of this flexibility, I join other scholars in adopting the term "queer" as an umbrella term for the many identities described in the acronym while also allowing room for other identities which may not be explicitly named in it.

37. See a similar approach in Warren Carter, "'The Blind, Lame, and Paralyzed' (John 5:3): John's Gospel, Disability Studies, and Postcolonial Perspectives," in

Disability Studies and Biblical Literature, ed. Candida R. Moss and Jeremy Schipper (New York: Palgrave MacMillan, 2011) 128–50.

38. Warren Carter, *John and Empire: Initial Explorations* (New York: T&T Clark, 2008).

39. Stefan Alkier, "Intertextuality and the Semiotics of Biblical Texts," in *Reading the Bible Intertextually*, ed. Richard B. Hays, Stefan Alkier, Leroy A. Huizenga (Waco, TX: Baylor University Press, 2009), 3.

40. Alkier, "Intertextuality," 5. See, for example, Mikhail Bakhtin, *Problems of Dostoevsky's Poetics*, ed. and trans. Caryl C. Emerson, introduction by Wayne C. Booth, THL 8 (Minneapolis: University of Minnesota Press, 1984).

41. Julia Kristeva, "Word, Dialogue, and Novel," in *The Kristeva Reader*, ed. Toril Moi, trans. Léon S. Roudiez and Seán Hand (New York: Columbia University Press, 1986), 35–36; quoted in Alkier, "Intertextuality," 6. See also Kristeva, *Revolution in Poetic Language*, EPS (New York: Columbia University Press, 1984).

42. For this reason, Kristeva eventually abandoned the term "intertextuality" for "transposition." Kristeva, *Revolution*, 59–60 in Alkier, "Intertextuality," 7.

43. See Richard B. Hays's critique in "Forward to the English Edition," in Hays, Alkier, Huizenga, *Reading the Bible Intertextually*, xi–xiii.

44. Alkier, "Intertextuality," 7.

45. Alkier, "Intertextuality," 8–9. Alkier analyzes these themes in Mark on pp. 13–21.

46. Alkier, "Intertextuality," 10–11.

47. For a review of literature, see Alicia D. Myers, "Abiding Words: An Introduction to Perspectives on John's Use of Scripture," in *Abiding Words: The Use of Scripture in the Gospel of John*, ed. Alicia D. Myers and Bruce G. Schuchard, RBS 81 (Atlanta: SBL Press, 2015), 1–20; Ruth Sheridan, *Retelling Scripture: "The Jews" and the Scriptural Citations in John 1:19–12:15*, BibS 110 (Leiden: Brill, 2012), 1–48.

48. Richard B. Hays, *Echoes of Scripture in the Letters of Paul* (New Haven: Yale University Press, 1989) Hays responds to his critics in *The Conversion of Imagination: Paul as Interpreter of Scripture* (Grand Rapids: Eerdmans, 2005) and finally settles on what he calls "figural reading" in his exploration of the Gospels, *Echoes of Scriptures in the Gospels* (Waco, TX: Baylor University Press, 2016), 1–6.

49. For an overview of classical rhetoric, including primary sources and terminology, see Hans Lausberg, *Handbook of Literary Rhetoric: A Foundation for Literary Study*, ed. D. E. Horton and R. D. Anderson, trans. M. T. Bliss, A. Jansen, and D. E. Horton (Leiden: Brill, 2008). For explorations in NT study, see C. Clifton Black and Duane F. Watson, eds., *Words Well Spoken: George Kennedy's Rhetoric of the New Testament*, SRR 8 (Waco, TX: Baylor University Press, 2008). For a quick overview on the Gospel of John, see Alicia D. Myers, "Rhetoric," in Estes and Sheridan, *How John Works*, 187–203.

50. Sheridan, "Persuasion," in Estes and Sheridan, *How John Works*, 207.

51. Kenneth Burke, *A Rhetoric of Motives* (Berkley: University of California Press, 1969), 261–62; Chaim Perelman and Lucie Olbrechts-Tyteca, *The New Rhetoric: A Treatise on Argumentation*, trans. John Wilkinson and Purcell Weaver (South Bend, IN: University of Notre Dame Press, 1971).

52. Richard Graff and Wendy Winn explore the communal awareness of identity in both Burke and Perelman and Olbrechts-Tyteca's theories. Burke emphasizes individual participation in groups as key to forming identity, while Perelman and Olbrechts-Tyteca focus on the ways epideictic rhetoric reinforces agreed upon "communal values" ("Kenneth Burke's 'Identification' and Chaïm Perelman and Lucie Olbrechts-Tyteca's 'Communion': A Case of Convergent Evolution?" in *The Promise of Reason: Studies in the New Rhetoric*, ed. John T. Gage [Carbondale, IL: Southern Illinois University Press, 2011], 108–9). The awareness of groups, rather than just individual identity, in these works resonates with ancient models of rhetoric, which were constructed in group cultures rather than modern individualistic societies of the Western world.

53. Perelman and Olbrechts-Tyteca, *The New Rhetoric*, 2 in John T. Gage, "Introduction" in Gage, *The Promise of Reason*, 3.

54. Perelman and Olbrechts-Tyteca, *The New Rhetoric*, 55 in Gage, "Introduction," 4.

55. Gage, "Introduction," 4–5.

56. Sheridan, "Persuasion," 207.

57. Graff and Winn, "Kenneth Burke's 'Identification,'" in Gage, *The Promise of Reason*, 104.

58. Gage, *The Promise of Reason*, 116–17.

59. Jean Nienkamp emphasizes the overlap of rhetoric and ethics writing, "[R]hetoric is inescapably based on values or value hierarchies of some sort, just as ethics is inescapably based on rhetorical deliberation about ends and actions. For this reason, rhetoric and ethics are two mutually enabling and effecting aspects of the same critical enterprise" ("RhETHorICS," in Gage, *The Promise of Reason*, 171).

60. Thus, Quintilian's famous phrase: "I am not saying that the orator must be a good man, but that *no one* can be an orator *unless* he is a good man" (*Inst.* 12.1.3 [Russell, LCL]). Of course, what is up for debate is precisely what makes a "good man" (*vir bonus*), something in which Quintilian himself invests a significant amount of time in his *Institutes on Oratory* (books 11–12). The gender constructions that undergirded ancient systems of rhetoric were extensive and are the subject of several recent studies, including those focused on NT works; see Maud W. Gleason, *Making Men: Sophists and Self-Presentation in Ancient Rome* (Princeton: Princeton University Press, 1995); Cheryl Glenn, *Rhetoric Retold: Regendering the Tradition from Antiquity through the Renaissance* (Carbondale: Southern Illinois University Press, 1997); Colleen M. Conway, *Behold the Man: Jesus and Greco-Roman Masculinity* (Oxford: Oxford University Press, 2008); Brittany E. Wilson, *Unmanly Men: Refigurations of Masculinity in Luke-Acts* (Oxford: Oxford University Press, 2015).

61. Perhaps it is not coincidental, therefore, that the rise in rhetorical studies of the Gospel of John has occurred at the same time (and often by the same authors and schools) as interest in Johannine ethics. See, for example, Jan G. van der Watt and Ruben Zimmerman, eds., *Rethinking the Ethics of John: "Implicit Ethics" in the Johannine Writings*, WUNT 291, CNNTE 3 (Tübingen: Mohr Siebeck, 2012); Sherri Brown and Christopher W. Skinner, eds., *Johannine Ethics: The Moral World of the Gospel and Epistles of John* (Minneapolis: Fortress, 2017).

Part 1

JOHN 1:1–18

NARRATIVE, SOCIOCULTURAL, INTERTEXTUAL, AND RHETORICAL READINGS

Chapter 1

Beginnings

Introducing the Narrative of the Word through the Prologue of John's Gospel

Sherri Brown

One of my favorite quotes about the narrative techniques in the Gospel of John is by Charles Giblin, who claims that "as every Irishman knows, the meaning of a story lies largely in the way it is told. For each storyteller wants himself [or herself] to be understood appreciatively through his [or her] own way of telling the tale, whether that tale is not as yet known or, and indeed preferably, if it already is. That is how the storyteller functions as a teacher."[1] He goes on to claim that the Fourth Evangelist is a consummate storyteller. Although Giblin's work focuses on the passion narrative (John 18–19), as a first page, the Prologue (John 1:1–18) is also fundamental to the storytelling, the teaching content, and the dramatic structure of the Gospel. Further, Jo-Ann Brant has shown that "the author of the Fourth Gospel plunders a trove of theatrical devices and conventions," particularly those of ancient Greek drama, in order to tell his tale.[2] Indeed, through the threshold of 1:1–18, audiences come to the body of the Gospel armed with the information in this Prologue—information only the narrator and audiences have. Although the enigmatic ideas of the Prologue may prove initially elusive, this intangibility is precisely what creates the tension that begs the question of the *how* of God's action in the world. The subsequent narrative *shows* what the Prologue *tells*.[3]

As distinct from their Greco-Roman religious counterparts, the Jewish and Christian traditions teach the covenant faithfulness of the one Creator God alongside the freedom of humankind to choose to live in right relationship with that God. The Fourth Evangelist is writing firmly within this tradition. However, by writing a gospel, he is also sharing good news and teaching that God has broken into history with a new act of covenant. God is faithful and consistent and, yet, has done something distinctive and new through Jesus as the Christ and Son of God. John's use of the poetic Prologue as a foundation for his Gospel that suddenly and definitively breaks into prose narrative can also be understood as a reflection of his theological perspective. The incarnation of the Word suddenly and definitively turns the custom and "truth" of the world on its ear.[4] According to John, God became human and dwelt among humankind in a new act of covenant, and John's Prologue is the beginning of the "word" that shares that story in a distinctive way.

THE ROLE OF THE PROLOGUE IN ANCIENT GREEK DRAMA

In both narrative and drama, prologues serve as a message before the body that become the key to appreciating the full force of the story to come, giving background that introduces the setting, previews the main characters, sets up the action, and establishes the primary themes of the work. We certainly see this in contemporary narratives. In ancient Greek drama, the prologue developed as the first component of the play that set forth the subject and protagonists of the drama before the chorus entered the stage. The speaker, who could be a god or human, a major or minor character, would typically address the audience more or less directly. The prologue, in open-air theaters without lights or curtains, would signal the beginning of the play by capturing the audience's attention and giving the historical and mythological background necessary for understanding the events of the drama at hand.

Much like the prologues in ancient Greek dramas, therefore, John's Prologue gives audiences a synthesis of events to come. It tells the *who* and the *what* of the people and events at hand but leaves open the *how*. Again, the subsequent drama *shows* what the Prologue *tells* since the story itself is necessary to understand how it all plays out. All of this becomes information audiences have that characters in the story *don't* have but likely wish they did as they struggle to grasp the person and mission of Jesus.[5] Thus, the Prologue puts the audience in a privileged position as it participates in the action of the story, watching and waiting, even hoping, for characters to catch on, as it were, and begin to grasp the fullness of what is at stake. As audience members identify with various characters, they can further make ethical judgments about them, thereby receiving some models for their own decision-making and rejecting others.

Euripides, the famous dramatist from Athens writing in the late fifth century B.C.E., is often credited with inventing, or at the very least "reinventing," the prologue for Greek drama. Jo-Ann A. Brant has offered a useful comparison of his work with that of the Fourth Evangelist.[6] She argues that "the audience then joins in a sort of collusion with the narrator by sharing the privileged knowledge and transcending the finite realm of normal human experience to view what normally cannot be seen: the workings of the cosmic order."[7] Through the Prologue, the Gospel's audience likewise "recognizes the implications of actions and the 'truth' that lies behind veiled or unwitting assertions" of later characters in the story. Plays often begin in the midst of some action such that the audience must be ready to step into its flow, and prologues allow members to do just that. Indeed, through points and counterpoints, the prologues of both Euripides and John strike the chords of tension with which the action begins.[8] The movement of the Prologue in the Gospel of John is toward the audience, toward the visible, toward incarnation, so as to bridge "the distance of time and place between the action of the play and the situation of the audience."[9] The Fourth Evangelist then employs the character of John the Baptist in particular to bridge that distance of time and place between the action of God in Jesus and the potential response of his audience. The characters of God and Jesus, likewise introduced in the Prologue, also hold steady across the narrative. In addition, all the major themes that play out across the Gospel are introduced in the Prologue. John the Evangelist thus adopts the conventions of Greek drama so pervasive in his world but reimagines them to tell his singular narrative of the God of Israel giving the gift of truth to humankind through the incarnation of the Son. We can now turn to a closer look at this key to interpreting the Gospel.

THE NARRATIVE FLOW OF THE PROLOGUE TO THE GOSPEL OF JOHN

Werner Kelber remarks, "both in life and in literature beginnings are consequential, but risky undertakings" that often create the central predicament of the coming story.[10] Further, beginnings are the manners by which the evangelists present keys to understanding what follows in their narratives.[11] That said, the structure of John's Prologue is elusive, and many have attempted to grasp it. The work of R. Alan Culpepper, however, is comprehensive in appreciating its oral features, including poetic parallelism, claims that build upon one another, and thematic repetition.[12] Recognizing the complexity of these verses, Culpepper is open to the fluidity of the evangelist's style but is nonetheless convinced that the framework of the Johannine Prologue is the chiasm, with seven corresponding elements that turn on the "pivot" in v. 12b.[13]

As a structuring technique, a chiasm is a placing crosswise of words, phrases, or concepts that may comprise whole passages as well as single sentences. This structure is called a *chiasm* because when the passage is diagrammed, the resulting graphic looks like the left side of the Greek letter *chi*, which resembles the Latin/English letter X. The words and phrases that are placed in corresponding positions could be verbatim, synonyms, or share themes. Often there are inversions of similar ideas rather than identical terms. Authors might use a chiasm in a story, letter, or speech in order to introduce the main point generally and then to give more and more information as they move toward their climax. Instead of concluding at that point, however, these authors revisit the initial information in reverse order to show how it has been affected by that climax. This means that the structure and content of a passage move from general to more and more specific claims that typically turn on a central assertion. This pivot is the climax of the passage's thematic presentation. According to Culpepper, the crux of the Prologue, and thus the focus of the narrative it introduces, is to teach that the mission of the Word of God who has become human is to empower those who receive and believe in him "to become children of God" (v. 12). As the Prologue to the Gospel, John 1:1–18 can thus be structured as follows:[14]

```
A    vv. 1–2    The Word in the Beginning with God
 B   v. 3       What Came to Be through the Word
  C  vv. 4–5    Life and Light in the Darkness
   D  vv. 6–8   John, Sent from God for Testimony
    E  vv. 9–10  The Light in the World
     F  v. 11    His Own Did Not Receive Him
      G  v. 12a   Receiving Him
       H  v. 12b   Becoming Children of God
      G' v. 12c   Believing Him
     F' v. 13    His Own of Born of God
    E' v. 14     The Word became Flesh in the World
   D' v. 15      John's Testimony
  C' v. 16       Gift upon Gift
 B' v. 17        The Gift of Truth in Jesus Christ
A' v. 18         The Son Reveals the Father
```

Since the Prologue is the key to unlocking the narrative discourse of John's Gospel, this "pivot" of Jesus Christ as the Word of God incarnate in the gift of truth who gives those who believe the power to become children of God must be the central thesis of John's telling of the good news. Studying the Prologue as an integral first page of John's narrative should follow this structure.

In the Beginning Was the Word (vv. 1–11)

The first words of the Gospel are identical to the opening words of Genesis. They serve to bring audiences not only to "the beginning" of this narrative but also to that of their sacred narrative of history, when God literally spoke creation into existence (Genesis 1).[15] By echoing this shared story of God's action in history, the Prologue grounds the story to come in the realm of the sacred Scripture of Israel. This literary intention is furthered with the fullness of the initial clause: "In the beginning was the Word (*logos*)." The evangelist's use of *logos* allows for rich and varied symbolism, evoking God's revelation in Torah as well as the broader voice of the Jewish and Greek sages throughout the diverse cultural milieu, and allowing for a fundamental identification of the Logos with the creative activity of God.[16] The "word" introduced here corresponds with God's word of creation in the beginning, now described as a being who is divine, eternal, and in relationship with God (v. 2).[17] Verse 2 parallels and affirms the claims of v. 1. In a poetic fashion, the evangelist teaches that as an independent being of the same divine essence as God, the Word is fundamentally oriented toward union with God. The expansiveness of these first verses prepares audiences for God's revelatory action in the story to come.

The chiasm pushes forward as the nature and role of the Logos is presented as the vehicle for creation (v. 3) who is the giver of life (v. 4) and stands fast in the darkness lighting the way for humankind (vv. 4–5). The evangelist introduces these themes of life, light, and its corresponding darkness, which will play out across the rest of the narrative, but also continues an exposition of Genesis 1 that echoes the eternal creative force of God. This presentation affirms what "came to be" (*egeneto*) through the Logos that always existed (*ēn*, v. 1). The final words of v. 5 further hint at the conflict to come between the Word of light and the darkness that exists among the people who are meant to be the caretakers of God's creation (Gen. 1:26–30). A physical threat to this newly characterized Word is implicated; nonetheless, in regard to the shining light, the darkness "did not overcome it" (v. 5). This leads to the introduction of John, the one who comes to give testimony and becomes the driving force to the Prologue's crux.

The first human being (*anthrōpos*) is introduced into the story as John (vv. 6–8).[18] We should clarify that, although the evangelist never calls him "the Baptist," this John is the same person that the other Gospels call "John the Baptist" (and not John the Evangelist). He is described as having come to be like the rest of creation, in distinction to the eternally existing Logos. This person, however, is also "sent from God" (v. 6), the only fully human character in the narrative identified as such. John, then, is special: he is sent into the world by God with a mission. Audiences are alerted that he is to be trusted. His mission is to testify by bearing witness (*martyrēsē*) to the light of the eternal Logos (vv. 7–8). As the witness sent from God, everything that John says about Jesus is true. Through the introduction of John and his role, the concept of "believing" in the Word is also introduced. John the human witness is carefully distinguished from the light, but his purpose is crucial to point to it and thus facilitate the process of believing (v. 7).

Focus then returns to the light, flowing from the final words that introduce John. The light is further characterized by way of truth (*to phōs to alēthinon*, v. 9). The "true light" whose reign reaches everyone was coming into the world. The incarnation foreshadowed here comes to pass in the counterpart to these verses, v. 14. The imminent conflict of the Gospel story is also reaffirmed, this time in terms of knowledge (v. 10; see v. 8). The Logos, instrumental giver of life and light in intimate relationship with God, comes into what is his own and is not received by these own people (v. 11). Giving, receiving, and rejecting in relationship thus become the operative interactivity of the incarnation of the Word.

Becoming Children of God: The Pivot of the Prologue (v. 12)

Audiences now arrive at the pivot of the Prologue (v. 12b) and the hinges upon which the pivot turns (vv. 12a and 12c).[19] The force of the entire Prologue is poised on the fulcrum of the mission of the Word to give them "power to become children of God" (v. 12).[20] The evangelist's syntax allows the central assertion of the Word's giving action to be framed by the introduction (v. 12a) and description (v. 12c) of the potential recipients of the gift of the Word. These verses are thus corresponding phrases that hinge the core assertion of v. 12b, the crux of the Prologue's message.[21] This crux also determines the rest of the corresponding elements that balance the Prologue.[22] The claim that those who receive the Word are given the power to become children of God and that one receives him in order to achieve this childhood by believing in his name is thus the heart of the Prologue (v. 12c).

Gift upon Gift: The Word Became Flesh and Dwelt Among Us (vv. 13–18)

The remainder of the Prologue thus sheds light on what it means to become "children of God" and how this could be the narrative and teaching *telos* (goal) of John's Gospel. Verse 13 supplements the description of the role of the "receivers" in this relationship by characterizing the role of God and the "how" of becoming God's children and also corresponds antithetically to v. 11 by describing spiritual birth as coming from above.[23] This notion is more fully articulated in the discourse of John 3 but is introduced here in terms of the mission of the Word. Because of the Word's coming into the world and the rejection by "his own" (v. 11), the nature the people of God likewise changes forever: heritage and race are rendered irrelevant to birth from God.[24] The Sinai covenant will be fulfilled, and a new covenant put in place.

The Prologue then returns to what God did to make this possible. Corresponding to the proclamation in vv. 9–10, that the "Word," characterized as "the true light" that was "coming into the world," v. 14 announces how the true light did come into the world, who the Logos becomes, and what is given in the process: "And the Word became flesh." These words announce an event made possible by the plan of God to re-envision the people of God as children of spiritual, not human, birth. Just as God's action in the covenantal giving of Torah changed the nature of God's relationship with creation, the incarnation of the Word, while very much in accord with that history, once again decisively alters the manner by which creation relates to God. Speaking inclusively from the perspective of the children of God, the Prologue proclaims the enfleshed Logos made his dwelling "among us."[25] The evangelist leaves no doubt as to the full humanity of the incarnate Word with the use of "flesh" to describe this in-breaking of God's action.

The visible and powerful manifestation of the glory of God dwelling in creation also harks back to the revelation of the glory of God to Moses on Mount Sinai (Exod. 34:15–16).[26] The verb *skēnoō* means literally to "pitch a tent" and the form here is generally translated as "lived" or "made his dwelling." The evangelist's verb choice, however, resonates with Exodus 33–40, where God renews the covenant with Israel mediated by Moses, and the people are told to make a tent (the Tabernacle, the *skēnē*,) so that God can live among them. After a lengthy description of the Tabernacle and its construction, Exodus 40 recounts the erection of the Tabernacle and the placement of the tablets of the Torah in the Ark of the Covenant and its setting in the Holy of Holies. Depicting the incarnation of the Word in terms of the *shekinah*, or dwelling presence of God, also preserves the Word's divinity as a new presence of God and God's covenantal activity in creation. This echo would not have been lost on the evangelist's first audience. In Jewish tradition, wisdom is ultimately accepted and manifested in Israel through the Sinai covenant. By contrast, the Gospel of John brazenly breaks new ground by claiming that God will send his preexistent Son to restore humankind to right relationship by gathering into one the scattered children of God through his rejection by his own people (see 11:45–54).[27] Since nothing in their shared tradition could prepare an audience for this bold new claim, the Prologue alone prepares the audience to follow the mission of Jesus in the Gospel and the evangelist's teaching through the Gospel.[28]

The glory of the incarnate Word is then described in the context of a father's uniquely begotten son who is *plērēs charitos kai alētheias*.[29] By translating the Greek word *charis* with its more widely held denotation of "an expression of good will, a gift, an unexpected favor," and reading the "and" as explanatory, thus allowing the second term, "truth," to clarify the first term, the phrase is rendered more clearly as "full of a gift which is truth."[30]

The Word, giver of light and life, now incarnate, is filled with a new gift, truth. The giving and receiving of this gift of truth is intimately connected to the power to become children of God (v. 12b) and thus to the crux of the mission of the incarnate Word.[31] In OT terms, this gift of truth would also entail the unified relationship with God that is produced by covenantal obedience. The remainder of the Prologue returns to where it began by continuing to elucidate this gift, integrating it into the life and being of the Word now made human.

This incarnate Word is then firmly grounded in history as the narrator returns to John, the human witness sent by God (v. 15; see vv. 6–8). In this role, John provides the first direct speech about the Word and the first direct speech of the Gospel. To assert both the correspondence of this verse to vv. 6–8 as well as the trustworthy nature of John's message, the evangelist places the narrator's major verbs about him thus far in the mouth of John and has him repeat them, thereby confirming in direct speech what the Prologue claimed for him.[32] Thus, John is the audience's accurate witness, but not the true light (i.e., not the protagonist). Robert Alter suggests, "Phrases or whole sentences first stated by the narrator do not reveal their full significance until they are repeated, whether faithfully or with distortions, in direct speech by one or more of the characters."[33] In performance, the technique affirms the integrity of this human witness. John testifies that the Word is the one who comes after him temporally but ranks before him. He further explains that this is so "because he was before me" (v. 15). With this historical grounding and temporal designation in place, the Prologue surges forward with the mission of the Word.

Continuing in the collective voice of the children of God, the narrator details the process of God's action in creation in terms of their reception of God's gifts (v. 16). Retaining the earlier understanding of *charis* as "gift," what God has done through the incarnate Word is give a gift upon a gift: *charin anti charitos*.[34] These gifts are illuminated in v. 17: "For the Law was given through Moses, the gift which is truth (*hē charis kai hē alētheia*) came to be through Jesus Christ." The gift of truth was given through the incarnation of the Word, who is finally identified in history as Jesus, who is the Christ (from the Greek word for "Messiah"). This gift of truth is likewise a gift of God that acts in history in covenant with creation. But one cannot "replace" the other. Rather, the gift of the Law is perfected in the gift of the incarnation. The giving of the gift of the Torah was God's covenantal activity at Sinai. The incarnation of the Word that is full of the gift of truth is God's covenantal activity in Jesus.

The final verse of the Prologue returns to the beginning (vv. 1–2) while elucidating the relationship of Jesus as "only Son" who is turned toward the Father, now in history (v. 18).[35] It is the Son who makes God known, revealing how humankind can become children of God. This is indeed a new covenantal move in history. Jesus, the Word of God made human, will make God known through his life and ministry. The remainder of the Gospel will dramatize the "how" of the covenantal claim of receiving and believing that the Prologue introduces. In essence, the new covenant gives the power to become children of God through receiving the gift of truth as revealed by Jesus Christ the only Son who is in perfect relationship with God the Father.

THE BEGINNING OF THE WORD: NARRATIVE THROUGH PROLOGUE IN THE GOSPEL OF JOHN

Raymond Brown suggests that the Fourth Gospel is "a gospel of encounters."[36] Characters "one after another" make "their entrance onto the Johannine stage to encounter Jesus, the light come into the world" and in so doing they judge themselves "by whether or not they continue to come to the light or turn away and prefer darkness."[37] John sets forth this nature of Jesus and his mission in the Prologue and witnessed by John the Baptist, who crosses from the Prologue into the narrative body of the Gospel. The dialectic sparked by the word of Jesus creates dramatic dialogical interactions that actively move his story to its fulfillment on the cross. The evangelist also provides a guide for audiences as they, too, journey toward the cross and beyond. The opening verses of the Gospel further share that Jesus gives power to those who receive and believe in him to become children of God (1:11–13). Believing thus becomes the fundamental commandment by which Jesus calls people to live. Jesus then goes on to teach, however, that this believing must not be based on signs alone but must be founded in the word of Jesus—both his being as the Word of God and the words of his teaching. Further, "belief" as a noun (*pistis*) does not occur in the Gospel, but forms of the verb "to believe" (*pisteuein*) occur regularly and often (98 times). Thus, faith in the Gospel of John is always an action and is rightly described in terms of a process, or better, a journey. Jesus facilitates these journeys of believing in those he encounters across his ministry. The body of the Gospel narrative ends as John tells his audience that this Gospel was written so that they may *go on believing* (20:30–31). This also becomes the summons to all who read the Gospel across the ages: to believe in the word of Jesus, Christ and Son of God, through John's story in the Gospel.

The Prologue to the Gospel of John is one of the most famous texts of the NT. It is poetic and beautiful, even while it is enigmatic and provocative. As a prologue, it sets the stage for all that is to come, introducing key characters (God, Jesus the Christ and Word of God, John the Baptist who witnesses to Jesus, the world, and Jesus's own people, the Jews) and key themes (word, life, light, dark, truth, knowledge, family, glory, and the revelation of God) of the Gospel. As such, it is indispensable information for audiences who launch into the body of the narrative. The chiastic structure of the Prologue further points toward the mission of the Word made human in this world and the hope of the new activity of God in truth: that everyone who encounters the Word may receive and believe in him, thus becoming the new children of God in the family formed by Jesus, the Christ and Son of God. Therefore, it is available to anyone and everyone, regardless of race, gender, or ethnicity. All humankind has to do is receive him and believe in his word (1:12).

NOTES

1. Charles Giblin, "Confrontations in John 18,1–27," *Bib* 65 (1984): 215.

2. Jo-Ann A. Brant, *Dialogue and Drama: Elements of Greek Tragedy in the Fourth Gospel* (Peabody, MA: Hendrickson, 2004), 16.

3. "Showing" and "telling" are the means by which narratives reveal character. See Wayne Booth, *The Rhetoric of Fiction*. 2nd ed. (Chicago: University of Chicago Press, 1983), 3–9. Tom Thatcher elaborates: "'Telling' occurs when the narrator makes direct evaluative statements or gives information not normally available in the readers' experience. 'Showing' occurs when the narrator offers selective information about the actions of the characters and allows readers to draw conclusions from them. By combining 'telling' and 'showing' the author enables readers to develop 'both intrinsic and contextual knowledge' of the characters"; ("Jesus, Judas, and Peter: Character by Contrast in the Fourth Gospel," *BSac* 153 [1996]: 435–48, here 435). See also W. J. Harvey, *Character and the Novel* (Ithaca: Cornell University Press, 1965), 32.

4. Robert Alter argues that highly structured epic poetry was the accepted oral and literary expression of polytheistic religions (think of the Greek poet Homer and his epic poems, the *Iliad* and the *Odyssey*, that tell of the history and religion of the Greek Empire). Therefore, that so many biblical authors from Judaism and developing Christianity chose to use prose narrative to tell their stories is a conscious break from that custom in an effort to say something different (*The Art of Biblical Narrative* [New York: Basic Books, 1981], 3–46, esp. 23–26). He is building upon Shemaryahu Talmon, "The 'Comparative Method' in Biblical Interpretation—Principles and Problems," *Congress Volume: Göttingen, 1977*, VTSup 29 (Leiden: Brill, 1978): 354.

5. Just think if Nicodemus (3:1–21; 7:45–52; 19:38–42), among many others, Jewish leaders and regular people alike, would have known the Prologue! Their decisions about Jesus could have been very different along the way.

6. Brant, *Dialogue and Drama*, 17–26.

7. Brant, *Dialogue and Drama*, 18; Mark Stibbe, *John as Storyteller: Narrative Criticism and the Fourth Gospel*, SNTSMS 73 (Cambridge: Cambridge University Press, 1992), 36–37.

8. Brant, *Dialogue and Drama*, 22.

9. Brant, *Dialogue and Drama*, 24–25.

10. "Transcendental and earthly beginnings, this double gesture of centering and decentering . . . creates the central predicament for the subsequent narrative," Werner Kelber, "The Birth of a Beginning: John 1:1–18," *Sem* 52 (1990): 121.

11. Morna Hooker, *Beginnings: Keys That Open the Gospels* (Harrisburg, PA: Trinity Press International, 1997), xiii. For the Prologue as the key to this Gospel, see 64–83.

12. R. Alan Culpepper, "The Pivot of John's Prologue," *NTS* 27 (1980): 1–31. D. A. Carson concurs that this is the most persuasive structure presented to date; *The Gospel according to John* (Grand Rapids: Eerdmans, 1991), 13. See also Culpepper's more recent work on the Prologue in "The Prologue as Theological Prolegomenon to the Gospel of John" in *The Prologue of the Gospel of John*, ed. Jan G. van der Watt, R. Alan Culpepper, and Udo Schnelle, WUNT 359 (Tübingen: Mohr Siebeck, 2016), 3–26, and the creation ethics of the Gospel founded therein in "The Creation Ethics of the Gospel of John," in *Johannine Ethics. The Moral World of the Gospel and Epistles of John*, ed. Sherri Brown and Christopher W. Skinner (Minneapolis: Fortress, 2017), 67–90. For other recent scholarship, see Charles Giblin, "Two Complementary Literary Structures in John 1:1–18," *JBL* 104 (1985): 87–103; Jean Irigoin, "La composition rythmique du prologue de Jean (I, 1–18)," *RB* 98 (1991): 5–50.

13. Culpepper's analysis is based upon (1) language; (2) conceptual parallels; and (3) content ("Pivot," 8–17).

14. This diagram presents Culpepper's structure with my titles to punctuate the flow and development of each element. For detail, see Sherri Brown and Francis J. Moloney, *Interpreting the Gospel and Letters of John: An Introduction* (Grand Rapids: Eerdmans, 2017), 163–77.

15. For the Prologue as a targumic exposition of Gen. 1:1–5, see Peder Borgen, "Observations on the Targumic Character of the Prologue of John," *NTS* 16 (1970): 288–95; Borgen, "Logos Was the True Light: Contributions to the Interpretation of the Prologue of John," *NovT* 14 (1972): 115–30. Similarly, see Daniel Boyarin, "The Gospel of the *Memra*: Jewish Binitarianism and the Prologue to John," *HTR* 94 (2001): 243–84, esp. 267.

16. *Logos* terminology has roots in the Jewish wisdom tradition as well as the Greek philosophical tradition; see Thomas Tobin, "The Prologue of John and Hellenistic Jewish Speculation," *CBQ* 52 (1990): 252–69. Derek Tovey suggests the *logos* functions as a "character-substitute" that prompts readers to wonder about the identity of this mysterious figure. The audience thus becomes determinative of the formative background of the *logos* concept; "Narrative Strategies in the Prologue and the Metaphor of ὁ λόγος in John's Gospel," *Pacifica* 15 (2002): 141.

17. Boyarin, "Gospel of the *Memra*," 255–59; Martin McNamara, "*Logos* of the Fourth Gospel and *Memra* of the Palestinian Targum: Ex 12:42," *ExpTim* 79 (1968): 115–17.

18. These verses, with their counterpart in v. 15, interject striking prose into the fluid hymn-like poetry of the rest of the Prologue, leading to the argument that they are interpolations to the *Vorlage* of the Prologue. John A. T. Robinson, for example,

refers to these verses as "rude interruptions" in "The Relation of the Prologue to the Gospel of John," *NTS* 9 (1963): 120–29. For the argument that these verses are an integral connection to the body of the narrative to follow, see Morna Hooker, "John the Baptist and the Johannine Prologue," *NTS* 16 (1970): 354–58. Culpepper concurs with Hooker and argues that the double articulation of John and his role is further evidence of the chiastic presentation of the Prologue ("Pivot," 12–13).

19. Culpepper, "Pivot," 15–17. The balance of the three phrases of v. 12 is lost in some English translations. The RSV, NRSV, and NIV, for example, present v. 12c in apposition to v. 12a and thus directly following it, reading v. 12acb: "But to all who received him, who believed in this name, he gave power to become children of God." By contrast, the evangelist's syntax allows the central assertion of the Word's giving action to be framed by the introduction (v. 12a) and description (v. 12c) of potential recipients of the gift of the Word. These corresponding phrases thus hinge the core assertion (v. 12b) which is the crux of the Prologue's message to audiences.

20. Ernst Käsemann also identifies this climax: "Verse 12 specifies the gift which is his to bestow and the goal of his redeeming effectiveness" ("The Structure and Purpose of the Prologue to John's Gospel," in *New Testament Questions of Today* [London: SCM, 1969], 151–52).

21. For correlation of these phrases (not identified as a chiasm), see Raymond E. Brown, *The Gospel according to John I–XII*, AB 29 (New York: Doubleday, 1966), 10.

22. The correspondence of receiving the Word to becoming children of God also suggests "while Israel, which had been given the Torah, nevertheless rejected the Logos, some others, not necessarily Israel by virtue of flesh-and-blood parentage, became children of God" by receiving the Logos (Boyarin, "Gospel of the *Memra*," 278). See also Charles H. Dodd, *The Interpretation of the Fourth Gospel* (Cambridge: Cambridge University Press, 1960), 271.

23. Carson, *John*, 126; Brown, *John*, 11; Frank Kermode, "St John as Poet," *JSNT* 9 (1986): 10.

24. John Pryor, "Covenant and Community in John's Gospel," *RTR* 47 (1988): 48. Heritage and ethnic identity have become irrelevant to birth from God.

25. This inclusive narration also draws the reader into the potentiality of becoming part of that group; see Clayton R. Bowen, "Notes on the Fourth Gospel," *JBL* 43 (1924): 22.

26. Brown, *John*, 34. Morna Hooker reads all of John 1:14–18 as midrash on Exod 33–34; "Johannine Prologue and the Messianic Secret," *NTS* 21 (1974): 40–58; esp. 53–56.

27. Brant, *Dialogue and Drama*, 19.

28. Brant, *Dialogue and Drama*, 19; Elizabeth Harris, *Prologue and Gospel: The Theology of the Fourth Gospel*, JSNTSup 107 (Sheffield: Sheffield Academic, 1994), 45.

29. Raymond Brown argues it evokes OT covenant love (Exod 34:6; *John*, 14). See also Andrew T, Lincoln, *The Gospel according to Saint John*, BNTC 4 (London: Continuum, 2005), 105.

30. Francis J. Moloney, *The Gospel of John*, SP 4 (Collegeville, MN: Liturgical Press, 1998), 45; *LSJ*, s.v. *cháris*; BDF §442.9, 16.

31. Andrew Osborn asserts that the NT use of the word means more than truth in utterance: "It refers to that truth in character which not only leads to truth in speech, but manifests integrity in action, together with a firm belief in that which is real and true as opposed to vanity and hypocrisy" ("The Word Became Flesh: An Exposition of John 1:1–18," *Int* 3 [1949]: 46). In OT terms, this also encompasses the relationship with God in covenantal obedience.

32. Jeffrey Staley, "The Structure of John's Prologue: Its Implications for the Gospel's Narrative Structure," *CBQ* 48 (1986): 252.

33. Alter, *Art of Biblical Narrative*, 182. Jo-Ann A. Brant (*Dialogue and Drama*, 77–78) would refer to this as *Redundant Narration*, a technique whereby the narrator uses language that refers to objects, time, and place, that is then also used by the characters in dialogue (usually verbatim). This technique confirms the veracity or integrity of those characters.

34. I continue following Moloney for the rendering of *charis* (*John*, 46). The preposition *anti* is translated *upon* to render the superabundance of grace, though this is questioned. For detail, see Ruth B. Edwards, "*Charin anti charitos* (John 1.16): Grace and Law in the Johannine Prologue," *JSNT* 10 (1988): 3–15. I retain the English *upon* to include the full range of meaning, since *anti* could denote "instead of," "for," or "on behalf of" in addition to the stricter "instead of" (BDAG, s.v. *anti*); and to avoid reference to replacement or supersessionism, a tragic misreading of the Fourth Gospel. As Boyarin asserts, "Jesus comes to fulfill the mission of Moses, not to displace it" ("Gospel of the *Memra*," 280). See the evidence in John Suggit, "John XVII.17: Ο ΛΟΓΟΣ Ο ΣΟΣ ΑΛΗΘΕΙΑ ΕΣΤΙΝ," *JTS* 35 (1984): 104–17.

35. Francis J. Moloney, "John 1:18 'in the Bosom of' or 'Turned Towards' the Father," *ABR* 31 (1983): 63–71.

36. Raymond E. Brown, "The Resurrection in John 20: A Series of Diverse Reactions," *Worship* 64 (1990): 194.

37. Brown, "Resurrection," 194.

Chapter 2

John 1 Beyond the Binary

Lindsey S. Jodrey

John's Prologue tells a cosmic tale of God's creative work by which the world came into being and God's revelatory work through the Word. The major point of conflict in the story is that the "darkness" is opposed to the "light" of God's revelation. John 1:5 reads, "The light shines in the darkness, and the darkness did not overcome it."[1] *Katalambanō*, here translated as "overcome," can refer to the physical realm, indicating that one person or entity obtains or overpowers another. But the verb can also refer to the cognitive realm, indicating that one person or entity understands or comprehends another. As elsewhere in this Gospel, a double meaning may be at work: the "darkness" does not understand the "light," but neither will the darkness win out.

The story hinges on a dualistic presentation of these two opposing forces, meaning that it presents darkness and light as separate spheres that frame existence in terms of divided and conflicting categories.[2] At first glance, the Gospel of John seems to affirm this dualistic perspective. For example, the light is set against the darkness (1:5), and the world above is altogether separate from the earthly world (3:3, 7, 31; 8:23; 17:16; 18:36). These categories also appear to establish divisions within and for the community: members of the "in group" who are from above and in the light and members of the "out group" who are not (1:5; 8:47; 14:17; 15:18–19; 17:14, 16). An interested reader of John's Prologue may notice this dualistic language and wonder how it functions within the story.

QUEERING THE APPROACH

In this chapter, I take up a sociocultural approach to this question. A sociocultural approach values the diverse social locations of readers and invites readers to bring their embodied experiences with them as they engage texts.[3] For my reading of John's Prologue, I intentionally allow my social location as a queer person to influence how I explore the biblical text. Anyone can put the lens of queer theory to work in reading the Bible. Those of us who have practice pushing against the boundaries imposed on various facets of our lived experiences and identities can bring that experience with us as we push against the boundaries of biblical scholarship.

Queer theory is inherently difficult to define, and purposefully so. The term *queer*, which more generally refers to something outside of the norm, has been used as a derogatory term to identify "homosexual" or effeminate men since the 1920s. This use of the term is based on the cultural construction of "heterosexuality" as the only valid sexual orientation and the subsequent construction of "homosexuality" as pathological—that is, deviant in a way that is harmful to self or society. This viewpoint, often called *heteronormativity*, also assumes a binary model of gender. In a binary model, gender is classified in two opposite and distinct forms: masculine and feminine. These gender classifications are then assumed to match one's genetic or biological sex—male or female—which is usually assigned at birth based on anatomical characteristics. Heteronormativity is the belief that a person's genetic sex determines (or should determine) many other facets of their life and being, including their behavior, appearance, and sexual orientation toward people classified as the opposite gender.[4] More recently, those who describe themselves as lesbian, gay, bisexual, transgender, queer, intersex, or asexual (LGBTQIA) have appropriated the term "queer" as a collective descriptor for the community of people whose gender identities or sexual orientations challenge the assumptions of heteronormativity.

On the heels of the Gay Liberation movement that was unfolding on the social landscape in the 1960s and 1970s, Lesbian and Gay Studies emerged in the academy to elevate the perspectives of those with "non-heterosexual" identities and to argue for the validity of these identities. Queer theory takes a different approach. Rather than arguing that gay, lesbian, or other identities are just as valid as "heterosexual" identities, queer theory questions the validity of the identity categories themselves. The term "queer theory" was designed to disrupt the field of Lesbian and Gay Studies. It was first used as the title of an academic conference hosted by Teresa de Lauretis at the University of California, Santa Cruz, in 1990. De Lauretis intended the term to be provocative; she was making a statement about the academy itself.[5] As she conceived of it, queer theory critiques several problematic elements of academic theory. Queer theory challenges purely theoretical ways of knowing, recognizing that theory is particularly problematic when it defines and controls elements of embodied existence like gender and sexuality. Queer theory also challenges the heterosexist assumptions that lie at the foundation of much of academic theory. It uses the tools of critical theory to push against the academic discourse that pretends to be disembodied while elevating some bodies as normative. Queer theory also refuses to remain in the theoretical realm, instead insisting that theory must be connected to the lived realities and experiences of people previously labeled as outside the lines.

The academy seemed to miss the irony and made queer theory a critical field of study almost immediately, bringing what was intended to be a subversive way of thinking under the domain of the very schools of thought it sought to resist. To call it "queer theory" was to approve queer ways of thinking. And so, in some ways, the potential of queer theory is limited by its existence as an academic discipline. Some prefer to talk about "queering" or "queer commentary," since these terms suggest an active and dynamic way of interpreting rather than a fixed "theory."[6] A queer reading, then, is an approach that uses a variety of methods in order to take up a new vantage point for old questions. Particularly, queer approaches are helpful when the discourse concerning a certain question has been problematically constructed upon the acceptance of false binaries. Queer approaches often push against discourses surrounding gender and sexuality, since these conversations often assume that straight and gay are two opposing categories, one normal and "good," the other deviant and "bad." Queer approaches question existing assumptions and trouble existing categories, and they often look for movement, tension, and fluidity where the discourse might be bound to static answers and polarized positions.

So why take a queer approach to John 1? Although John's Prologue does not explicitly deal with issues of sexuality, its dualistic language seems to affirm a worldview built on the foundation of binary categories. The binary finds explicit expression in the metaphor of light versus darkness (1:5). This metaphor is linked to a worldview that affirms two opposing realms. The Prologue begins in the divine realm, outside of time, where the Word (who is divine) creates a second realm, "the world." Although the world was created by God, the Prologue describes the world as separate from God, not knowing or accepting the Word (1:10–11). What is interesting for this queer reading is that this constructed worldview has implications for identity. It categorizes people into "insiders" or "outsiders," and draws a sharp dividing line between the two. This chapter will "queer" the discourse surrounding John's dualism by pushing against these categories and exploring how the dynamic function of the dualistic language is queer. I argue that John's Gospel does not affirm the dualistic categories it presupposes; rather, John's story queers the dualism of its conceptual world, presenting the "good news" that light shines into the darkness, breaking down the boundary between the divine realm and the "world" and disrupting the division between insiders and outsiders. In this queer reading, the forces of revelation, incarnation, and love trouble and transgress these dividing lines.

QUEERING THE PROLOGUE

The Prologue as Guide

When we think about John's Prologue, we might imagine a reader sitting down and opening their Bible to the first pages of the Fourth Gospel, but the vast majority of people in the ancient world were illiterate and would experience texts as hearers rather than readers.[7] Because of this, ancient rhetoricians understood structure to be one of the most important features of a text, and today's interpreters recognize that attention to structural elements is an important step in interpretation. Structure can illuminate the rhetorical situation, correct mistakes within the history of interpretation, and generally clarify meaning.[8] The beginning of a text is essential for an audience of hearers. It sets the stage for what is to come and gives the audience the ideological framework they need to understand the complexities and tensions that will arise in the rest of the story.[9] The Prologue, then, is an essential piece for any interpretive approach that looks for the underlying ideologies present in or provoked by a text.[10]

John's Prologue includes the first eighteen verses of the Gospel's first chapter. The Prologue poetically recounts the story of Jesus, the divine Word, who came down from his place with God to enlighten the world and offer life. Although rejected, he accomplished his mission to reveal God to the world. This poetic tale is then carried out in the story of Jesus, and many themes introduced in the Prologue can be traced throughout the Gospel. The Prologue reflects a dualistic philosophical framework that sees the world as divided into sets of binary categories—the world above versus the world below (8:23; 17:16; 18:36), light versus darkness (1:5, 9; 12:35–36). These images also demarcate an "in group" of those who are born from above or who are in the light and an "out group" of those born from below or who are in darkness.[11]

Much of the scholarship on Johannine dualism focuses on the origin or background of that framework—whether inherited from early Jewish apocalyptic thought, the Qumran community, or various elements of a Gnostic worldview that influenced early Judeo-Christian beliefs. Emphasis on the background of this dualistic language can lead readers to assume that the function of dualism in John mirrors the function of the dualism in other contexts. For example, one might see John reflecting the flesh-versus-spirit binary of Middle Platonism and later Gnostic thought, in which all things bodily are considered inherently evil and opposed to the spiritual "good." Or one might see John reflecting the ethical dualism of Qumran, which sees people divided into predetermined categories of insiders or outsiders.[12] As Jörg Frey has argued, however, John's dualistic motifs differ drastically from the strict dualism found in other literature of the time. Because of this, interested readers should consider the function of John's dualism on its own terms, rather than only comparing it to existing framework.[13] In the remainder of this chapter, I will articulate how John's story, when taken on its own terms, actually subverts the dualistic framework it seems to accept.

Revelation as Transgression

Although queer theory is difficult to define, there are several markers of "queerness" that describe it as a resistant way of being.[14] One such characteristic is *transgression*. While in religious circles, one might think of "transgression" as a "sin," the word comes from the Latin roots for "across" and "go" and is used to describe an action that crosses a line. In what sense is transgression a mark of queerness? As discussed above, "queer" became a slang descriptor for "homosexual" in the 1920s, used to mark those who didn't fit socially defined categories of gender or sexual orientation as "other," to devalue them as strange or out of bounds. Queer theorists, however, prefer to understand *queer* as a verb. To queer something is to challenge it. Rather than passively being deemed "out of bounds," the bodies and lived experiences of those deemed "queer" can oppose the very lines that have been drawn around them. The value of transgression invites queer people to question and challenge the lines drawn between "normal," which is deemed good, and "queer," which is deemed bad.

John's Prologue presents a dividing line between the divine realm and the "world." The divine realm is associated with God and the light; the world is associated with ignorance and darkness. The Prologue says that the world does not know the Word (1:10c), and the Gospel story goes on to show that the world hates Jesus because he testifies against it, that its works are evil (7:7). The world is the realm of the non-believing religious leaders as distinct from the heavenly realm of Jesus (8:23). The world is the realm in which judgment takes place (12:31). The world does not receive the Spirit of truth because it cannot see the truth (14:17–19). Just as the world hated Jesus, it will hate the disciples (15:18–19). Much of John's story describes the world in negative terms as the realm of human life that stands as the opposing counterpart to the divine realm, hostile to Jesus.

At the same time, the narrative movement of the Prologue transgresses this dividing line. Verses 1–4 contain nine verbs that indicate past action, including the Greek imperfect, aorist, and perfect tenses. But in v. 5, where the contrast between light and darkness is made explicit, the tense of the verb suddenly changes. Rather than using a tense that would indicate past or completed action, the author uses the present tense: "The light shines in the darkness." This move to the present tense happens again in v. 9: "The true light, which enlightens everyone, was coming into the world." The present tense calls attention to these two movements in which the Word transgresses the dividing line between the divine realm and the world. These movements are not "once upon a time." The use of the present tense in Greek describes an action that is ongoing and continuous. John does not present light and darkness as fixed opposites in a static state; rather, John uses the metaphor of light to present the Word as a revelatory force that actively and continuously breaks into the darkness.[15]

The incarnational movement of the Word radically challenges the line between the divine realm and the world.[16] The Word, called "the true light," embodies the divine realm. In the incarnation, the Word also embodies the human realm of the world: "And the Word became flesh and lived among us" (1:14a). The result is that those in the world now have a way to "see" or understand God. Through the powerful work of revelation, the Word has made God known. The queer work of the incarnate Word in John's Prologue is revelation, transgressing the dividing line between the divine realm and the world in order to make God known.[17]

Love as Resistance

One important element of queer theory is its link to the real, embodied experiences of people. With this value in mind, readers will notice that the world in John is not simply a "realm"; it is a group made up of people. Light and darkness are not merely theoretical "realms"; these categories describe and define people—those who are "in" and those who are "out." A second mark of queerness, *resistance*, can be helpful in describing how these categories of "insider" and "outsider" function in John's story.[18] The very term "queer" inherently challenges the stability of categories that are often assumed to be fixed or essential, including markers of identity. Much of the dualistic language in John mirrors that of highly sectarian groups (like the community at Qumran) who held to a strict boundary between those within the community and those outside of it.[19] For many of these groups, a member's status was predetermined and fixed. However, John's story insists that these two categories are not fixed and that one's status is not set. Rather, the transgressive work of the Word in bridging the gap between the divine realm and the world also has the effect of making the dividing line between insiders and outsiders permeable. In queering the divide between the divine realm and the world, the Word also queers the categories of insider and outsider.

If a reader looks beyond this allegedly binary opposition, they will notice that the Prologue first describes the world in positive terms, as the creation of God (1:10b), or at least in neutral terms, as the realm of human life or the realm into which Jesus is coming (7:4; 11:27; 12:19). It is true that the world is often characterized as hostile, but the world is also the object of God's work (3:16). The Prologue does not reinforce the dualism that paints a negative view of the world; rather, it tells the story of God's work to break down the dualism. As the Johannine Jesus explains, "I came not to judge the world, but to save the world" (12:47). Jesus prays for the world (17:20–21) and sends the disciples into the world so that the world may believe and no longer be separate from God (17:15–23).[20] Jesus was sent to enlighten the world (1:9), to take away the sin of the world (1:29), to give life to the world (3:16–17; 6:33, 51), to save the world (4:42; 12:47), and to invite the world to join in the love he shares with God (14:31; 17:23).

This range of meaning is not haphazard. It reveals a dynamic movement within the story of the Gospel, a rhetorical trajectory where the world that was positive in relation to God as God's creation becomes a hostile entity opposed to God when Jesus presents himself on earth and encounters rejection. But, as the Gospel shows, God works to break down the dualism presented by this opposition. The story insists on the flexibility of these identity categories and presents the opportunity for a person to leave the realm of outsiders to join the community.[21] This decision, in fact, is the purpose of the Gospel: "But these are written so that you may believe that Jesus is the Messiah, the Son of God, and that through believing you may have life in his name" (20:31). This dynamic opportunity is narrated throughout the story as people who encounter Jesus are invited to believe and move from the realm of darkness to the light.[22] This purpose was also announced in the Prologue: "But to all who received him, who believed in his name, he gave power to become children of God" (1:12). It is divine love for the world that drives God's work in the Gospel (3:16; 13:1; 15:13; 17:23, 26). The queer work of God in the Gospel is resistance, divine love pushing against the binary categories of insiders and outsiders.

QUEERING BIBLICAL INTERPRETATION

This chapter is an example of queer biblical interpretation in three ways. First, it is queer because it features the interpretive perspective of a person who identifies as queer.[23] Second, it is queer because it uses queer theory to engage the academic discourse around the function of John's dualistic language. Third, this chapter is queer because it pushes against convention, examining a biblical text that does not deal explicitly with gender or sexuality. As Teresa Hornsby and Ken Stone demonstrate in their important volume *Bible Trouble*, "Queer reading does not just spell 'trouble' for gender and sexuality. It also 'troubles' the norms of biblical scholarship."[24] This queer reading shifts the discourse from asking what the Bible has to say about human sexuality to asking how queerness, in terms of identity and critical theory, might inform biblical interpretation.

In this chapter, I bring my experiences as a queer reader and as a critical reader interested in the rhetorical function of texts to my exploration of John's Prologue. As a queer reader, I am constantly aware of socially constructed categories and consistently reminded how important it is to question these categories. As a critical reader interested in the rhetorical force of texts, I am constantly curious about what the text is *doing*. My curiosity led me to employ queer theory to consider the rhetorical function of John's dualistic language. The queer values of transgression and resistance emerged as helpful tools for my reading, suggesting that John's story does not affirm the dualistic categories it presupposes. The Fourth Gospel queers the dualism of its conceptual world, presenting the good news that the queer force of revelation transgresses the boundary between the divine realm and the world, and the queer force of divine love resists the division between insiders and outsiders. More than a "queer approach" to John's Prologue, this chapter notices and elevates the queer dynamics ever-present in John's Gospel story.

NOTES

1. All translations are from the NRSV unless otherwise noted.

2. Defining "dualism" in a technical sense within philosophy or the history of religions is too large a task for this chapter. The dualistic language in John does not present a true binary as in the radical dualism that sees two forces as coequal and coeternal. John's dualistic language is diverse. It resembles different types of dualism at various points. What is important for this chapter is that the dualistic language seems to present fixed categories that are defined in opposition to one another. At times John's dualistic language resembles cosmic dualism (which presents the categories of good/evil, light/darkness), spatial dualism (above/below, heaven/earth) and theological dualism (divine/human). See Stephen C. Barton, "Johannine Dualism and Contemporary Pluralism," in *The Gospel of John and Christian Theology*, ed. Richard Bauckham and Carl Mosser (Grand Rapids: Eerdmans, 2008), 7–8.

3. George Aichele et al., *The Postmodern Bible* (New Haven: Yale University Press, 1995), 15.

4. For more, see Michel Foucault, *The History of Sexuality: An Introduction*, trans. Robert Hurley (New York: Vintage Books, 1978). See also Sean Burke, *Queering the Ethiopian Eunuch: Strategies of Ambiguity in Acts 8* (Minneapolis: Augsburg Fortress, 2013), 39–40.

5. David M. Halperin, "The Normalization of Queer Theory," *Journal of Homosexuality* 45 (2003): 340.

6. Burke, *Queering the Ethiopian Eunuch*, 42. See also Judith Butler, *Bodies that Matter: On the Discursive Limits of "Sex"* (New York: Routledge, 1993), 228; Ian Barnard, *Queer Race: Cultural Interventions in the Racial Politics of Queer Theory*, Gender, Sexuality, and Culture 3 (New York: Lang, 2004), 10–14.

7. For more on the oral/aural context of biblical texts, see Richard A. Horsley, *Hearing the Whole Story: The Politics of Plot in Mark's Gospel* (Louisville: Westminster John Knox, 2001), 7, 70; and Bruce W. Longenecker, *Rhetoric at the Boundaries: The Art and Theology of New Testament Chain-Link Transitions* (Waco, TX: Baylor University Press, 2005), 49–55.

8. See Quintilian's *Inst.* 11.2.34–38. For more on this topic, see Michael R. Whitenton, *Hearing Kyriotic Sonship: A Cognitive and Rhetorical Approach to the Characterization of Mark's Jesus*, BibS 148 (Leiden: Brill, 2017).

9. Gérard Genette, *Paratexts: Thresholds of Interpretation* (Cambridge: Cambridge University Press, 1997), 197; see 161. See also Mikeal C. Parsons, "Reading a Beginning/Beginning a Reading: Tracing Literary Theory on Narrative Openings," *Sem* 52 (1990): 11–31 and the important contributions by Tannehill and Struthers Malbon in that volume.

10. See, for example, the chapters by Sherri Brown and Jo-Ann A. Brant in this volume.

11. See also John 3:18–21, 36; 5:24, 29; 8:23–24, 47; 12:35–36; 14:17; 15:19; 17:9, 14, 16, 25.

12. Raymond E. Brown, "The Qumran Scrolls and the Johannine Gospel and Epistles," in *The Scrolls and the New Testament*, ed. Krister Stendahl (New York: Harper & Brothers, 1957), 190; Barton, "Johannine Dualism and Contemporary Pluralism," 13.

13. Jörg Frey, "Johannine Dualism: Reflections on Its Background and Function," in *The Glory of the Crucified One: Christology and Theology in the Gospel of John*, trans. Wayne Coppins and Christoph Heilig, Baylor-Mohr Siebeck Studies in Early Christianity 6 (Waco, TX: Baylor University Press, 2018), 101–67.

14. Patrick S. Cheng, "Contributions from Queer Theory," in *The Oxford Handbook of Theology, Sexuality, and Gender*, ed. Adrian Thatcher (Oxford: Oxford University Press, 2015), 154–59. In addition to the two discussed here, Cheng mentions social construction and identity without essence as markers of queerness.

15. Harold W. Attridge, "The Gospel of John and the Dead Sea Scrolls," in *Text, Thought, and Practice in Qumran and Early Christianity: Proceedings of the Ninth International Symposium of the Orion Center for the Study of the Dead Sea Scrolls and Associated Literature*, ed. Ruth Clements and Daniel R. Schwartz, STDJ 84 (Leiden: Brill, 2009), 116–17.

16. Barton, "Johannine Dualism," 13–15.

17. Others have also noticed this dynamic in John. Barton calls it a "deconstruction of dualism" (Barton, "Johannine Dualism," 15). See also Barton's references to similar descriptions by Charlesworth and Barrett. Other authors consider the rhetorical function of certain features that cut against John's dualism. For example, Colleen

Conway considers how characterization is gendered in John's Gospel, noting that female characters present an ambiguity that confounds strict divisions of belief and unbelief. Colleen M. Conway, *Men and Women in the Fourth Gospel: Gender and Johannine Characterization*, SBLDS 167 (Atlanta: SBL Press, 1999). Susan Hylen considers ambiguous characters who resist classification and demonstrate fluidity that challenges fixed categories like "believer" or "unbeliever." Susan Hylen, *Imperfect Believers: Ambiguous Characters in the Gospel of John* (Louisville: Westminster John Knox, 2009). This chapter uniquely uses the language of queer theory to articulate the rhetorical function of John's dualistic language.

18. Cheng, "Contributions from Queer Theory," 157–58, goes further, describing this marker as "resistance to binaries." In the realm of sexuality and gender, the binary distinctions (male/female, heterosexual/homosexual) are very clear. Once one leaves the realm of sexuality, it can be helpful to broaden the scope of resistance beyond strict binary opposites to include any categorical structure that leaves no room for ambiguity, flexibility, or movement between two sides.

19. See Jaime Clark-Soles, *Scripture Cannot Be Broken: The Social Function of the Use of Scripture in the Fourth Gospel* (Boston/Leiden: Brill, 2003).

20. Kobus Kok, "As the Father Has Sent Me, I Send You: Towards a Missional-Incarnational Ethos in John 4," in *Moral Language in the New Testament: The Interrelatedness of Language and Ethics in Early Christian Writings*, ed. Ruben Zimmermann and Jan G. van der Watt, with Susanne Luther, WUNT 2/296 (Tübingen: Mohr Siebeck, 2010), 168–93.

21. See John 6:37–45; 12:32. Brown, "Qumran Scrolls and the Johannine Gospel and Epistles," 191.

22. See John 12:46; see also 3:16, 36; 5:24; 6:35; 8:12. So argues Charlesworth, "A Critical Comparison of the Dualism in 1QS 3:13–4:26 and the 'Dualism' Contained in the Gospel of John," in *John and the Dead Sea Scrolls*, ed. James H. Charlesworth (New York: Crossroad, 1990), 95.

23. Cheng, "Contributions from Queer Theory," 159.

24. Teresa J. Hornsby and Ken Stone, eds., *Bible Trouble: Queer Reading at the Boundaries of Biblical Scholarship* (Atlanta: SBL Press, 2011), x.

Chapter 3

Revealing the Fuller Word*

Craig S. Keener

One could illustrate the value of intertextuality for John's Prologue in a number of ways, even if we limit discussion to texts directly relevant to John's own milieu. Given the limitations of space, I focus on two related intertextual issues here: a broader one, concerning John's background for the Logos, or "Word," and specific reference to a biblical passage that John 1:14–18 evokes.

These intertextual issues are closely related in the Prologue's climax: God revealed God's character in a limited manner in the first giving of the Law at Sinai, but God reveals God's character now most fully in the enfleshed Word, especially as glorified in the cross. Thus, for John, the grace and truth present in a less visible way at the giving of the Law climax fully in the Word's incarnate ministry and ultimately death. In addition to primary references from antiquity, I draw where possible on older, classical Johannine scholarship[1] to illustrate the wide and long-term character of the observations I offer here, though here, as elsewhere in scholarship, consensus remains elusive. (Scholars commonly draw on Wisdom as a background for John's Prologue, but less often on Torah.)

JEWISH CONTEXTS FOR JOHN'S LOGOS

Hellenistic philosophy likely does provide some of the context for how a Diaspora audience could have appropriated John's Logos.[2] Although John writes with less metaphysical concerns and on a much less elite intellectual

---

* Chapter 3 contains material from Craig S. Keener, *The Gospel of John: A Commentary* (Grand Rapids: Baker Academic, 2003). Used by permission of the publisher.

level than Philo, one need look no further than Philo to imagine how authors could reenvision the Jewish conception of divine Wisdom in terms of Logos for a Hellenistic audience.[3] Philo influenced and especially reflected the Diaspora Jewish milieu where John's Gospel was published. Philo's Logos and the synthesis that it reflects warrant more extensive treatment than is possible in this chapter.[4] Suffice it to say here that the early Christian movement, like its Jewish contemporaries, often communicated earlier Jewish conceptions in imagery intelligible for a Diaspora audience. Given John's explicit reference to the OT (1:17) and Jesus's Jewish context (1:11), my focus here is on specifically Jewish intertexts, but these do not exclude Hellenistic associations for John's Diaspora audience.

Personifications and even hypostatizations of Wisdom and the Word circulated before direct Hellenistic influence.[5] Not all proposed Jewish influences are equally relevant for John. For example, some scholars have long suggested that the targumic circumlocution of Memra influenced John's imagery;[6] but given its limitation to Targumim, which are later in date, this connection is highly unlikely.[7] Instead, even though OT depictions of the Word do not fully explain John's Prologue, OT personifications of the Word or expressions of its activity in creation provide a helpful backdrop. Some ancient Israelite texts could easily be understood as identifying the divine word in creation with the divine word of Scripture (Ps. 33:4, 6, 9, 11). First Enoch 14:24, from the second century B.C.E., might personify the Word. A clearer passage appears in the Hellenistic Jewish work Wis. 18:15: God's all-powerful Logos comes down from heaven to slay the firstborn immediately before the exodus.[8] More fully, observers have long noted that almost everything John says about the Logos—apart from its incarnation as a particular historical person—Jewish literature already affirmed concerning divine Wisdom.[9] Wisdom, which came from God's mouth, could be identified with the Word (Sir. 24:3; Wis. 9:1–2).

Wisdom usually functions as mere personification rather than as a person (e.g., Prov. 8:1–36; Sir. 15:2). In some texts, however, it may assume hypostatic form, especially in the widely used works of Ben Sira (Sir. 1; 24) and Wisdom of Solomon (Wis. 9:4). Wisdom descended from heaven (Bar. 3:29–30; see John 3:13), is a special object of God's love (Wis. 8:3; see John 3:35; 5:20), and sits by God's throne (Wis. 9:4; see Rev. 3:21; 5:6). Those who proclaimed Jesus used Wisdom and Logos Christology long before John's Gospel (see, for example, 1 Cor. 1:24, 30; 8:6; 2 Cor. 4:4; Col. 1:15; Heb. 1:1–3).[10] Given John's comparison of Jesus with Moses and the Law in John 1:17, one connection particularly relevant to John's Prologue is the ancient Jewish connection between divine Wisdom and Torah (Sir. 15:1; 19:20; 39:1); some passages even seem to identify the two (24:23; 34:8; 39:1). The identification is clearer in Bar. 3:29–4:1 and in the philosophically informed 4 Macc. 1:16–17, and apparently flowered in the Torah-centric later rabbis.[11]

Eldon Jay Epp has meticulously documented the coalescing of the attributes of Torah and Wisdom in Jewish literature.[12] Although most of his sources for the Torah come from later, rabbinic sources, the earlier sources illustrate the antiquity of the general identification, and rabbinic sources naturally dominate because of their focus on Torah. Thus Wisdom and Torah are both preexistent; both Wisdom and Torah are related to God in a unique way; both Wisdom and Torah played a significant role in creation; both Wisdom and Torah are eternal; both Wisdom and Torah are related to life, light, and salvation; both Wisdom and Torah appear in the world or among people; both Wisdom (Prov. 8:6–8) and Torah are associated with truth; and both Wisdom and Torah are associated with glory. The cumulative force of such parallels suggests that sages assimilated Wisdom and Torah.

By the second century and probably earlier, rabbis personified the Torah, largely replacing personified Wisdom.[13] Early Christians could also mine texts about the Law going forth again, only this time from Zion rather than from Sinai (Isa. 2:2–4). In the context of a new exodus, God likewise would inaugurate a new covenant, writing God's Laws on the hearts of God's people so they would break them no longer (Jer. 31:31–34; Ezek. 36:27). John's Jewish audience would, therefore, be at least somewhat familiar with such an image. An image that draws on connotations of Wisdom, the Word, and Torah allows him to communicate his conception of the divine, eternal revelation of the Father, but it is ultimately Jesus's identity as a human being (1:14) that concretizes the abstract personification as a person in history.

JOHN AND THE FINAL WORD?

As noted above, echoes of Wisdom and Torah language recur throughout the Prologue. "In the beginning" in John 1:1 clearly evokes Genesis 1; less clearly, some also suggest an echo of the traditional gospel account (see Mark 1:1; Matt. 1:1). It is possible, however, that John might also play on fuller nuances in postbiblical Wisdom language since early Jewish wisdom texts recognized the preexistence of Wisdom and the Word or the Torah. Jewish sources sometimes call the Logos and, eventually, Torah, "the beginning." Jesus's special relationship with the Father in John 1:1b–2 (see, for example, 8:29, 35–38) may resemble an image relevant to (though not necessarily derived from) Wisdom (Wis. 8:3; 9:9).[14] More clearly, Wisdom is also involved in creation, as in John 1:3. Jewish people often attributed creation to Wisdom (e.g., Wis. 7:22; Sir. 24:3–12; *2 En.* 30:8; 33:3; t. Sanh. 8:9) and to Torah (m. Avot 3:14; Sipre Deut. 48.7.1.). In Philo, God formed the universe through the Logos (*Creation* 20, 26, 31; *Migr.* 6.); God made the world as a copy of the divine image, the Logos being the archetypal seal imprinted on them (*Creation* 16, 26, 36).

Even earlier than Philo, Judean thinkers saw God's prior design for creation rooted in knowledge or wisdom.[15] According to Genesis 1, God spoke the world into being, and John's contemporaries continued to celebrate this OT pattern.[16] For example, one second-century rabbinic title for God was "the One who spoke and summoned the universe into being."[17] Other texts directly connect creation by God's word with creation by divine wisdom (Wis. 9:1–3) or Torah.[18] Moreover, pre-Johannine Christians already understood Jesus as the agent of creation (1 Cor. 8:5–6; Col. 1:15–17), sometimes in language quite similar to Logos or Wisdom traditions.

Some Jewish people spoke of Wisdom's rejection on earth (*1 En.* 42:1–3), just as the world rejects Jesus in John 1:10. God provides the light for all humanity in Jesus's incarnation (1:9), just as in Jewish tradition God provided the light of Torah to all nations at Sinai.[19] Just as the nations rejected Torah, however, so the world rejects the Word made flesh (1:10). But whereas in this line of Jewish tradition Israel alone among the nations accepted Torah,[20] here even the Word's own people reject him (1:11). That God's chosen people who celebrated Torah rejected Torah in flesh constitutes a "foundational irony of the gospel . . . at the outset."[21]

JOHN'S LOGOS AS TORAH

Some scholars suggest that John, playing on the link between Torah and Wisdom, presents the Logos of its Prologue as Torah.[22] Such a link helps to explain the climax of the Prologue in 1:17–18. According to the most common reconstructions, John's primary audience consists of predominantly Jewish Jesus-followers who had been rejected by non-Christian Jewish communities for their faith in Jesus.[23] Some synagogue leaders may have charged them with the sorts of offenses that surface in the writings of second-century rabbis: they believe that the charismatic, messianic Jesus movement has departed from proper understanding of the Torah (particularly from strict monotheism).[24]

John responds that not only does following Jesus entail true observance of Torah, but also that Jesus himself is God's Word. Now that the fullest revelation of the Word has come, therefore, no one can genuinely follow God's message revealed in the Torah without following Jesus. Jewish language about divine mediation through Wisdom, Torah, and God's Word provides John a culturally intelligible (albeit limited) means to communicate Jesus's divine character, supremacy, and perfect relationship to the Father while maintaining Jewish monotheism.

A neutral term like *logos* could draw on associations with personified Wisdom already offered in Hellenistic Judaism, without compromising its bridge to the Torah, which was even more explicitly recognized as God's Word.[25] John's choice of the Logos (embracing also Wisdom and Torah) to articulate his Christology was brilliant: no concept better articulated an entity that was both divine yet distinct from the Father. (That some Diaspora Jewish writers had already expressed these Jewish conceptions as Logos presumably further facilitated John's use of this designation.) Finally, by using this term, John could present Jesus as the epitome of what his community's critics claimed to value: God's word revealed through Moses. Jesus was thus the supreme revelation of God; the Torah had gone forth from Zion.

John, however, implies more than Jewish Wisdom or Torah language normally indicated in the various writings mentioned above. In contrast to the preexistent creation of Wisdom or Torah in most Jewish sources, John's affirmation that the Word "was" (rather than "became," as in 1:14) may imply its eternal preexistence.[26] Nevertheless, it was easier to stretch Wisdom or Logos language beyond its conventional usage than to try to communicate Jesus's identity without any recognizable precedent or cultural bridge. Paul had earlier used a similar point of contact in Col. 1:15–20 with Wisdom or Logos with terms like "image" and "firstborn."[27]

Thus, far from committing apostasy from Torah, John's ideal audience is faithful to the fullest embodiment and revelation of God's Word also found in Torah. As Rodney Whitacre shows, Jesus's opponents in the Fourth Gospel repeatedly claim loyalty to Moses and Torah. By contrast, the Gospel reverses their accusations, showing that Jesus, rather than his opponents, is faithful to the Law (see, for example, 5:39, 45; 7:19).[28] John has a very high view of Scripture (e.g., 10:35; 13:18; 17:12); "It is his opponents' use of it in their rejection of Jesus that he finds completely unacceptable."[29] As a fuller embodiment of divine revelation also found in Wisdom/Torah, Jesus is far greater than Moses, the mediator of Torah. Such a rhetorical and theological move is extraordinary. As W. D. Davies notes, "This personification of Torah in Christ goes beyond anything which we have found in the Jewish sources: there is no premonition of a Messiah becoming in himself the Torah."[30]

The final statements of John's Prologue (1:17–18), therefore, contrast Jesus as the enfleshed Logos with God's Word as Torah. The grace and truth present in the Law were more fully revealed in Jesus (1:17); the glory of the Law restrained for human weakness was now fully unveiled in Jesus of Nazareth (1:18). Some other commentators have also long noted that John's point in the Prologue is ultimately a direct comparison with Torah.[31] Verse 17, with its description that "the Law was given through Moses, grace and truth came through Jesus Christ," is not unnaturally abrupt, any more than the mention of Torah in Ben Sira 24:23, precisely because the identification of Torah with Wisdom and the Word could be assumed.

THE NEW SINAI (JOHN 1:14–18)

Although the larger environment informs how John deploys the imagery in his Prologue, a particular background shared by John and his audience dominates in 1:14–18. Many scholars have observed such points of contact between Exodus 33–34 and John 1:14–18,[32] even if they do not all agree on the connection between John's Logos and Judaism's Torah that explicitly climaxes in this section (1:17–18). In Exodus 33–34, in the context of giving Torah from Mount Sinai a second time, God reveals God's own character to Moses. Many individual echoes in the Prologue could evoke other passages that also echo Exodus, but their accumulation leaves the specific allusion beyond reasonable doubt. Both contexts address:

- The coming of God's Word (Exod. 34:1–4; John 1:14)
- God dwelling among God's people (Exod. 33:14–15; John 1:14)
- God revealing God's glory (Exod. 33:18, 22; John 1:14)
- The glory is "abounding in covenant love and faithfulness" (Exod. 34:6) or "full of grace and truth" (John 1:14)
- No one can see God (Exod. 33:20; John 1:18)

In Exodus, even Moses could not see God fully (Exod. 33:20–23); in John, however, God's heart is revealed fully in Christ (1:18). In this way, the "grace and truth" in Christ is greater than the grace and truth already revealed in the Law (1:17).

Just as God "tabernacled" with God's people in the wilderness, God's Word tabernacled (*eskēnōsen*) among the witnesses of the new exodus accomplished in Jesus (1:14).[33] The widely known work of Ben Sira noted that Wisdom's tabernacle dwelt in Jacob (Sir. 24:8).[34] Especially after 70 C.E., when Diaspora Judaism no longer had a central temple to look to, Jesus as the locus of divine dwelling could constitute a powerful challenge to competing versions of Jewish faith.[35]

As God revealed God's glory to Moses in Exodus 33–34, "full of grace and truth," so here God reveals the divine glory in Jesus to the disciples, whose mission is now to announce the more glorious new covenant. In Exodus 33–34, "glory" functions as a revelation of God's character, as is implied in Exodus 33–34 (see especially 33:19; 34:6–7). As in the Hebrew Bible (Isa.

60:1–3), Judaism continued to associate an ultimate revelation of "glory" with the eschatological time.[36] Although John's eschatology is primarily realized, we may nevertheless understand his point eschatologically: the climactic revelation of glory has occurred in Christ, as Torah has been revealed again in a new covenant (Isa. 2:2–3; Jer. 31:33).

Elsewhere in this Gospel, Jesus's glory is revealed in signs (2:11; 11:4, 40), but the ultimate expression of glory is the complex of events that includes Jesus's death (12:16, 23, 28; 13:31–32; cf. 21:19), resurrection, and exaltation (see 7:39; 12:16; 17:1, 5).[37] His glory thus climaxes in the cross, where God's covenant love and faithfulness come to their ultimate expression (12:23–24). This glory thus becomes the ultimate revelation of "grace and truth": where the world's hatred for God comes to its ultimate expression, so also does God's love for the world (3:16). The critics of John's target audience might regard the cross as proof that Jesus was not the Messiah, but John regards Jesus's humiliation as the very revelation of God: his entire enfleshment, and especially his identification with humanity in his mortality and death, constitute the ultimate revelation of God's grace and truth revealed to Moses.[38]

Because Jesus revealed his glory in ways obscure to the elite but evident to the eyes of disciples (2:11; a continuing paradigm: 14:21–23), those who actually beheld his glory were those who came to believe him (11:40). The first-person plural probably suggests that, in contrast to the view of many scholars, John includes himself among the eyewitnesses (see 19:35; 1 John 1:1–4; 4:6, 14). Whereas many commentators compare Jesus in the Fourth Gospel with Moses,[39] it is actually particularly his witnesses who are analogous to Moses, and Jesus is the glory that Moses witnessed on the mountain. Jesus's eyewitnesses mediate a revelation greater than that of Moses (see 2 Cor. 3:7–18; Mark 9:2–7; see also Isaiah in John 12:41; Isa. 6:1–4).

God's revealing God's own character[40] in Exod. 34:6 as *"abounding in covenant love and faithfulness"* translates naturally into John's Greek expression "full of grace and truth."[41] Although the Septuagint (the common Greek translation of the OT) rarely renders the Hebrew term here as "grace" (*charis*), John or his sources could translate directly from Hebrew at times.[42] Early Christian literature typically employs *charis* in this sense, making it the natural term for John to apply. Although the phrase "covenant love and faithfulness" recurs frequently in the Hebrew Bible and similar language appears elsewhere in Jewish texts,[43] the accumulation of allusions to Exodus 33–34 in John 1:14–18 leaves little doubt as to the object of John's allusion. When God revealed God's own character of grace and truth at Sinai, it was incomplete; Moses saw only part of God's glory (Exod. 33:20–23; John 1:18). But what was an incomplete revelation of grace and truth through Moses was completed through Christ (1:17).

In 1:17, therefore, John again alludes to Exodus 33–34.[44] God's character of grace and truth was revealed with the giving of Law (Exod. 34:6) but was made fully available to humanity ultimately through Christ. Observing the climactic comparison in v. 17, some commentators have suggested not only a deliberate allusion to grace and truth present at the giving of Torah, but that John declares that these attributes were present in Christ and *not* in the Law.[45] This suggestion, however, goes too far, ignoring the sense of continuity suggested by the omission of an explicit adversative. Rather than opposing Torah, Christ is the full embodiment of Torah, completing what was partial (but actually present) in Torah. The lack of adversative conjunction here does not eliminate the contrast (compare the lack of adversatives in 1:18; 2:9, 10; 7:36), but it also does not permit us to exaggerate the force of the contrast.[46] Context must dictate the *force* of contrast. As in m. Avot 2:7, the contrast of John 1:17 is between something good and something better.

Jesus the Messiah thus embodies the hope of Judaism; John does not encourage his community to forsake its Jewish past, but to recognize that in following Christ, the embodiment of Torah, his community fulfills the highest ideals of their heritage. Conversely, their Jewish opponents, synagogue leaders who claim to speak for the Jewish community, have unwittingly rebelled against the ultimate embodiment of Torah. Far from opposing Torah, John identifies it with Jesus and declares that only followers of Jesus submit to its ultimate eschatological expression. In accordance with this understanding, John argues that Moses and the Law testify to Jesus (1:45; 5:45–47). Those who contend with Jesus on the basis of the Law (7:49; 9:28–29; 18:31; 19:7) actually misunderstand (7:23; 8:17; 10:34; 15:25) and disobey (7:19, 51) the Law themselves. In contrast to Abraham (mentioned eleven times in the Gospel), John's mentions of Moses (twelve times) generally are at pains to subordinate Moses as an agent and a witness. John consistently portrays Jesus as the true gift to which Moses's gifts of Torah, manna, and lifting up the serpent point.[47] The believers' opponents appeal to Moses as their witness (9:28–29), but he is a witness against them (5:45–46).

BEHOLDING GOD'S FACE IN CHRIST (JOHN 1:18)

In Exodus, Moses could not see all God's glory because God declared that no one could see God's face and live (Exod. 33:20).[48] John declares first the sense in which that affirmation remains true: "No one has beheld God at any time" (1:18). The rest of this Gospel continues to maintain the Father's invisibility to the world (5:37; 6:46; see 1 John 4:12, 20). But in 1:18 that affirmation is also qualified: the specially beloved, incarnate God has fully revealed God's character, so that the one who has seen him has seen the Father (14:9).

Indeed, the postresurrection Jesus also remains invisible to the world, but not to his disciples (14:21–23; 16:16–19, 22; 20:18, 25).

Greek and Roman sources sometimes emphasize God's invisibility.[49] Judean[50] and Diaspora Jewish[51] tradition emphasize it more consistently, even if some visionaries claimed to envision God's glory in mystical experiences. Jewish writers still affirmed Scripture's teachings both that God spoke with Moses face to face[52] and that Moses could not see all God's glory.[53] In Jesus, however, John affirms that believers see God's glory in a fuller way than did Moses.

CONCLUSION

This chapter focuses on two intersections between John's Prologue and its contemporary Jewish milieu. First, John's Logos, or Word, evokes Jewish conceptions of Wisdom, Word, and Torah. In the primary literary and theological canon that John shares with his ideal audience, the most obvious "Word of God" was Torah itself (Ps. 119:43, 160). By comparing Moses with Jesus the enfleshed Word in John 1:17, John presents Jesus as the fullest embodiment of God's Word also revealed in Scripture. Second, through multiple allusions, John 1:14–18 directly evokes the glorious revelation of God's gracious and faithful character in Exodus 33–34, a context in which God gave the Law again to Israel. In Exodus, even Moses could see only part of God's glory. By contrast, John suggests that God's heart is fully unveiled to believers in God sharing our humanity—and ultimately our mortality.

NOTES

1. A secondary benefit may be some samples of earlier critical Johannine reception history.

2. See Craig S. Keener, *The Gospel of John: A Commentary*, 2 vols. (Grand Rapids: Baker Academic, 2003), 1:340–47; see Ed L. Miller, "The Logos of Heraclitus: Updating the Report," *HTR* 74 (1981): 174–76. For divine Law and *logos*, see Diogenes Laertius 7.1.88; Marcus Aurelius 7.9.

3. See Harry Austryn Wolfson, *Philo: Foundations of Religious Philosophy in Judaism, Christianity, and Islam*, 4th rev. ed., 2 vols. (Cambridge, MA: Harvard University Press, 1968), 1:226–94, esp. 253–61; see also 325–32; Erwin R. Goodenough, *An Introduction to Philo Judaeus*, 2nd ed. (Oxford: Basil Blackwell, 1962), 102–6; A. W. Argyle, "Philo and the Fourth Gospel," *ExpTim* 63 (1952): 385–86; Donald A. Hagner, "The Vision of God in Philo and John: A Comparative Study," *JETS* 14 (1971): 81–93.

4. See Keener, *John*, 1:343–47.

5. See Martin Hengel, *Judaism and Hellenism*, trans. John Bowden, 2 vols. (Philadelphia: Fortress, 1974), 1:154–55.

6. See, for example, C. F. Burney, *The Aramaic Origin of the Fourth Gospel* (Oxford: Clarendon, 1922), 38.

7. "A blind alley," as C. K. Barrett, *The Gospel According to St. John: An Introduction with Commentary and Notes on the Greek Text*, 2nd ed. (Philadelphia: Westminster, 1978), 153, puts it.

8. For later rabbis, see Helmer Ringgren, *Word and Wisdom: Studies in the Hypostatization of Divine Qualities and Functions in the Ancient Near East* (Lund: Häkan Ohlssons Boktryckeri, 1947), 163–64; see Justin, *Dial.* 130.

9. J. Rendel Harris, *The Origin of the Prologue to St. John's Gospel* (Cambridge: Cambridge University Press, 1917), 43; C. H. Dodd, "The Background of the Fourth Gospel," *BJRL* 19 (1935): 335; Eric May, "The Logos in the Old Testament," *CBQ* 8 (1946): 438–47.

10. See, for example, Harris, *Prologue*, 57–62; Ben Witherington III, *Jesus the Sage: The Pilgrimage of Wisdom* (Minneapolis: Fortress, 1994), 249–94.

11. See Hengel, *Judaism*, 1:169–71; for example, Sipre Deut. 37.1.3.

12. Eldon Jay Epp, "Wisdom, Torah, Word: The Johannine Prologue and the Purpose of the Fourth Gospel," in *Current Issues in Biblical and Patristic Interpretation: Studies in Honor of Merrill C. Tenney Presented by his Former Students*, ed. Gerald F. Hawthorne (Grand Rapids: Eerdmans, 1975), 133–36. While some sources are late, the early sources indicate the antiquity of this general tendency of thought.

13. See Sipre Deut. 345.2.2; Ringgren, *Word*, 123.

14. See Torah in Gen. Rab. 1:1.

15. Jub. 2:2; see 1QS 3.15; 11.11; 4Q402 f3ii.12–13; 4Q415 f9.6; later, Torah in Gen. Rab. 1:1.

16. Judith 16:14; 4Q422 1.6; 4 Ezra 6:38; 2 Bar. 21:4; 48:8; *Sib. Or.* 1.9; 19; 3:20; 2 Pet 3:5; Sipre Deut. 330.1.1.

17. For example, Mek. Shirata 3.44–45, 49–51; 8.88; 10.29–31; Mek. Amalek 3.154–55; Mek. Bahodesh 11.111–12; Mek. Nezikin 18.67–68; t. B. Qam. 7:10; Sipre Num. 78.4.1; 102.4.1; 103.1.1; Sipre Deut. 33.1.1; 38.1.3–4; 49.2.2; 343.8.1.

18. For example, m. Avot 5:1; see Samaritans in John Bowman, *Samaritan Documents Relating to Their History, Religion & Life*, POTTS 2 (Pittsburgh, PA: Pickwick, 1977), 1–3.

19. In addition to Noahide Laws given to the nations; see, for example, Mek. Bahodesh 6.90; Sipre Deut. 343.4.1; b. Sanh. 59a.

20. Mekilta Bahodesh 5 (in Ephraim E. Urbach, *The Sages: Their Concepts and Beliefs*, 2nd ed. trans. Israel Abrahams, 2 vols. [Jerusalem: Magnes, 1979], 1:532); Sipre Deut. 343.4.1.

21. R. Alan Culpepper, *Anatomy of the Fourth Gospel: A Study in Literary Design* (Philadelphia: Fortress, 1983), 169.

22. See, for example, Epp, "Wisdom"; Jacobus Schoneveld, "Torah in the Flesh: A New Reading of the Prologue of the Gospel of John as a Contribution to a Christology without Anti-Judaism," *Immanuel* 24/25 (1990): 77–94; Craig S. Keener, "The Function of Johannine Pneumatology in the Context of Late First-Century Judaism"

(PhD diss., Duke University, 1991), 240–54; S. J. Casselli, "Jesus as Eschatological Torah," *TJ* 18 (1997): 15–41.

23. See already William Wrede, *The Origin of the New Testament*, trans. James S. Hill (New York: Harper & Brothers, 1909), 83–84; earlier still, M. von Aberle, "Über den Zweck des Johannesevangelium," *TQ* 42 (1861): 37–94.

24. See m. Sanh. 4:5; Sipre Deut. 329.1.1; 331.1.2; Justin *Dial.* 10; R. Travers Herford, *Christianity in Talmud and Midrash* (Clifton, NJ: Reference Book Publishers, 1966), 308–15.

25. For example, Deut. 17:11; Ps. 119:9, 11, 16–17, 67, 89, 101, 105, 133, 140, 148, 158, 169, 172; Isa. 2:3; Mk 7:13; Tg. Isa. on 1:2.

26. Mathias Rissi, "Jn 1:1–18 (The Eternal Word)," *Int* 31 (1977): 396; Raymond E. Brown, *The Gospel According to John*, 2 vols., AB 29–29a (Garden City, NY: Doubleday, 1966–1970), 1:4.

27. Compare, for example, Philo *QG* 4.97.

28. Rodney A. Whitacre, *Johannine Polemic: The Role of Tradition and Theology*, SBLDS 67 (Chico, CA: Scholars Press, 1982), 33–63. On Jesus and the Law, see also Severino Pancaro, *The Law in the Fourth Gospel*, NovTSup 42 (Leiden: Brill, 1975).

29. Whitacre, *Polemic*, 68.

30. W. D. Davies, *Torah in the Messianic Age and/or the Age to Come*, JBLMS 7 (Philadelphia: Society of Biblical Literature, 1952), 93.

31. Edwyn Clement Hoskyns, *The Fourth Gospel*, 2nd rev. ed., ed. Francis Noel Davey (London: Faber & Faber, 1947), 159; T. Francis Glasson, *Moses in the Fourth Gospel* (Naperville, IL: Allenson, 1963), 26; Epp, "Wisdom," 141; Longenecker, *Christology*, 40; Everett F. Harrison, "A Study of John 1:14," in *Unity and Diversity in New Testament Theology: Essays in Honor of George E. Ladd*, ed. Robert A. Guelich (Grand Rapids: Eerdmans, 1978), 35.

32. For example, Marie-Emile Boismard, *St. John's Prologue*, trans. Carisbrooke Dominicans (London: Blackfriars Publications, 1957), 135–45, esp. 136–39; Jacob J. Enz, "The Book of Exodus as a Literary Type for the Gospel of John," *JBL* 76 (1957): 212; Peder Borgen, *Bread from Heaven: An Exegetical Study of the Concept of Manna in the Gospel of John and the Writings of Philo*, NovTSup 10 (Leiden: Brill, 1965), 150–51; Anthony Hanson, "John I.14–18 and Exodus XXXIV," *NTS* 23 (1976): 90–101; Harrison, "John 1:14," 29; Henry Mowvley, "John 1.14–18 in the Light of Exodus 33.7–34.35," *ExpTim* 95 (1984): 135–37.

33. Boismard, *Prologue*, 48–49; survey of background in Mary L. Coloe, *God Dwells with Us: Temple Symbolism in the Fourth Gospel* (Collegeville, MN: Liturgical Press, 2001), 31–63. Jesus thus becomes the new temple; see 2:19–21; 4:21–24; 7:37–39; 10:36; 14:2–3.

34. With Geerhardus Vos, "The Range of the Logos-Title in the Prologue of the Fourth Gospel," *PTR* 11 (1913): 404; J. Rendel Harris, "The Origin of the Prologue to St. John's Gospel," *The Expositor*, 8th ser., 12 (1916): 147–60, 161–70, 314–20, 388–400, 415–26. See Wisdom in Bar 3:37; Philo, *Leg.* 3.46; *Congr.* 116; the *logos* in *Post.* 122.

35. See Coloe, *Temple Symbolism*, 11 and throughout.

36. For example, CD 20.25–26; 1QM 12.12; *Sib. Or.* 3:282. Some eschatological glory texts refer to a new exodus (e.g., Isa. 40:5; 2 Macc. 2:7–8; Ps. Sol. 11:6).

37. Often pointed out, for example, W. Nicol, "The history of Johannine research during the past century," *Neot* 6 (1972): 16; Gary M. Burge, *The Anointed Community: The Holy Spirit in the Johannine Tradition* (Grand Rapids: Eerdmans, 1987), 132–33.

38. See 1 Cor. 1:23–25; Phil 2:8; Robert Kysar, "The Contributions of the Prologue of the Gospel of John to New Testament Christology and their Historical Setting," *CurTM* 5 (1978): 360.

39. For example, Howard M. Teeple, *The Mosaic Eschatological Prophet*, SBLMS 10 (Philadelphia: Society of Biblical Literature, 1957); Glasson, *Moses*.

40. For John, "glory" includes "divine nature" (Robert G. Bratcher, "What Does 'Glory' Mean in Relation to Jesus? Translating *doxa* and *doxado* in John," *BT* 42 [1991]: 401–8).

41. With many, for example, Barrett, *John*, 167; Epp, "Wisdom," 138; Boismard, *Prologue*, 54–56; earlier and on the phrase more generally, see Moses Stuart, "Exegetical and Theological Examination of John 1:1–18," *BSac* 7 (1850): 316.

42. For John's composite text-types, see in general, Edwin D. Freed, *Old Testament Quotations in the Gospel of John*, NovTSup 11 (Leiden: Brill, 1965).

43. See James H. Charlesworth, "A Critical Comparison of the Dualism in 1QS III,13–IV,26 and the 'Dualism' Contained in the Fourth Gospel," *NTS* 15 (1969): 415, citing 1QS 4.4–5; cf. Wis. 3:9; 15:1.

44. So also others, for example, Boismard, *Prologue*, 62.

45. C. H. Dodd, *New Testament Studies* (Manchester: Manchester University Press, 1967), 141–42; Dodd, *The Interpretation of the Fourth Gospel* (Cambridge: Cambridge University Press, 1965), 82, 295, citing Midr. Ps. 25:10.

46. Harrison, "John 1:14," 35.

47. Wayne A. Meeks, *The Prophet-King: Moses Traditions and the Johannine Christology*, NovTSup 14 (Leiden: Brill, 1967), 292.

48. Many concur that 1:18 echoes Exod 33:20, see, for example, Peder Borgen, "God's Agent in the Fourth Gospel," in *Religions in Antiquity: Essays in Memory of Erwin Ramsdell Goodenough*, ed. Jacob Neusner, SHR 14 (Leiden: Brill, 1968), 145; Boismard, *Prologue*, 64; Epp, "Wisdom," 137; Glasson, *Moses*, 25.

49. Greek views seem to have varied; see, for example, Xenophon *Mem.* 1.4.9; Epictetus *Diatr.* 1.6.19; Plutarch *Is. Or.* 9, *Mor.* 354D; *Is. Or.* 75, *Mor.* 381B.

50. For example, 1QS 11.20; Sipra Vayyiqra Dibura Denedabah pq. 2.2.3.2–3. This could apply even despite partial throne revelations (*1 En.* 14:19, 21).

51. Aristobulus frg. 4; Philo, *Names* 7; *Creation* 69; *Spec. Laws* 1.47; 2.165; Josephus *Ag. Ap.* 2.191; *Sib. Or.* 3.12, 17; Rom 1:20; 1 Tim 1:17; see further Hagner, "Vision," 82–84; Marie E. Isaacs, *The Concept of Spirit: A Study of Pneuma in Hellenistic Judaism and its Bearing on the New Testament*, HeyM 1 (London: Heythrop College, 1976), 30.

52. LAB 11:14; see Sipra Vayyiqra Dibura Denedabah pq. 2.2.3.3; Philo, *Names* 8; *Spec. Laws* 1.41; cf. John 14:8.

53. Sipre Deut. 357.19.1; b. Ber. 7a; Meg. 19b.

Chapter 4

Ambiguity as a Rhetorical Strategy in the Prologue to John's Gospel

Jo-Ann A. Brant

John's Prologue brims with material with which to engage in rhetorical criticism. It satisfies the classical expectations for an *encomium* (a composition of praise): Jesus comes from the best of origins, has accomplished divine deeds, embodies virtue, and is superior to others worthy of praise.[1] Its many figures of speech are ready to be identified and their charm, to be discussed.[2] Sherri Brown has demonstrated that the Prologue plays an important role as an introduction to the Johannine narrative. A case can also be made that it plays a critical role in the rhetorical aims of the Gospel. The Prologue directs the energy of the audience toward cooperation—a sense of shared interests—by immediately making good on the implicit promise of a speech of praise not simply to tell them what they already know but to do so in a way that inspires trust and plumbs the depths of their convictions. In doing so, John prepares the audience to hear a reshaping of prior understandings and imagery by which followers of Jesus make sense of the their benefactor's identity and with which they identify themselves.[3] Jonathan Pratt describes the audience of speeches of praise as "hungry for arguments that support their most firmly held convictions, enhance their status in the eyes of outsiders, or simply pay due honor to those they believe deserve it. Failure to do these things with panache will diminish the status of the speaker."[4] This chapter focuses on the Johannine gambit of utilizing ambiguity (multiplicity of meanings), a bold move but one calculated to generate a cooperative space in which he can play his hand in ways that may be unfamiliar to his audience without violating their sense of fair play. Unintentional ambiguity is simply loose writing; intentional ambiguity is strategy. Where historical criticism has seen problems to eliminate by pinning down intended meaning, rhetorical criticism sees evidence of intended effect. Ambiguity allows John to stir the minds of his audience so that they become engaged in the play of meanings and awaken to a new or a renewed appreciation of the divine gifts that they have received.

Before proceeding further, I should lay my own cards on the table. This analysis will depend upon a number of presuppositions. First, the Prologue is designed as an introduction to the Gospel and not a stand-alone piece affixed to the narrative. Secondly, the intended audience is one primarily filled with individuals habituated to believing that Jesus is the Messiah but who may not necessarily agree with each other on what that signifies. Thirdly, the intended audience is one that listens to a reading or recitation of the Gospel and not a silent reader. Fourthly, I will analyze the Prologue as a piece of epideictic rhetoric, Aristotle's catchall category for speeches that are neither *symbouleutic* (deliberative), such as those given in the context of a governing body deliberating over policies and doctrines, nor *dicanic* (judicial), those given in a courtroom in which a jury or judge decides the innocence or guilt of an individual. Epideictic speeches in the form of *encomium* or panegyric praise or through vituperation criticize their subject in the context of religious and civil ceremonies such as funerals, welcoming convocations, and crown speeches. They are designed to provide language on behalf of the audience. The goal of such rhetoric is to galvanize a common identity by both shaping and increasing the intensity of shared commitments that become the foundation for subsequent decisions and actions.[5] Finally, I begin with a high estimation of the intentionality of the Prologue and the Gospel's rhetorical craft that is not limited to the techniques taught in classical handbooks. As a result, I do not limit myself to prescriptions of ancient teachers of rhetoric but also seek investigative tools from modern scholars of rhetoric. Ancient teachers and philosophers often discuss ambiguity as a difficulty or defect and seldom as a helpful device (e.g., Aelius Theon, *Prog.* 81–83). Aristotle suggests that people use equivocal words when they are pretending to have something to say (*Rhet.* 1407a). However, modern scholars tend to be more generous in their assessment of the possible purposes for ambiguity.

The first five verses of the Prologue, set before and during creation of the cosmos, move the discourse to abstract concepts whereby shared beliefs can be invoked without the danger of disagreement provoked by more concrete language. The choice of the word "*logos*" (word) to denote the subject of the Gospel sends scholars off on the hunt for precedents and the philosophical and scriptural contexts by which one can best determine the perimeter in which to comprehend the word's definition and to try to imagine what was intended by *logos*. What, or rather who, John means by *logos* is suggested through allusion until v. 17, when Jesus is explicitly named. As a piece of rhetoric, the ambiguity of referent avoids the specificity that scholars crave to allow each member of the audience to hear the same word but to fill it with the richness that various prior associations afford. Edward Sapir calls the sort of symbolically charged language that appears in the Prologue "condensation symbols" that, in the words of David Zarefsky, "serve to 'condense' into one symbol a host of different meanings and connotations which might diverge if more specific referents were attempted."[6] Given that John will present bold claims about Jesus's christological status and a narrative that seeks to undercut any dissention or doubt, it seems likely that any intended audience for the Gospel is conceived as including people who might privately dissent or lack certainty. By moving the discourse to a higher abstract level, the speaker generates a cognitive space that allows a sense of unity without requiring the particular agreement that the clarity of plain speech expects. Poetry, by inviting a positive emotional and aesthetic response, helps gloss over any potential disagreements. Paul Ricoeur explains the objective of poetry with reference to metaphor as an effort not to persuade but rather to purge feelings of pity and fear.[7] In the case of the Prologue, John may be borrowing this power of poetry for the rhetorical purpose of reducing any anxiety his audience might feel in reframing Jesus's narrative, with a view not to what Jesus proclaimed about the kingdom of heaven, but about what he proclaims about himself.

Abandoning clarity at the beginning of the Prologue also substantiates that what follows is inspired. All speeches and literary works must begin with the rhetorical act of persuading an audience to pay attention. Aristotle encourages the speaker to use metaphor to this end noting how it provides an "out-of-the-ordinary air" that inspires a pleasurable cognitive state of wonder. He compares this to the pleasure brought by the curiosity felt about people from foreign lands (*Rhet.* 1404b8–11). By situating *logos* in creation and the realm of God, the Prologue solicits fascination. Scholars who have argued that the Prologue was an independent composition affixed to the Gospel have pointed to the fact that *logos* as a signifier for Jesus does not appear in the narrative. The context prior to and during creation, however, calls for *catachresis*, the adaptation of an available term to describe something for which no actual term exists. Once the Logos becomes incarnate, John turns to proper names, metaphors, and relationships.

Socrates, in Plato's *Ion* (533–534), describes the poet as subject to divine madness or inspiration and not to knowledge or truth. The sort of inspiration to which I refer above does not deprive John of his wits. It is the sort of inspiration to which Shakespeare refers in Sonnet 18 when he writes self-consciously about poetry, "Shall I compare thee to a summer's day? Thou art more lovely and more temperate."[8] The subject inspires the language of the poet rather than the poem serving to enhance the qualities of its object. The self-consciousness of Johannine poetic rhetoric surfaces more explicitly when the narrator uses the first-person plural: "And the Word became flesh and lived among us, and we have seen his glory, the glory as of a father's only son, full of grace and truth" (1:14, see also 1:16). A comparison to the beginning of Luke highlights how style helps build cooperation before proceeding with a narrative. Luke composes an impressive periodic sentence (1:1–4) in which he favorably compares himself to others who have *epecheirēsan* (attempted) to write orderly accounts based upon traditions handed down from witnesses from the beginning by claiming that his (successful) orderly account is built on careful investigation from the very first. Initial cooperation rests upon trust not in Luke's skill as an investigator but in his competency in constructing a complicated sentence. Luke's contention that he will present an orderly account would make poetry a mismatched style. John's Prologue, in contrast, does not introduce a narrative so much as its subject, Jesus. The incarnation provokes the author to try to match the glory of Jesus's presence with the sublimity of his prose.

Epideictic rhetoric relies heavily upon amplification, an elaboration of the subject to emphasize its importance, and as such, is an argument that the subject is worthy of praise.[9] When the audience already holds the subject in high esteem, the amplifications prove that the speaker is doing the subject justice as well as arouse the emotions of the audience in a way that honors the subject (see Cicero, *Part. or.* 15.52). The first sentence of the Prologue uses the stylistic pattern of *anadiplōsis* (doubling back) by repeating the word at the end of a clause at the beginning of the next clause. The second clause amplifies the first and the third amplifies the second. Together with v. 2, the pattern forms a chiasm.

1. In the beginning was the *logos*
   And the *logos* was with God
   And the *logos* was God.
2. This [*logos*] was in the beginning with God. (author's translation)

Theos, in the clause "and the *logos* was God," has no article and as a result generates ambiguity as to whether the reference is to God or God's nature. The catachresis of *logos* and the metaphor of light serve as signifiers of Jesus's divine status and, through their association with creation and life and the allusion to Gen. 1:1, evoke positive associations for the audience. By beginning with *en archē*, John lays claim to the prestige of Genesis for the Logos—anything ancient is worthy of respect—and then in v. 3 he uses an antithetical parallelism to emphasize the scope of the Logos's role in creation: "All things came into being through him, and without him not one thing came into being." The beneficiaries of his deeds are "all people" (see also 1:4, 6, 16). The words "first," "all," and "only" are key words in many forms of amplification. Quintilian notes that "what is particularly agreeable to an audience is anything that a man can be said to have been the first, or among the very few, to have done" (*Inst.* 3.7.16 [Russell, LCL]).

In order for ambiguity to work as a strategy it does need to be bounded. In the final strophe of the Prologue's opening, John's use of *katelaben* limits ambiguity to two choices: the darkness fails either to overcome the light or to comprehend the light. In this case, a listening ear has time to appreciate the play on two sensible meanings. In the act of weighing out meaning, the audience participates in the reading by exercising choice and awaiting confirmation or correction.[10] John limits speculations about to what *ho logos* (the word) can refer by containing it within the creation narrative in Genesis and the conventions of Jewish wisdom discourse. Biblical allusions in modern political speeches seek to persuade audiences that the politician shares their values. For example, in the 2016 American presidential campaign, Hillary Clinton told the National Baptist Convention, "Yes, we need a President who will do justice, love kindness, and walk humbly with our God" (Mic. 6:8).[11] By beginning with the allusion to Gen. 1:1 followed by creation and wisdom motifs, John signals that Scripture will play an authoritative role in the narrative and can then be treated as part of an ethos shared by text and audience.[12]

Other elements of the Prologue that also contribute to the construction of the insider status for the audience include the references to John the Baptist, the world, Moses and the Law. Mention of the Baptist and Moses falls under the heading of amplification insofar as they function as comparisons (*synkrisis*). Scholars debate whether or not the comparisons seek to diminish the status of these two precursors, but following the logic of rhetorical strategies, it is probable that John uses their high status to step up his claims about Jesus. Aristotle recommends that, "One should make comparison with famous people for the subject is amplified and made honorable if he is better than [other] worthy ones" (*Rhet.* 1368a38 [Kennedy]). This strategy is employed in the modern context with great frequency by the travel industry. One *TripAdvisor* review of the ruins of Herculaneum reads, "Imagine the best of Pompeii, but in more detail."[13] A visitor to a hotel at the Grand Canyon writes, "Imagine the best—and then be surprised at even better."[14]

The shift from the *logos* to John the Baptist in 1:6–8 serves a number of purposes. Aelius Theon advocates the judicious use of digressions to "give the hearer's mind a rest" (*Prog.* 80 [Kennedy]).[15] In his discussion of the use of fable as *chreia* (or an anecdote), John of Sardis notes the problem with fable: "Who will be persuaded that something is true which is not true by nature?" (*Prog.* 35). The mythic language of 1:1–5 calls for a quick shoring up with reference to shared history. In the context of a discussion of courtroom rhetoric, Quintilian has both good and bad things to say about the digressions that lawyers habitually add immediately after the statement of facts. He disapproves when digressions merely flaunt the speaker's talents and approves if they are brief and serve as the conclusion of the statement and the beginning of the proof (*Inst.* 4.3.1–5). John's digression performs the function of a *paradeigmata* (a historical precedent) and type of anecdote known as a *chreia* (see Theon, *Prog.* 96). In this case, it fulfills the role of a proof by supporting the *action*, not the *content*, of vv. 1–5—the *identification* of Jesus as the Logos and light coming into the world—with the testimony of John. The addition of the negative epithet, "He himself was not the light" (1:8), makes clear that John is not being compared with Jesus but with the narrator. The narrator implicitly asserts that he is not the first to make such claims (see Theon, *Prog.* 116). Ian H. Henderson observes, "In a world in which idiosyncrasy was not only rhetorically dangerous, a speaker could nonetheless realize some of the benefits of pointedly projecting a salient characterization, by rhetorically projecting the socio-linguistic risk onto a carefully chosen chreia protagonist."[16] John admits an element of ambiguity into 1:6–8 by omitting the positive epithet "the Baptist" with which to identify to which John he refers. The lack of any other specific information to tie this John to the Baptist indicates that there is a tacit assumption that the audience is "in the know" about who is intended as if to say, "You know who I am talking about." For the reference to work, the audience must be well acquainted with John the Baptist and hold him in high regard. The allusion presumes upon and fosters a close narrator-author relationship, a community of knowledge and experience, by briefly sharing the warm of a deeply meaningful memory.

The Gospel of John similarly relies upon a shared meaningful memory in his quick summary of the life of Jesus (1:10–11), but whereas the emphasis has been on a universalism in vv. 1–9, this summary turns the included audience into an exclusive audience. The "all people" of 1:4 and the "everyone" of 1:9 becomes the world that does not know him: "He came to what was his own (*ta idia*), and his own (*hoi idioi*) did not accept him" (1:11). The CJB translation adds "homeland" after *ta idia*, and the NRSV adds "people" after *hoi idioi*, to make the references more distinct and explicit. The play on words with the simple shift of pronouns from *ta* to *hoi* and the addition of an *omicron* to *idia* is classified as a witticism in classical rhetoric (Cicero, *De or.* 2.256; *Rhet. Her.* 4.29, 32). Quintilian warns his students to be guarded against the use of this device but concedes that if the play is not forced it adds natural charm (*Inst.* 9.3.73–74). Verse 11 is either a simple repetition for emphasis or a narrowing of focus from the general, the world, to the particular, Jesus's ethnic identity, presumably Jewish. Seen within the strategy of ambiguity, the use of *periphrasis* (speaking around the subject) allows the audience to determine the intended population at this point. The narrative will eventually identify particular Jewish groups who reject Jesus: his brothers (7:5); some disciples (6:66); the Pharisees (9:13–34; 11:57); and the priests (11:57; 19:15). The narrator will frequently refer to *hoi Ioudaioi* as a homogeneous group who with one voice reject Jesus (2:18–20; 5:16–18; 7:13; 9:22; 10:31–39; 18:40;

19:7; 19:38; 20:19), and Jesus will describe those who reject his as children of the devil rather than of Abraham (8:39–47). The Prologue discursively generates "the other" without being explicit about the identity of those who do not receive Jesus and without succumbing to juxtaposing the positive language used for the "we" with negative metaphors, hyperbole, or another figure of speech. At this point, John is more interested in constructing a cooperative audience engaged in the rhetoric of praise than vituperation.[17] Nevertheless, avoiding the explicit name of an opponent can be a rhetorical strategy for showing disdain. Cicero famously avoided naming Publius Clodius Pulcher, who had forced him to go into exile for a year. For example, on one occasion he referred obliquely to his enemy as one of "those who were hostile to me out of hatred for the republic I had saved" (*Red. pop.* 21).[18] *Ta idia* and *hoi idioi* are not true periphrasis but rather an omission comparable to the phrase, "Will the gentleman yield," still used in many modern legislative bodies. While politely saying, "Shut up and sit down," it encodes the speaker's criticism of the other's lack of restraint as well as his or her own discipline in showing self-restraint by being polite.

The rhetoric of division receives more attention in modern analysis than in the classical handbooks. Kenneth Burke points to two possible functions for the emphasis of division that can be applied to the summary of Jesus's earthly ministry. First, it provides a means by which those in the audience can sharpen their identity. The second function follows from the first. Identification becomes a compensation for division.[19] If the latter is operative in the Prologue, these verses signify that the parting of the ways of church and synagogue is a source of pain that shapes the Gospel narrative and using restrained terms keeps the focus on the positive emotions associated with that identity. While at this point, the rhetoric is not pointed, it is important to note that there is what Celeste M. Condit calls a "dark side" to epideictic rhetoric to which all readers have an ethical obligation to attend.[20] Andreea Deciu Ritivoi contends that epideictic discourse "lies on the verge of propaganda" by creating a mythical and glorious "us" that calls justification for exclusion of a mythically constructed "them."[21] It is impossible to know precisely the full implications of this rhetoric for John's first audiences but we do know that the "dark side" of this aspect of epideictic rhetoric has had ugly consequences for many Jewish communities and as a result alarms many modern readers.

The language of belonging, particularly to a family, permeates the remainder of the Prologue. Jesus is the *monogenēs* (only son), the only one to have seen God (1:14, 18), and thus capable of making God known (1:18). *Monogenēs* is a very curious word. Hesiod uses the term in his advice that one should have only one son so as to increase the family's wealth (*Op.* 376), but one could designate who that son might be. The early patristic writers introduced the notion that Jesus was begotten in order to eliminate any chance that

John is referring to a lower Christology such as divine adoption. Those who accept Jesus receive "the power to become children of God" (*exousian enesthai tekna theou*; 1:12). *Tekna theou* belongs to the broad category of familial metaphors that serve to bond an audience together by evoking the values—perhaps chief of which was honor—and emotions associated with families that foster a sense of social well-being. The choice of *tekna theou* (children of God) rather than *huioi theou* (sons of God; see Gal. 3:26) may reflect John's need to preserve the distinction between Jesus as the Son of God and his followers. In 1 John 3:1–3, the author appeals to his reader as God's children in order to inspire confidence in their purity by virtue of their intimacy with God and hope for the future. The emphasis upon intimacy is evident in the reference to Jesus's position "close to the Father's heart" (1:18, NRSV). In the amplification on "children of God" in v. 13, John uses anaphora, the repetition "not of" (*ouk ex*) at the beginning of successive clauses about the causes of human procreation—something highly valued by the ancient audiences—followed by "but of God" (*all ek theou egennēthēsan*). Once more, John uses something that is considered very good to offer something better. The anaphora serves not just to please but also to encode the strength of the narrator's convictions that what Jesus offers is a gift worth receiving (see *Rhet. Her.* 4.12.19).

The sudden introduction of the first-person plural pronoun in v. 14, if understood as an inclusive "we," anchors the audience more firmly within the exclusive category of children of God. The "we" can be received multiple ways and it seems plausible that the author exploits this ambiguity. Inclusive of the audience, it makes the implicit claim that the author can speak on behalf of those present, thereby, evoking consensus by aligning the audience with the authorial voice. In her study of the rhetoric of Athenian citizenship, Victoria Wohl calls the first-person plural the "syntax of political fantasy" evident in Thucydides's version of Pericles's funeral oration when Pericles consistently uses the word "we" to claim the virtues of past Athenians for all Athenians (*Hist.* 2.39).[22] The same rhetorical construction of an ideal social identity is evident in the preamble to the American Constitution: "*We the People* of the United States, in order to form a more perfect union, establish justice, insure domestic tranquility, provide for the common defense, promote the general welfare, and secure the blessings of liberty to ourselves and our posterity, do ordain and establish this Constitution for the United States of America." While the audiences of the Gospel have not directly witnessed Jesus's words and deeds, as part of a shared social identity, they can lay claim to the experiences and authority of past witnesses.

Taken as an exclusive allusion to the witness of the author, the use of "we" is an appeal to authority. On the lips of a political figure, "we" can signify an individual who embodies the state as is the case when Queen Victoria reportedly snapped, "We are not amused," in response to a piece of spicy gossip. In the Prologue's case, the authority is that of a witness and the "we" serves as an amplification. Credibility relies upon more than one witness. In addition, the exclusive first-person "we" signifies that what is being promoted is both possible and pleasant (see Aelius Theon, *Prog.* 116). Rhetorical handbooks from antiquity to the modern classroom teach that relevant knowledge is necessary for establishing a speaker's authority but are not sufficient and should be complemented with virtue and goodwill (see Aristotle, *Rhet.* 1378a112). In modern speeches, this is often achieved with a simple expression of gratitude for being invited to speak and explaining how the audience can benefit from what is about to be said. The Prologue establishes the narrator's authority by making clear that by receiving the Jesus the Gospel presents, the audience receives a blessing.

In the culmination of the Prologue, forms of the word *"charis"* play a prominent and significant role in what Adele Reinhartz calls "a rhetoric of desire and fulfillment."[23] Jesus is "full (*plērēs*) of grace (*charitos*) and truth (*alētheias*)" (1:14), "from his fullness we have all received, grace upon grace (*charin anti charitos*)" (1:16), "grace (*charis*) and truth (*alētheia*) came through Jesus Christ (1:17, NRSV)." In the Christian tradition, *charis* is translated with the theologically charged term "grace," but in ancient Greek literature, *charis* connoted a kindness done or a generous gift or the gratitude with which the gift is received. As such, *charis* is an ambiguous signifier. The word *"charis"* appears nowhere else in the Gospel; therefore, interpretations have been heavily influenced by Pauline usage, which accounts for 100 of the 155 times the word appears in the NT. Paul uses the word to refer to God's gift of Jesus that frees humanity from sin. In its one-time appearance in the General Epistles, it is used as a greeting (2 John 3). If we look at its context within the Prologue, the generous gift to which vv. 15–17 refers includes both the Logos and the power to become children of God.[24]

The phrase *charin anti charitos* generates scholarly debate. The first *charis* could signify Jesus's gift and the second, the gift of the Sinai covenant, so that the phrase can mean "a generous gift [Jesus] in replacement of an earlier generous gift [the Law]" or more positively "one generous gift [Jesus] after another generous gift [the Law]." Translators generally ignore the possibility that the repetition of *charis* permits another translation: "*charin* (gift) in return *charitos* (gratitude)." Recently, David Konstan has demonstrated that Aristotle, in his discussion of *charis* as a form of pathos that rhetoric seeks to awaken (*Rhet.* 2.7), speaks not about kindness but gratitude.[25] Even if *charitos* should not be translated as gratitude, by virtue of repeatedly naming that which has been received as *charis*, the speaker expresses gratitude. The vehemence of the prose expresses the joyful appreciation with which the Prologue receives the Logos as God's gift and the ability to become children of God as Jesus's gift. Verses 12–17 provide an energetic contrast to the lack of gratitude with which the world and his own received him.

Western philosophical tradition gives rise to a discussion—alien to most societies and traditions—whether gratitude is a problematic sentiment because it presumes a form of indebtedness to the giver. Aristotle's ideal virtuous individual declined gifts from human beings to avoid indebtedness (*Eth. nic.* 61124b11–12). Auguste Comte (1798–1857) coins the term "altruism" to describe the ideal motive for kindness, concern for others without any regard for oneself.[26] Anders Nygren, in *Agape and Eros* (1930), argues that God's love (*agapē*) and, therefore, the love expressed as Christians, desires nothing in return.[27] His definition of *agapē* becomes extremely influential in Christian thought through the remainder of the twentieth century and still seems to hang on tenaciously. Recently, classicists and NT scholars have returned to the ancient Greco-Roman and early Christian sources to recover an attitude toward gratitude that would have informed early Christian authors and their interpreters. In both Greco-Roman and Jewish societies, gratitude is treated as a supreme virtue. Solomon Schimmel, in examining the treatment of gratitude and its expressions in the Hebrew Bible and later rabbinic literature finds that "the sentiment of gratitude is central to the very relationship between God (YHWH) and the people of Israel."[28] Cicero claimed that gratitude was the greatest virtue from which all others followed (*Planc.* 33 see also *Off.* 1.47–48). His *De officiis,* in which much of his thought on gratitude is scattered, is appropriated into Christian thought by Ambrose, Augustine, and Jerome and was the second book to roll off Gutenberg's press after the Bible. Where early Christian writers differ from Cicero is that they reject the system of debts that enslaved some and maintained a hierarchical system of patronage.[29] Recently, the field of cognitive psychology, gratitude has become a disposition that is to be fostered in order to promote well-being and sociologists have examined how the chain of reciprocal gift-giving motivated by gratitude creates social cohesion and community.[30] In the simple act of inviting gratitude, the Prologue promotes the joy and strengthens the social bonds of followers of Jesus within his audience.

The final line of the Prologue begins with an absolute claim: "No one has ever seen God," which is quickly corrected, "It is God the only Son, who is close to the Father's heart, who has made him known" (1:18). As a Christological assertion it provides an appropriate *inclusio* with the first line of the Prologue, but as a rhetorical act following the discussion of *charis*, it is something more. The tally of gifts bestowed by Jesus includes creation, the power to become children of God, and the knowledge of God. In contrast, Paul writes, "For now we see in a mirror, dimly, but then we will see face to face. Now I know only in part; then I will know fully, even as I have been fully known" (1 Cor. 13:12). For Paul, complete knowledge of God is an eschatological gift. John presents knowledge as a gift of the incarnation.

Ambiguity can be problematic when it leads to misunderstanding and misguided action. In the context of Abbott and Costello's routine "Who's on first," in which a statement about a player with the last name *Who* is taken as a question, the consequences of ambiguity are humorous. In some contexts, the consequences of ambiguity can be horrific. On December 28, 2014, AirAsia flight QZ8501 crashed after the pilot instructed the copilot to "pull down" intending the plane to descend.[31] The copilot responded by pulling the control yoke toward himself sending the plane soaring upward and causing it to stall. Using ambiguity as a strategy in rhetoric could result in unwanted uncertainty about meaning that throws the audience into doubt about how to respond. The uncertainty that ambiguous elements in the Johannine Prologue admits into the process of communication does not endanger the clarity of the call to receive Jesus and trust in his name or that an appropriate response is to listen to the story that is about to be told with a sense of joyful gratitude. Justice Antonin Scalia once quipped, "The main business of a lawyer is to take the romance, the mystery, the irony, the ambiguity out of everything he touches."[32] Much of modern scholarship reflects the same sort of training as Scalia's lawyer by treating ambiguity as a choice limited to one option. One of the virtues of rhetorical criticism is that, while unmasking the strategies that John employs to persuade, it frees the reading audience to enjoy ambiguity's charm.

NOTES

1. For a thorough analysis of the rhetorical topoi used to construct the person of Jesus in the Prologue, see Alicia D. Myers, *Characterizing Jesus: A Rhetorical Analysis on the Fourth Gospel's Use of Scripture in its Presentation of Jesus*, LNTS 458 (London: Bloomsbury/T&T Clark, 2012), 61–75.

2. For a breakdown of the stylistic features, see Dan Nässelqvist, "Stylistic Levels in Hebrews 1.1–4 and John 1.1–18," *JSNT* 35 (2012): 44–52.

3. See Jeffrey Walker, *Rhetoric and Poetics in Antiquity* (Oxford: Oxford University Press, 2000), 9.

4. Jonathan Pratt, "The Epideictic *Agōn* and Aristotle's Elusive Third Genre," *AJP* 133 (2012): 191.

5. See Michael Schandorf, "A Gesture Theory of Communication" (PhD diss., University of Illinois at Chicago, 2015), 197–210.

6. David Zarefsky, *President Johnson's War On Poverty: Rhetoric and History* (Tuscaloosa, AL: University of Alabama Press, 1986), 10–11, citing Edward Sapir, "Symbolism," *Encyclopaedia of the Social Sciences*, ed. Edwin R. A. Seligman (New York: Macmillan, 1934), 492.

7. Paul Ricoeur, *The Rule of Metaphor* (Toronto: University of Toronto Press, 1981), 12.

8. *Shakespeare's Sonnets*, ed. Barbara A. Mowatt and Paul Werstine (New York: The Folger Shakespeare Library, 2004), 39.

9. Laurent Pernot, *Epideictic Rhetoric: Questioning the Stakes of Ancient Praise* (Austin: University of Texas Press, 2015), 87.

10. Jeanne Smith Muzzillo, "Positive Effects of Ambiguity When Created by Rhetorical Devices: To Be or Not to Be," *ETC* 67 (2010): 453–54.

11. Steve Kraske, "Here's What Hillary Clinton Said Thursday in Kansas City," *Kansas City Star*, September 8, 2016; https://www.kansascity.com/news/local/news-columns-blogs/the-buzz/article100787652.html.

12. See Myers, *Characterizing Jesus*, 62.

13. "Imagine the Best of Pompeii, But in More Detail," *TripAdvisor*, January 23, 2013; https://www.tripadvisor.com/ShowUserReviews-g670330-d195507-r150433924-Ruins_of_Herculaneum-Ercolano_Province_of_Naples_Campania.html.

14. "Imagine the best—and then be surprised at even better," *TripAdvisor*, March 12, 2011; https://www.tripadvisor.com/ShowUserReviews-g303492-d1201905-r99930836-Cachoeira_Inn-Armacao_dos_Buzios_State_of_Rio_de_Janeiro.html.

15. All quotations from the *Progymnasmata* are taken from George A. Kennedy, *Progymnasmata: Greek Textbooks of Prose Composition and Rhetoric* (Atlanta: SBL Press, 2003).

16. Ian H. Henderson, *Jesus, Rhetoric and Law* (Leiden: Brill, 1996), 86.

17. For a thorough discussion of the rhetoric of disaffiliation in John, see Adele Reinhartz, *Cast Out of the Covenant: Jews and Anti-Judaism in the Gospel of John* (Lanham, MD: Lexington/Fortress Academic, 2018), 67–92.

18. Author translation.

19. Kenneth Burke, *A Rhetoric of Motives* (Berkeley, CA: University of California Press, 1969), 150.

20. Celeste M. Condit, "The Functions of Epideictic: The Boston Massacre Orations as Exemplar," *CommQ* 33 (1985): 289.

21. *Paul Ricoeur: Tradition and Innovation in Rhetorical Theory* (Albany: State University of New York Press, 2006), 97.

22. Victoria Wohl, "Rhetoric of the Athenian Citizen," in *The Cambridge Companion to Ancient Rhetoric*, ed. Erik Gunderson (Cambridge: Cambridge University Press, 2009), 171.

23. Reinhartz, *Cast Out of the Covenant*, 3–22.

24. See Sherri Brown, *Gift upon Gift: Covenant Through Word in the Gospel of John*, PTMS144 (Eugene, OR: Pickwick, 2010), 88.

25. David Konstan, "The Emotion in Aristotle *Rhetoric* 2.7: Gratitude, not Kindness," in *Influences on Peripatetic Rhetoric: Essays in Honor of William W. Fortenbaugh*, ed. David C. Mirhady (Leiden: Brill, 2007), 239–44.

26. Auguste Comte, *System of Positive Polity*, 4 vols., ed. Edward Spencer Beesly, trans. John Henry Bridges, Frederic Harrison, Richard Congreve, Henry Dix Hutton (London: Longmans, Green, and Co., 1875–77).

27. Anders Nygren, *Agape and Eros*, trans. Philip S. Watson (London: SPCK, 1953), 210.

28. Solomon Schimmel, "Gratitude in Judaism," in *The Psychology of Gratitude*, ed. Robert A. Emmons and Michael E. McCullough (Oxford: Oxford University Press, 2004), 39.

29. See Jeremy Engels, *The Art of Gratitude* (Albany: SUNY Press, 2018), 54–56, 76–77.

30. Aafke Elisabeth Komter, "Gratitude and Gift Exchange," in *The Psychology of Gratitude*, ed. Robert A. Emmons and Michael E. McCullough (Oxford: Oxford University Press, 2004), 19.

31. Kate Lamb, "AirAsia Crash: Crew Lost Control of Plane after Apparent Misunderstanding," *Guardian*, December 1, 2015; https://www.theguardian.com/world/2015/dec/01/airasia-crew-actions-caused-jet-to-lose-control-say-crash-investigators.

32. Remarks given at Juilliard School "Symposium on American Society and the Arts," September 22, 2005, quoted in Antonin Scalia, *Scalia Speaks: Reflections on Law, Faith, and Life Well Lived* (New York: Crown Forum, 2017), 43.

Part 2

JOHN 10

NARRATIVE, SOCIOCULTURAL, INTERTEXTUAL, AND RHETORICAL READINGS

Chapter 5

The Parable of the Sheepfold
A Narrative Reading of John 10
Dorothy A. Lee

A narrative reading of the Fourth Gospel approaches the text primarily as a literary artifice. The narrative is deciphered at a surface (though not superficial) level, without direct attention to the history lurking behind the text or the future beckoning in front of it. The core question is: how is the text shaped and molded as narrative?[1] The question recognizes the interconnection between form and meaning, structure, and content. Form is not a shell or wrapper to be peeled away and discarded to reveal the essence of meaning. In this sense, "the medium is the message" and, while it can be helpful to paraphrase them, the contents can never ultimately be torn from their container.[2] A narrative approach thus explores the contours of the text from within its own form.

There are three steps to such a narrative reading. The first involves analyzing the text in its locale in the Gospel's overarching tale, in this case, John 10; without this initial step, the smaller units become isolated from their place in the plot to which they intrinsically belong. The second step involves narrowing in on the structure in order to identify the literary devices employed by the narrator in recounting the story. These devices include imagery, metaphor and symbolism,[3] plot, point of view and implied reader,[4] and characterization, irony, and rhetoric.[5] The third step engages the theological meaning of the text as it emerges from within its crafted form. In this chapter, I will use these three steps to provide a narrative reading of John 10.

CONTEXT

The immediate context, on the one side, is the feasts of Judaism (John 5–10) where the narrative operates around four festivals associated with the temple, their significance directed toward the Johannine Jesus. The series begins with the Sabbath (John 5) and the divine work and rest, manifested in the "signs and works" of Jesus's ministry; the second is Passover, with its memorial of exodus, the manna, and the paschal lamb (John 6); the third is Tabernacles, recalling the exodus with the core rituals involving light and water (John 7:1–10:21); and the fourth is the Feast of Dedication celebrating the reconsecration of the temple in the second century B.C.E. (John 10:22–49).[6]

On the other side of John 10 is the raising of Lazarus, the last scene in the first half of the Gospel, bringing Jesus's public ministry to a climax and setting in motion his impending passion, death, and resurrection. It presages a new movement in the plot—the crossing over from public to private, from arrival to departure, from life-giving ministry to life-giving death (John 11–12).[7] Here as elsewhere, the divisions of John's Gospel are pliable; always there is overlap and interlinking, connections that look forward and back, interweaving one story into another. The two last "signs" of the public ministry of Jesus, the giving of sight and raising from the dead, embody dramatically the core motifs of light and life that emerge first in the Prologue (1:4–5).

The narrative of John 10 thus forms a kind of bridge between the two "signs," introducing at the same time new imagery that heightens both the revelation and the hostility it evokes. But it also forms a conduit between Tabernacles and Dedication (though it jumps several weeks),[8] displaying the close links with John 9 and its Tabernacles themes, as well as launching the Feast of Dedication to buttress the Gospel's Christology within the broader narrative.

NARRATIVE STRUCTURE

Jesus's teaching in the opening verses of John 10 shapes the ensuing drama of hostility, retreat, and faith. Verses 1–18 are integral to the story and not a separable "discourse" that can be winkled from its narratorial shell. In order to identify the narrative profile, we begin by sketching a pattern that will establish the sequence of events. This structure moves in three distinct phases, marked by time difference and change of locale. The first two scenes consist of Jesus's expanding self-revelation followed by the increasingly negative response of his hearers, and it concludes in the third scene with Jesus's own response and that of those who believe in him:

Scene 1

    Parable of sheepfold (10:1–6)
    Jesus as gate (10:7–10)

Jesus as shepherd (10:11–18)
Response: division of opinion (10:19–21)

Scene 2

Setting: Feast of Dedication, winter, temple (10:22–23)
Dialogue: Jesus as shepherd (10:24–31)
Dialogue: charge of blasphemy (10:32–39)

Scene 3

Response of Jesus: retreat (10:40)
Response of faith (10:41–42)

This structure assumes that, despite controversy over its genre and the meaning of *paroimia* (10:6),[9] Jesus's opening scenario is a parable rather than an allegory, image-field, or vague "figure of speech." If we include all the Gospel sayings of Jesus labeled "parables," we find no sharp disjunction between the Synoptic *parabolai* and the Johannine *paroimiai*; both have similar (though not identical) features. A helpful definition of parable in all four Gospels includes three elements: it is a *narrative* that is *fictional* and *realistic*, and it centers around a *metaphor* that takes on symbolic meaning.[10] This definition is as true for the Johannine parables as for the Synoptic ones.[11] The parable of John 10 is a fictional and realistic narrative as it recounts a credible scenario in Palestinian farming practice:

(A)   The thief sneaks into the fold over the wall;
    (B)   The shepherd, known to the gatekeeper, enters via the gate and the sheep follow his familiar and trusted voice;
(A^1)   The thief is a stranger the sheep do not follow, running from his unfamiliar voice.

The parable then becomes metaphorical, as its enlargement in the ensuing verses make plain.[12]

Within this structure, the narrative flows in a characteristically Johannine fashion. It begins with a foundational image, which is the parable (vv. 1–5); misunderstanding (v. 6) leads to an unfolding of the symbolic meaning (vv. 7–18); the revelation leads to a struggle for understanding on the part of Jesus's interlocutors (vv. 19–21); this struggle turns to rejection of the symbolic meaning through dialogue, with two attempted acts of violence (vv. 22–39); and finally Jesus withdraws indicating the total rejection of him, while others comes to faith (vv. 40–42).[13]

There is one further aspect to the structure. The narrative of John 10 also consists of a series of images divulged in typically Johannine oppositions that unfold in dialogue with the group called *Ioudaioi* ("Jews" or "Judeans").[14] These set out in antitheses that capture John's moral and spiritual dualism:

- thieves and robbers vs. shepherds
- illegitimate vs. legitimate entry into sheepfold
- voice of stranger vs. voice of shepherd
- gate/shepherd vs. thieves and robbers
- shepherd vs. hired hand
- shepherd vs. wolves
- scattering vs. ingathering
- snatching vs. protecting

Many of these images have their root in OT imagery of God as the true shepherd of Israel, God's flock, and the critique of the false leaders/shepherds which connects John 10 back to John 9 (Ezekiel 34).[15] But there are also paired images that do not stand not in opposition but work together as a synthesis:

- gatekeeper and shepherd
- sheep and shepherd
- sheepgate giving access to pasture and protection
- sheep of this fold and sheep of other folds
- Father and Son

The narrative seems initially to delineate a stark contrast between those who belong and those who do not: there is no grey area, no in-between; everything seems black or white, ostensibly in the list of contrasts. Yet there is also some ambiguity within the dyadic framework. Those who become Jesus's opponents are at first of divided mind, suggesting an initial openness to faith on the part of some. Jesus also speaks of "other sheep" who belong to another sheepfold (10:16) and the ambiguity of their identity leaves room for something less dogmatic and defined. The imagery may be proffered in polarities, but the dialogue remains accessible, intimating a potential for convergence where such divisions no longer exist.

Scene 1:

a) *Parable*

There is no formal narrative opening to the first scene in John 10. Jesus continues his words to the religious authorities from 9:39–41 where he describes his presence as that of light, both illuminating and also critically exposing. Here it is not the blindness of the authorities with which Jesus takes issue—blindness in his hands can, after all, be cured—but their erroneous assumption (in John's view) of possessing sight. At the same time, John 10:1 leaves behind the imagery of blindness and sight, darkness and light, and opens a new set of images around shepherding and the sheepfold, although its first reference is to the attempt of the thief to jump the wall. There is thus both continuity and discontinuity between John 9 and John 10.

The narrative begins with a solemn saying that frequently occurs in John's Gospel on the lips of Jesus: "Very truly I say to you" (*amēn amēn legō hymin*, 10:1a). The formula communicates for the narrator (as also for the Synoptics) a commanding sense of divine authority in the expanding revelation.[16] This is a common rhetorical device in John's Gospel, strengthening the weight of Jesus's more significant utterances. The thief contrasts markedly with the shepherd who can come and go as he likes through the gate, known and recognized by the gatekeeper. The sheep also recognize the voice of the shepherd whom they follow in and out by the sheepgate.

It may seem strange, given its everyday familiarity, that the parable is not immediately understood (10:6). Yet this is characteristic of parables. They entail interpretation to reveal their reference, which is sometimes provided by Jesus himself in the Synoptics, while at other times it remains implicit; indeed sometimes the purpose is to obfuscate or obscure (e.g., Mark 4:11–12). Johannine parables, by contrast, are generally accompanied by their meaning which is unfurled in the encircling narrative, drawing out the associations for Jesus and the community of faith (e.g., 3:11–15; 15:1–11; 16:19–22).

b) *Gate*[17]

The second part of the first scene (10:7–18) draws out the metaphorical and symbolic meaning in a way that is uniquely Johannine, turning the pastoral imagery into a cluster of symbols that enunciate John's theology. This is in keeping with John's parables, most of which turn on specific symbols that are substantial and bearers of meaning.[18] Like the first section, the opening verse is prefixed by the solemn, "Very truly I say to you" (10:7). The two core symbols of the parable which are now elucidated are the *gate (thyra)* and the *shepherd (poimēn)*, each of which John will clarify in turn. They comprise two of the seven, metaphorical *egō eimi* ("I am") sayings of the Fourth Gospel,[19] which convey an intimate divine association. Along with the solemn *amēn amēn* sayings in which the parable and its meaning are encased, they communicate a transcendent sense of identity and authority that becomes embodied precisely in the symbols, just as the divine Word (Logos) becomes "flesh" (*sarx*, 1:14) in the Johannine Jesus.[20] The "I am" sayings with their imagery disclose symbolically the central theme of the Gospel which is eternal life (*zōē aiōnios*): life in the light of Jesus's resurrection.[21]

The two core symbols of gate and shepherd work together around the imagery of the sheepfold. While overlapping, they are not identical in meaning. John uses the imagery of the gate to depict the egress and ingress of the sheep on a daily basis. They are assured of pasture in the day as they leave the sheepfold in the morning and of security from predators and warmth from the cold in the evening as they return to the sheepfold. The gate gives them dual access to nurture and safety, fulfilling the conditions needed for their survival and thriving.

The "I am" saying, used twice, identifies Jesus explicitly as the sheepgate (10:7–10). In the terms of the symbolism Jesus gives access to both nourishment and safety to his "sheep"—those who belong to him: "If anyone enters in through me they will be saved and will come in and go out and find pasture" (10:9). Jesus is the source of their life: their nurture and safety. Indeed, the narrator describes it as life "in abundance" (*perisson*), which implies an excess, an overflowing, a superfluity: life that overcomes death, both literally and metaphorically (10:10). On either side of this narrative are examples of those who receive such access to life: the man born blind (9:1–41) and Lazarus (11:1–44).

In order to strengthen the point, Jesus—using the polarities we have noted—contrasts the gate in these verses with the "thieves and bandits." There is a pattern of interweaving around the two "I am" sayings:

A   Jesus ("I am"): the gate for the sheep (v. 7)
        B   Thieves and bandits: strangers to the sheep (v. 8)[22]
A^1 Jesus ("I am"): the gate, giving nurture and safety (v. 9)
        B^1 Thief: bringing destruction and death (v. 10a)
A^2 Jesus: bringing abundant life (v. 10b)

In this cyclical pattern, the destructive elements (B, B^1) are enclosed by Jesus at the beginning and end (A, A^2), who is also the centerpoint (A^1), reinforcing the Johannine theme that the life he offers outmaneuvers the forces of death and destruction. They are not equal powers contending in battle, but the resurrection life of the Johannine Jesus triumphs over death at every turn (see 1:5).

Once again the parable provides a commentary on the two Johannine "signs" which surround it. The authorities mistreat the man born blind, abusing and dismissing him (9:34), while the Jerusalem authorities, following the raising of Lazarus, plot Jesus's death (11:45–53). Though they see themselves as true shepherds of the flock, in the Johannine narratorial worldview, the religious leaders act as thieves and bandits whose only intent is to harm and destroy. The safety and security provided within the metaphorical fold protects the sheep from precisely such as these.

c) *Shepherd*

The existence of the sheepgate is a form of metonymy, where a part that is loosely connected serves to signify the whole. It implies, in other words, the whole system of shepherding, including the person responsible for the sheep. In the parable itself, the gatekeeper is mentioned only in passing (10:3); it is the shepherd who is now the focus of attention following the symbol of the gate. Past readings of John 10 have associated the shepherd with pastoral care and compassion for the sheep. But that is not quite how the symbolism works. The gate comes first, as it does in the parable (10:1–2a), serving the pastoral function. The shepherd symbol gathers up and takes the same imagery further (10:11–18).

The expansion of the symbolism becomes immediately apparent in the "I am" statement (10:11). Jesus's words now move in a surprising direction. The shepherding image, which lies behind that of the gate, has already been alluded to in the parable itself: the shepherd's voice is known and trusted by the sheep and they will follow it (10:2–4). But now the shepherd is described as "good" (*kalos*) because he will "lay down his life for the sheep"; his readiness to die is precisely where his "goodness" lies. The imagery is interwoven in a chiastic pattern of contrasts:

A   Jesus: good shepherd, ready to die for his own (v. 11)
    B   Hired hand: does not own sheep, will not protect them against wolf (vv. 12–13)
A^1 Jesus: good shepherd, knows his own and will die for them (vv. 14–15)

At the same time, the imagery is puzzling. How will dying for the sheep protect them from ravening wolves? Admittedly, the employee's precipitate departure leaves the sheep vulnerable as prey; but the death of the shepherd will not protect them either in the long run. With this imagery, both employee and shepherd will forsake the sheep, even if the one is indifferent and cowardly while the other a hero. The Johannine symbolism will counter this, however, stretching the parable beyond its limits, since no shepherd is expected to die for his flock. At the same time, the Father is now explicitly included, and a parallel drawn between the intimacy Jesus shares with the Father, and his own relationship to "the sheep."[23] This is an exceptional shepherd because behind him, in a unique and intimate way, stands the Johannine God.

In the meantime, the shepherd has a further function: to gather in and unite "other sheep" who belong to "other folds" (10:16). Who are these other sheep: Gentiles, non-Johannine Christians, people of other faiths?[24] The narrator does not say to whom or what it refers at this point, although the coming of the Greeks to see Jesus later in the narrative points in the direction of the Gentiles (12:20–21). In the end, the "world" will go after Jesus (12:19) and he will open his arms on the cross to embrace "all things" (12:32).[25] The passion and resurrection are implied in this reference to the ingathering by the shepherd which is directly connected to the cross.

The last two verses both reiterate and extend the significance of the shepherd symbolism. They are preceded by a further reference to the Father whose love is described as both the source and consequence of Jesus's loving and self-giving mission (10:17a; see 3:16–17).[26] Indeed, the Father stands at the beginning and end of these chiastic verses:

(A)   Father's love given to Jesus
    (B)   Jesus's dying and rising
(A¹)   Father's authority given to Jesus

Jesus's identity, life, and mission are shown here to be embraced by the Father, enfolded in the divine purpose. That makes all the difference. It is not so absurd that the shepherd should die for the sheep, because he will not actually be abandoning them. He will also rise again for them; indeed, his dying will bring about his resurrection, which he accomplishes himself: "I myself lay down my life in order that I might take it up again" (10:17b). The capacity to gather in "all things" is based on the cross which means that, far from deserting the sheep, the resurrection enables Jesus to gather them and everyone else into the embrace of the Father. The goodness of the shepherd has taken the reader in an unexpected direction that amplifies the imagery: Jesus will give life to the sheep by dying and rising for them. The last sentence points to Jesus's divine authority over life and death that enables him to do this (10:18; see 5:19–29).

d) *Division*

The parable, with its symbolic explication, results in conflict among Jesus's hearers who are now mentioned explicitly for the first time (10:19–21). There is division of opinion among them (*schisma*), as a consequence of Jesus's self-revelation. It is a typically Johannine persuasive device to offer only two ways of responding to Jesus: either he is demon-possessed, and therefore under the power of sin—a "sinner"—or he is a genuine miracle worker, and therefore truly "from God" (9:31–33). A similar alternative is present also in the previous narrative where the authorities dispute the identity of the man born blind among themselves, while the man himself sees Jesus's work as divine rather than sinful (see 9:25–33).

This somewhat stylized alternative functions as a literary device for the implied audience who is summoned to make up their own minds about Jesus's identity. No other possibilities for explaining Jesus's behavior are given, because the narrator is not attempting a neutral presentation of Jesus but a rhetorical narrative that is geared toward eliciting faith. The reader is invited to identify with the sheep of the fold who recognize and confirm Jesus's true identity. The Johannine alternative is to side with those who will call for his death and ally themselves with the forces of destruction and darkness.

Scene 2:

a) *Dedication*

Scene 2 appears to move in a different direction, since it presupposes a change of time and a new feast, but it also flows out of the parable and its christological explication. In this sense, the parable works rather like the "signs" in the Fourth Gospel which often lead to considerable dialogue and debate (e.g., 6:25–65). Furthermore, the feast itself also functions symbolically and christologically, as do the other festivals in this section of the Gospel. The word used for the Feast of Dedication (*Hanukkah*) is *"egkainia"* which means literally "renewal."

The issue is that of Jesus's identity, which follows directly from the parable and is linked to the Feast of Dedication, raising the question of whether Jesus will be the one to renew and redeem Israel from its oppressors.[27] Jesus's claims, both explicit and implicit, are messianic, evoking an authority and status that are divinely bestowed. This identity is reinforced by the Johannine implications of the festival: as "the visible evidence of God's presence," the temple is fulfilled in Jesus himself who is "the living presence of God among his people."[28]

b) *Dialogue: Shepherd*

The scene is in two parts, each concluding with an attempted act of violence against Jesus. The division of opinion is no longer apparent: Jesus's interlocutors at this point have become a hostile group, a point reinforced by the portentous verb: they now "encircled" him (*ekyklōsan*, v. 24). Using the imagery of the parable, Jesus interprets their hostility as the sign of their non-belonging: they fail to hear and recognize the shepherd's voice, and thus to follow him, indicating that they are not of God's people, whatever they claim to be.

At the same time, the conflict evokes further revelation by Jesus. The "life in abundance" of the parable (10:10), which describes the nurture and protection of the flock, is now extended explicitly to indicate "life eternal" (*zōēn aiōnion*, 10:28), a protection that, for the narrator, no hostile force of darkness can eradicate. This gift is given, paradoxically, through Jesus's death and resurrection (see 11:25–26). Yet Jesus goes on to clarify that he does not offer this of himself but it is given to him from the Father by virtue of his identity (5:19). To belong to Jesus, in Johannine terms, is thus to belong to God. The sheep, safe within the fold, are an image of the people of God, safe within divine hands (10:29). In the sense of his mission, the Johannine Jesus and the Father are united, emphasizing that Jesus's saving work is in fact the work of God (10:30).

Whereas the first response of Jesus's auditors is incomprehension (10:6) and the second response a division of opinion (10:19–21), the third response is that of violence: they take up stones to execute him (10:31). The conflict is escalating. The irony is that, in the Johannine worldview, unbelief and enmity work as effectively as faith and understanding in unfolding the revelation. It is Jesus's claim of a unique relationship with God that is the impetus for the hostility, which itself arises out of incomprehension. Capital punishment in the form of stoning is the penalty for, among other crimes, blasphemy (Lev. 24:10–23).

c) *Dialogue: Blasphemy*

At the same time, the response of Jesus's adversaries impels the next part of the dialogue, in which Jesus defends himself against the charge of blasphemy. Jesus's initial rejoinder is to point to the "good works" he has done, indicating that his mission has divine origins and that his work is "from God" (10:32). But the real issue is not here: it lies in the messianic claims Jesus makes for himself in relation to the Father (10:33), the claims which underlie his ministry and which his ministry, in Johannine terms, validates. Undergirding his mission is John's Sabbath Christology, his belief that Jesus holds authority to carry the work that is uniquely divine (5:19–20).

The relationship between who Jesus is (his identity) and what he does (his works) has a balancing structure in these verses:

A works (v. 32)
   B identity (vv. 33–36)
A^1 works (vv. 37–38a)
   B^1 identity (v. 38b)

This complementary design conveys eloquently the point Jesus is making to his opponents: that his works authenticate his identity and arise from his identity, so that the two are ultimately fused. At the same time, Jesus speaks of the works as having a mediating function that can facilitate believing: they can serve as a first step on the tangled footpath to faith. This, in fact, is precisely the experience of the man born blind whose firsthand experience of Jesus's work in giving him sight enables him to move from ignorance (9:12) to full faith (9:25–33).

Jesus's apologia to his opponents for his challenging self-identification is based on the first part of Ps. 82:6: "You are gods, children of the Most High, all of you" (John 10:34). The argument is generally viewed as moving from the lesser to the greater: if the Scripture can refer to certain human beings as "gods," there is nothing inherently blasphemous in Jesus using the title "Son of God" (10:35–36). Taken alone, this may seem a weak argument for Jesus's status in this Gospel, particularly in view of John's Sabbath Christology and the intimate connection between Father and Son; not to mention Jesus's own emphatic *"my* Father" at various points in the narrative (2:16; 5:17; 8:19; 14:2; 15:1; 20:17), including our own narrative (10:18). But the appeal to OT Scripture, which for the narrator is fulfilled in Jesus,[29] functions as a provisional means to enable faith in the opponents: like the appeal to the works of his ministry, Jesus suggests ways in which those who struggle can move closer to faith and understanding.

At the same time, the use of Psalm 82 is also a statement of the community's identity, and not just of Jesus himself. "You are gods" is both an address and an invitation to the opponents and the audience of the Gospel to take on a new identity as "children of God" (1:12–13) and therefore as "gods."[30] Jesus's alienated enemies are summoned to move to a radically new identity in union with him and therefore with the Father.

Note also the allusion, in all this disagreement and conflict, to the Feast of Dedication. Jesus describes himself as one whom the Father has both "consecrated" (*egiasen*) and "sent" (10:36). Yet this sublime identity, bringing the feast to its fullness, is not appreciated by Jesus's opponents; indeed, it is actively rejected. The dialogue ends no better than at first. This time the opponents, far from being convinced by Jesus's self-defense and progressing toward belief, are aroused to fury by the avowal of his identity and try to "snatch" him (*piasai*, 10:39). Here Jesus's adversaries may appear at first to be acting like their Maccabean forebears in resisting idolatry, but the Johannine Jesus is speaking as the true temple who is entirely dedicated to God (2:17–21). As elsewhere, Jesus escapes the violence (see 8:59). The hostility has intensified: in the first case, they wanted to stone him from a distance; now they move closer to lay physical hands on him, most likely to arrest him and drag him before the authorities.

Scene 3:

a) *Response of Jesus*

Jesus retreats from Jerusalem and the temple, in part out of self-defense, but mainly because his "hour" has not yet arrived, the "hour" of his departure as directed by the Father (12:23; 13:1), when he will indeed surrender himself to the authorities and drink the cup placed in his hands (18:11). Significantly, he travels to the locale associated with John the Baptist's baptizing (Perea, 1:28), on the other side of the Jordan and beyond the reach of the Judean powers. It is also by implication a place of refuge and comfort for the Johannine Jesus, the place where he was first attested to by the Baptist and where the first disciples gathered around him (1:29–42).

b) *Response of Faith*

The new location is also a place of believing response to Jesus. Despite the rising tide of hostility, the narrative ends on an unexpectedly positive note, with many who "came to him" (10:41a) and who "believed in him" (10:42). Their progress from "coming" to Jesus to "believing" in him occurs, once again in this Gospel, through John the Baptist who is the faithful witness to Jesus (10:41b). With his life in danger, Jesus stands within the community—the "flock"—of those who believe in him, who hear and recognize his voice, and who bear witness to him, over against the Jerusalem authorities. It is a place of oasis for Jesus before the conflict recommences in earnest in the following narrative (11:45–57).

CHARACTERIZATION

The way the central characters are portrayed is also an important feature of Johannine narrative.[31] Some of Jesus's opponents, the *Ioudaioi*, are depicted as initially willing to be open to Jesus's revelation and many of them, in the following narrative, will come to faith (11:45): "Jesus was not only able to penetrate the hostile attitude of his opponents but also to win some over (whether publicly or secretly)."[32] In John 10, however, hostility is quickly roused by the risk Jesus poses to their religious power and influence. In a competitive spirit, they assume the arrogance of Jesus's claims, but they are not ready to call into question their own. The desire to kill Jesus discloses, in the terms of Johannine polemic, that they are children, not of God nor of Abraham, but "of the devil" (8:39–44). This portrait of the *Ioudaioi* groups them into one, despite the believing of many in the following narrative. It is thus somewhat stylized and schematic, a literary device to present the reader with the only alternative to authentic faith.

The same group also functions as a foil to Jesus. Where their desire is for destruction and harm (evident also in their treatment of the man born blind), the desire of the Good Shepherd is to give life, nurture, protect, and gather into one. Whereas the *Ioudaioi* want to safeguard their power and status, the Johannine Jesus is self-giving and will lay down his life for others. Yet his efforts to win his opponents to faith sit somewhat uneasily alongside his forthright pronouncements about their lack of faith and exclusion from the people of God. His characterization is depicted, in other words, in enigmatic terms as both calm and confrontational, kindly and yet uncompromising; so that his hard-hitting declarations of truth, despite his efforts to ease them toward faith, are in part responsible for their belligerent response to him. Yet this characterization of Jesus and of the *Ioudaioi* functions as a narratorial—rather than "realistic" or psychological—device to persuade the reader to move from one faction to the other, from the community of the religious leaders to that of the Shepherd.[33]

CONCLUSION

A narrative reading of John 10 lays bare the literary devices to show how the narrative divulges its symbolic meaning. Despite rebuff, the Johannine Jesus as the Gate and the Shepherd discloses himself through the texture of the narrative and gathers to himself the sheep who belong to him. The polemical nature of the story does not suppress the revelation but, on the contrary, intensifies it, pointing back to the story of the man born blind and forward to the raising of Lazarus where conflict also furthers the revelation, leading ultimately to the cross as the high point of Johannine revelation (19:33–37). A narrative reading enables the reader to enter the story, identify with the characters, and experience the imagery at an affective level, firing the imagination in the cause of Johannine faith. Sensitivity to the literary features has the capacity to disclose the shape and intent of the narrative, along with the rhetorical means it employs to persuade the reader.

NOTES

1. See especially R. Alan Culpepper, *Anatomy of the Fourth Gospel: A Study in Literary Design* (Philadelphia: Fortress, 1983); also James L. Resseguie, "A Narrative-Critical Approach to the Fourth Gospel," in *Characters and Characterization in the Gospel of John*, ed. Christopher W. Skinner, LNTS 461 (London:

Bloomsbury/T&T Clark, 2013), 3–17, and Jo-Ann A. Brant, "The Fourth Gospel as Narrative and Drama," in *The Oxford Handbook of Johannine Studies*, eds. Judith M. Lieu and Martinus C. de Boer (Oxford: Oxford University Press, 2018), 186–202.

2. Further on this, see Dorothy A. Lee, *The Symbolic Narratives of the Fourth Gospel: The Relationship of Form and Meaning*, JSNTSup 95 (Sheffield: Sheffield Academic, 1994), 23–35.

3. On the imagery and symbolism of the Fourth Gospel, see Dorothy A. Lee, "Imagery," in *How John Works: Storytelling in the Fourth Gospel*, ed. Douglas Estes and Ruth Sheridan, RBS 86 (Atlanta: SBL Press, 2016), 151–70, and Lee, "Symbolism & 'Signs': in the Fourth Gospel," in Lieu and de Boer, *Johannine Studies*, 259–73.

4. The implied reader or audience exists within the text; real readers, by contrast, experience the narrative in multiple, unpredictable ways; see Edward W. Klink III, "Audience," in Estes and Sheridan, *How John Works*, 245–48.

5. On the role of rhetoric in shaping characterization and the place of irony within it, see Alicia D. Myers, "Rhetoric," in Estes and Sheridan, *How John Works*, 197–202.

6. Jan A. Du Rand, "A Syntactical and Narratological Reading of John 10 in Coherence with Chapter 9," in *The Shepherd Discourse of John 10 and its Context: Studies by Members of the Johannine Writings Seminar*, ed. Johannes Beutler and Robert T. Fortna, SNTSMS 67 (Cambridge: Cambridge University Press, 1991), 94–115.

7. On the connection of John 10 to its wider narrative context, see Ulrich Busse, "Open Questions on John 10," in Beutler and Fortna, *Shepherd Discourse* (who sees the narrative of the sheepfold commencing at 9:39), 6–9.

8. On John's intricate understanding and use of time in the Gospel (in contrast to modern assumptions), see esp. Douglas Estes, "Time," in Estes and Sheridan, *How John Works*, 41–57.

9. John Painter, "Tradition, History and Interpretation in John 10," in Beutler and Fortna, *Shepherd Discourse*, 56–58.

10. Ruben Zimmermann, *Puzzling the Parables of Jesus: Methods and Interpretation* (Minneapolis: Fortress, 2015), 137–50.

11. Zimmermann, *Puzzling the Parables*, 333–60. See also Craig S. Keener, *The Gospel of John: A Commentary*, 2 vols. (Peabody, MA: Hendrickson, 2003), 1:797–98.

12. The lack of further reference to the gatekeeper indicates that it is not an allegory, since allegories see parallels in every aspect of the original story.

13. Lee, *Symbolic Narratives*, 12–15, 228–30.

14. Considerable disagreement exists on the significance of the phrase; see, for example, Adele Reinhartz, "The Jews of the Fourth Gospel," in Lieu and de Boer, *Johannine Studies*, 121–37.

15. Note also the parallel with John 15:1–18 which uses the parallel OT image of the vine for God's relationship with Israel (e.g., Isa. 5).

16. The form of these solemn sayings of Jesus is also found in the Synoptic Gospels, with a single *amēn*, "truly"; only John has a double *amēn*. They occur most frequently in Matthew (31x) and John (25x) and least often in Luke (6x).

17. A couple of manuscripts have "shepherd" here instead of "gate," but this is unlikely to be original (Francis J. Moloney, *The Gospel of John*, SP 4 [Collegeville: Liturgical Press, 1998], 309).

18. Further on this, see Dorothy A. Lee, *Flesh and Glory: Symbol, Gender and Theology in the Gospel of John* (New York: Crossroad, 2002), 9–28.

19. The others are the bread of life (6:35), the light of the world (8:12), the resurrection and the life (11:25–26), the way, the truth and the life (14:6), and the true vine (15:1). Each is dependent on the absolute use of "I am" in other Johannine contexts which identify Jesus as the divine Word (4:26; 6:20; 8:28, 56; 13:10; 18:5, 8). See Rudolf Schnackenburg, *The Gospel according to St John*, trans. Cecily Hastings, 3 vols. (London: Burns & Oates, 1980), 2:79–89.

20. Lee, *Flesh and Glory*, 29–64.

21. Michael J. Gorman, *Abide and Go: Missional Theosis in the Gospel of John* (Eugene, OR: Cascade, 2018), 48–51.

22. That John cannot be referring to all previous OT leaders and prophets is clear from the status given elsewhere in the Gospel to ancestral figures such as Moses (e.g., 5:45–46); see Andrew T. Lincoln, *The Gospel according to St John*, BNTC 4 (London: Continuum, 2005), 295–96.

23. The same parallel exists between the Beloved Disciple and Jesus at the Last Supper, and the Father and the Son (1:18; 13:2); Lincoln, *St John*, 378–79.

24. Marianne Meye Thompson, *John: A Commentary*, NTL (Louisville: Westminster John Knox, 2015), 227.

25. The text of the NRSV has "all people" at this point, but the original text may well read "all things" (there is only the difference of one letter between the two readings). Similarly, the NRSV translates "all flesh" (17:2) as "all people," ignoring the fact that "flesh" can have a wider meaning than human beings. Further on this, see Lee, *Flesh and Glory*, 43–45.

26. See Francis J. Moloney, *Love in the Gospel of John: An Exegetical, Theological, and Literary Study* (Grand Rapids: Baker Academic, 2013), 37–69.

27. Thompson, *John*, 231.

28. Francis J. Moloney, *Signs and Shadows: Reading John 5–12* (Minneapolis: Fortress, 1996), 144, 150.

29. See Rekha M. Chennattu, "Scripture," in Estes and Sheridan, *How John Works*, 171–81.

30. See Andrew J. Byers, *Ecclesiology and Theosis in the Gospel of John*, SNTSMS 166 (Cambridge: Cambridge University Press, 2017), 191–96.

31. It is important not to read modern, psychological themes into ancient characterization; further on this, see Christopher W. Skinner, "Characterization," in Estes and Sheridan, *How John Works*, 115–32.

32. Cornelis Bennema, *Encountering Jesus. Character Studies in the Gospel of John* (Milton Keynes: Paternoster, 2009), 44.

33. Further on the theme of persuasion in the Johannine narrative, see Ruth Sheridan, "Persuasion," in Estes and Sheridan, *How John Works*, 213–23.

Chapter 6

Jesus the Good Shepherd
John 10 as Political Rhetoric
Warren Carter

Elsewhere, I have examined the intertextuality between the good shepherd passage in John 10 and the condemnation of Israel's leaders in Ezekiel 34.[1] In that companion piece, I rejected a reading of both Ezekiel 34 and John 10 as spiritualized or religious rhetoric, emphasizing that both, in the contexts of their larger narratives, counter sociopolitical leaders who misuse their power. In contrast to spiritualized readings, both texts envision divine purposes that create a very different sort of societal life. As a consequence, Jesus the good shepherd emerges not as a religious leader but as one who manifests somatic and societal Johannine "life of the age" (eternal or "age-ly" life, kingdom/empire of God) marked by abundance, somatic wholeness and security.

In this chapter, recognizing that any text interacts with a wide spectrum of cultural artifacts, I examine another intertextuality, namely between John's good shepherd passage and the long Greek and Roman political tradition of kings and emperors as good shepherds. I first reject spiritualized-religious, christological readings of the image, and second, elaborate the tradition of Greek kings and Roman emperors as good shepherds in order to argue that the intertextuality among these texts frames John 10 as political rhetoric and creates both contest and mimicry in the construction of Jesus as the good shepherd.

SPIRITUALIZED-RELIGIOUS RHETORIC

Most commentators read the good shepherd discourse of John 10 as religious rhetoric.[2] They draw on Hebrew Bible and early Judaism traditions such as Ezekiel 34, Zechariah 11, Psalms 23 and 100, and *1 Enoch* 89–90 concerning God the shepherd and Israel the sheep. Commonly, they approach John

10 as allegorical rhetoric to concentrate on the intimate spiritual relationship between Jesus the good shepherd and the sheep. John's Jesus identifies himself as the "good shepherd" (10:11, 14), the sheep are the people of God—Israel—though in supercessionist Christian readings, the sheep become a church community that shares in intimate relationship with God revealed by Jesus. The passage contrasts the good shepherd's care for the sheep with "bad" shepherds described as "a thief and bandit/brigand" (10:1, 8, 10), the stranger (10:5), and the hired hand (10:12). Their "badness" includes a voice the sheep do not know and from whom they flee (10:5), their failure to understand the good shepherd (10:6), their stealing from and destroying the sheep (10:10), and their failure to protect the sheep (10:12–13).[3] In the context of chapter 9, these bad shepherds are identified by the interchangeable terms of the Pharisees (9:13, 15, 16, 40), and the *Ioudaioi*/the Jews (9:18, 22; 10:19). The distinguishing characteristic of these characters is, according to this reading, their rejection of Jesus. So one commentator observes, "'The Jews' . . . have rejected Jesus and rejected all who move toward his revelation. . . . Their claims to be the leaders of God's people are false. They are thieves and robbers, purveyors of a messianic hope of their own making.'"[4] Evoking the intertext of Ezekiel 34, this commentator constructs them as false shepherds in contrast to Jesus who "has come that the sheep may have life more abundantly (Ezek 34:25–31)." This life comprises intimate relationship with God.

These moves ensure John's Gospel is read as religious rhetoric, a religious text involved in a religious dispute with religious leaders. Three factors, however, indicate that this Christological interpretation of the John 10 passage as religious/spiritual rhetoric is not convincing.

First, these "bad shepherds," variously identified as *Ioudaioi*/Jews/Pharisees, are not adequately described as "religious leaders" who have not believed in Jesus.[5] They are constructed in the Gospel narrative as part of an alliance of Judean societal leaders that includes the chief priests based in the Jerusalem temple and that exercises political, economic, religious, and societal power in dependent partnership with and accountable relationship to Roman rule over Judea. Alliances between the central governing power and local leaders were a common Roman ruling structure.[6] The structure is evident in the Gospel, for example, when the Jews/*Ioudaioi* send priests and Levites from Jerusalem to investigate John (1:19–28); when the chief priests and Pharisees, also identified as the Jews/*Ioudaioi*, use temple police in an attempt to arrest Jesus (7:32–35, 45–49); when the Jews/*Ioudaioi*, Pharisees, and chief priests plot to put Jesus to death out of fear of Roman intervention (11:45–53); and when soldiers and police from the chief priests and Pharisees accompany Judas to arrest Jesus (18:3–14). In 19:12, this alliance of colonized leaders goads the governor, "If you release this man, you are not Caesar's friend." They expect the governor to uphold his part of the alliance:

"Everyone who makes himself a king sets himself against Caesar." Three verses later, they make the amazing confession of loyalty to their imperial overlord in the form of the Roman governor, "We have no king but the emperor."

This textual construction accurately inscribes and participates in one of Rome's preferred governing patterns which made ambivalent alliances between Rome and local provincial elites, sharing power, fostering competition, and rewarding loyalty. Josephus, for example, calls the temple-based, Jerusalem-located chief priests "the leaders of Judea" (*Ant.* 20.249), yet attests Rome's appointment of the chief priests (*Ant.* 18.33–35, 95), its guardianship of the chief priestly garments in the Antonia fortress (*Ant.* 15.403–8; 18.90–95; 20.6–14), the alliance of chief priests and leading Pharisees (*Life* 21), and Roman supervision of temple-based festivals—so prevalent in John's Gospel—such as Dedication (10:22) which celebrated victory over the imperial aggression of Antiochus IV Epiphanes. Josephus comments that "it is on these festive occasions that sedition is most apt to break out" (*J.W.* 1.88)[7] and he observes the increased presence of Roman troops in Jerusalem who "watch the people and repress any insurrectionary movements" (*J.W.* 5.244; also 2.224; *Ant.* 20.106). The Gospel's construction of these leaders participates in these imperial dynamics.

Moreover, the presentation of the bad shepherds in the widely recognized intertext of Ezekiel 34 confirms the societal-political role and rule of these shepherd-leaders.[8] Ezekiel 34 is not to be read as spiritualized rhetoric; its sociopolitical context and content are to be taken seriously. The text explains judgment on Israel's leaders carried out by means of sixth-century Babylonian imperial aggression and offers a new future for Israel from God's intervention.

The rhetoric is condemning as God judges the shepherds of Israel, the elite leadership, because they preside over and maintain a societal structure which benefits themselves but harms the people. These bad shepherds feed and clothe themselves but do not feed the sheep/people (34:2, 3, 8, 10 [2x], 18, 19, 28). They neglect the people and have not "strengthened the weak . . . healed the sick . . . bound up the injured . . . brought back the strayed . . . sought the lost . . . but with force and harshness you ruled them" (34:4). Repeatedly they are charged with making the sheep sick, not feeding them, failing to protect them, and scattering them. The intertext casts its light on the John 10 scene as John's Jesus condemns Israel's Rome-allied leaders as false or bad shepherds, hirelings, thieves, and robbers,[9] whose societal structures and practices damage and exclude people like the man born blind (9:22) and destroy the sheep (10:10), even as they pursue their own well-being at the expense of the sheep (10:12–13). The intertext of Ezekiel 34 exposes the unjust and sinful nature of their rule and declares God's verdict of judgment on it. And repeatedly God declares God will take over these shepherding-ruling duties through a Davidic agent (Ezek. 34:10, 13–14, 23, 27, 29), intervening to save and shepherd the people by gathering, protecting and feeding them, and healing the sick (34:11–22). An eschatological age of peace or wholeness comprising security, abundant fertility, physical wholeness, and God's presence will follow (34:25–30).

It is simply not adequate, I argue, to reduce Ezekiel 34's rhetoric to spiritualized-religious rhetoric about Jesus providing spiritual life. This Hebrew Bible intertext is political, material, somatic, societal; it is about social structures, about human interaction and flourishing; and it offers a vision of human life so very different from that served up by destructive imperial structures. Reading along lines of power highlights issues of societal structures rather than religious disputes.

Religious or spiritual rhetoric is also inadequate to understand Jesus as the good shepherd. Jesus's self-identification with the divine name "I am" and the title "good shepherd" (John 10:11, 14) allies him with the vision of divine purposes set out in contrast to the societal practices of the bad shepherds in Ezekiel 34. The previous Gospel narrative shows him to reveal God's presence and life-giving and just purposes in words and actions (4:34). His signs of turning water into abundant wine (2:1–11), providing much bread (6:1–14), healing the sick (5:2–15; ch. 9), and judging an evil imperial world (4:19–20; 5:22; 7:7) identify him as the divinely commissioned shepherd of the people enacting God's life-giving and just purposes in feeding and healing people. His actions, like those of the "bad shepherds" in Ezekiel 34 and the alliance of leaders in the Gospel, are somatic, political, material, and societal, but whereas the Gospel frames the actions of the blind and sinful rulers, thieves, and brigands as self-serving, self-enriching, and destructive (9:40), it constructs Jesus's actions as transformative and life-giving. The man born blind, now healed by Jesus, represents both *their* destructive, and *his* life-giving, actions.

GREEK KINGS AND ROMAN EMPERORS AS GOOD SHEPHERDS

I turn now to another intertext evoked by identifying Jesus as the good or noble shepherd and suggest that rhetorically the term contrasts Jesus not only with these Jerusalem-based, Rome-allied rulers of Judea, but also creates an ambivalent intertextuality with the emperor himself, paralleling, resisting, and mimicking imperial rhetoric concerning imperial rule. That is, I am broadening the intertexts usually evoked for John 10 beyond Ezekiel 34 and other Hebrew Bible texts to texts omitted from the discussion. And secondly I am taking them on their own terms as political rhetoric and not spiritualizing them as religious rhetoric.

Some have protested my previous explorations of John's Gospel in relation to Roman power.[10] Christopher W. Skinner complains that I deal only superficially with the "synagogue expulsion" theory, erroneously claim the Gospel's origin to be in Ephesus, and that I emphasize "less prominent features of the narrative" to make my argument of intertextuality between the Gospel and Roman imperial power.[11] None of these arguments engages in any depth the central claim that John's Gospel, read in an imperial provincial capital such as Ephesus, interacts with the visions, structures, practices, and personnel of Roman power. It is hard to dismiss claims of imperial intertextuality when the Gospel's main character is crucified by a Roman governor and his allies, an event connected to every aspect of the Gospel. Readers of the Gospel in a city like Ephesus inevitably found intertextuality between the Gospel and Roman power that was very visible in the city.[12]

In a strongly worded critique marked by significant misunderstandings, Moloney rejects the whole enterprise.[13] The claim that my work, if on target, would "marginalize" much Johannine scholarship from the last 150 years is a regrettable overstatement that ignores the developing nature of all critical scholarship and posits a false alternative between Jewish and imperial concerns. Jewish people, like the audience of John's Gospel, negotiated Roman power as chapter 2 of *John and Empire* demonstrates.[14] Likewise, Moloney's charge that I misconstruct the Gospel's origins simply misses my interest in the Gospel's reception and intertextuality, not its sources (excepting the appendix). The book demonstrates throughout considerable Roman presence in Ephesus, something indisputably recognized by archaeological and classical studies of the city. It addresses the question of possible intertextualities between this Roman presence and the Gospel's story of Jesus whom the Gospel presents as being sent from and sanctioned by God, just as Rome claims the same for itself, and crucified by the Roman governor and his allies.

In this chapter, I set a dimension of the Gospel's presentation of Jesus as the good shepherd in relation to another aspect of this Roman imperial world. There was a long tradition of imaging rulers and leaders as shepherds not only in Israel's traditions such as Ezekiel 34 or Moses, David, or God (Ps 23),[15] but also in Mesopotamia and Egypt,[16] and among Greeks.[17] So, for example, Homer describes Agamemnon as "shepherd of the peoples" (*poimeni laōn*; *Il.* 2.84–86, 243, 254; *Od.* 3.156; 4.24) and uses the same phrase to describe Dryas the warrior (*Il.* 1.263). Xenophon (*Mem.* 3.2) explicates Homer praising Agamemnon as a good king and warrior to mean that in both roles as a good shepherd he cared for his flock in ensuring necessary supplies and safety for the good life of his people. Xenophon also uses the analogy of herders controlling animals in relation to the rule of Cyrus the Persian (*Cyr.* 1.1.2–5).

Plato employs the image of the shepherd as the ruler who is concerned with the good of and justice for the flock (*Rep.* 1.343–45) and who, in relation to the actions of officials and agents, is distressed at rearing dogs who are to help with managing the flocks only to find that they behave as wolves in attacking and harming the sheep (416A).

Oswyn Murray points out that the description of "the king as shepherd of the people" becomes a "commonplace" post-Homer.[18] He argues that the image was useful in arguments that favored rule by kingship as "natural" whereby humans should live in conformity with nature: "The family possesses one head, the father; the shepherd controls his flocks, the captain a ship, the general an army."[19] The image participated in and evoked a long and multivalent discourse concerning the ideal king and kingship (*peri basileias*) which identified the characteristics, virtues, and roles the shepherd-king should display. Foremost was the king as brave, dominating, and manly, who gained and secured power, wealth, and glory in victorious military action. Kingship derived from displays of might whereby a king constituted his own legitimacy in declaring himself to be king and vindicated it in successful conquests of land, people, and resources.

M. M. Austin emphasizes the economic corollary of this kingly act, namely that economic exploitation follows subjection.[20] The domination of people, land, and resources meant the king acquired not only military glory but also wealth as a crucial resource that enabled the king to be, in Austin's words, a "giver as well as a receiver of wealth."[21] Wealth secured soldiers, but kingly beneficence also generously benefited and rewarded followers and "friends" in various material ways, thereby securing their loyalty and augmenting the king's status and power.

Frank William Walbank identifies further characteristics and roles of this shepherd-king.[22] The king must protect his people as their "savior" (*soter*) and "benefactor" (*euergetes*) who preserves the lives of his subjects. He is a champion of civilization against barbarism, securing peace and justice to improve people's lives. As a benefactor, he is to be affectionate, generous, and magnanimous toward his subjects. That is, he must use his wealth to benefit friends, relieve the needy among his subjects, and defend against enemies. He is to be pious toward the gods, wise, intelligent, reasonable, and able to control himself by avoiding excessive and hedonistic behavior. Subjects express gratitude by offering cultic honors to both the particular god/s/goddesses who protect and bless the king as well as to the king himself.

Walbank argues that the *Letter of Aristeas* 187–294 is the "best surviving source" for this discourse about the shepherd-king.[23] At a series of banquet scenes spanning seven days, the Egyptian king Ptolemy II questions his Jewish guests about matters related to ruling a kingdom. A long list of kingly virtues, with numerous repeated items, emerges. Piety and the imitation of God's just, merciful, and generous ways are pervasive for these Jewish scribes (200–1). They also construct the king, with various nuances and combinations, as a doer of justice (189, 192, 209, 212, 216, 267, 292). To do justice includes merciful treatment (188, 192, 207–8) and obedience to the Laws (240, 279), displaying love and concern for the people's lives and well-being including health and food (189–90, 225, 228, 240, 245, 259, 263, 265, 271), showing self-control or moderation (209, 211, 222–24, 237, 253–56, 277–78, 284–85), generosity (226–27, 230), wisdom and good judgment (207–8, 255, 260), maintaining good family bonds (196, 238, 241–42, 248, 250) and relations with others (267–70, 272, 276, 280–83, 286, 289–92), exhibiting equanimity (197) and courage (199), using wealth well (205), being truthful and incorruptible (206, 209), doing good works (230–31), able to listen (239), and ensuring the peace and security of the people (291–92).

The legacy of this Hellenistic kingship ideal continues in the Roman Empire, though under a name other than kingship, in understanding the emperor and/or his delegated officials to rule for the benefit of the flock.[24] Suetonius, for example, has the emperor Tiberius reject a provincial governor's request for increased taxes by cynically saying, "It was the part of a good shepherd to shear his flock not skin it" (*Tib.* 32). Dio Chrysostom (56.16.3) has Bato, son of the leader of the Dalmatian's revolt against Rome, explain the revolt to Tiberius: "You Romans are to blame for this; for you send as guardians of your flocks, not dogs or shepherds, but wolves." Philo has the imperial adviser Macro refer to Emperor Gaius Caligula as the "sovereign of earth and sea" and "a shepherd and master of the flock" (*Legat.* 44, 52).[25] Philo describes the joy of inhabitants of the empire at the news of Gaius's supposed return to health and the transformation of "living without any governor, or protector, or Lawgiver, to be now established under the care of a governor to be a sort of shepherd (*nomei*) and leader of a more domesticated flock" (*Alleg. Interp.* 20).

In his discourses on kingship, addressed to Emperor Trajan, Dio Chrysostom draws on this long Hellenistic political-philosophical tradition about kingship, influenced by Homer, to emphasize that kings/emperors should care for and guard the people as shepherds care for sheep (*Or.* 1.13, 15–20). He admonishes that the king should be "a shepherd of his people not . . . a caterer and banqueter at their expense" (1.13). Throughout, Dio Chrysostom's discourses on ideal shepherd-kingship emphasize the king's divine origin and sanction (1.11–12, 38–40), regard for the welfare of his subjects (1.12–14, 17–26), moral character and self-control (1.12–14), authority over people (1.14), piety with respect for the gods (1.16), military ability (1.27–32; 2.34), skill in rhetoric (2.19–27, 34), praise from the people (1.33), displays of courage and justice/righteousness (*dikaiosynēn* 2.54), rule with justice (*dikaiōs*) and equity (*kalōs*; 1.45), and emulation of Zeus in bringing people together (1.38–41). Kings personify key masculine qualities of military expertise and prowess, domination, strength, piety, wealth and benevolence, self-control, mercy, and justice.[26] In his Fourth Discourse on kingship, Chrysostom reminds the Emperor Trajan that the business of an emperor is to be a "shepherd of peoples" who is to "oversee, guard and protect flocks, not . . . to slaughter, butcher and skin them."[27] Such intertexts emphasizing the king/emperor as a good shepherd who provides for his sheep/subjects highlight the misleading nature of Rudolf Bultmann's claim that in John 10 "there are no traces whatsoever of the kingly figure."[28]

INTERTEXTUALITY: POLITICAL RHETORIC AND JESUS THE GOOD SHEPHERD

I am not arguing that such kingly discourse, or Chrysostom's writing in particular, is the *source* or the image of Jesus as the good shepherd in John 10. Rather, I position this rhetoric, part of a tradition that depicts the benevolent shepherd-king/emperor who is concerned for the well-being of his flock/subjects, as intertexts for John 10, though, not surprisingly, they have been given little attention by scholars pursuing isolated, individualized "religious" readings.[29] When the good shepherd in John 10 is placed in this cluster of intertexts, particularly those that declare the emperor to be a good shepherd, several questions emerge.

First, what happens when both Jesus *and* the emperor are declared to be good shepherds?

The question immediately foregrounds matters of societal vision and structures. An extensive body of scholarship has elaborated significant levels of poverty, material deprivation, and social misery throughout the Roman Empire. Classicist Peter Garnsey argues that in relation to the pervasive "food insecurity and poor health" of the Roman world, "food was power" and that "for most people, life was a perpetual struggle for survival."[30] Various obstacles—limited varieties of food, poor nutritional quality and quantities of food, transportation and storage challenges, limited purchasing power, market prices, irregular employment, urban overcrowding, and so on—meant many experienced malnutrition and, with a diet deficient in numerous vitamins and minerals, this resulted in diseases of contagion and of deprivation.[31] Steven Friesen and Bruce Longenecker have developed poverty or economic scales that provide a vertical "map" of the Roman Empire to highlight that while shepherd-ruling figures belong to the top 2 or 3 percent of society with high status, wealth, and considerable societal influence,[32] most non-elites, those in levels five through seven of the Friesen-Longenecker poverty scales (some 70–80% of the population!) faced a constant daily challenge of securing adequate supplies of nutritionally viable food. A wide range of stressors left somatic and psychological damage on non-elites,[33] and high death rates and short life spans in the twenties were pervasive.[34]

Interestingly, and ironically, imperial rhetoric proclaimed that Rome had healed a sick world—a claim trumpeted, for example, by Philo, Josephus, Tacitus, and Aristides among others.[35] Augustus had established, so it was claimed, the "golden age" marked by familial order, social harmony, military dominance, morality, Rome's eternity, and of course fertility and abundance, at least as poets such as Virgil (*Aen.* 1.278–82; 6.788–93) and Horace (*Carmen saeculare*) would have people believe. Statius writes later that it was Domitian who reestablished this age (*Silvae* 4.1.17–37).

John's Gospel, however, is not convinced. Its disabled bodies (4:46–52; 5:2–5; 6:2; 9:1–41) reveal the lie that the imperial world effects wholeness and healing. To the contrary, the Gospel shows Rome's world—of which the "bad shepherds," that is, the alliance of Jerusalem leaders, the kings and emperors, are representatives, rulers, and beneficiaries, and the world over which they exercise dominion—to be a sick place detrimental to the life and well-being of most of its residents. Jesus's healings and feedings, then, are acts that roll back and repair imperial damage in creating whole/healed bodies.[36]

These factors that recognize the miserable and life-threatening "living" conditions of various sections of the dominant poor suggest one interaction of the claims of various figures to be the good shepherd is certainly that of challenge or contest or contrast. Despite a long tradition that emphasized the ruler's responsibility to provide for the well-being of the sheep, despite imperial rhetoric to have healed the sick world, despite Augustan claims to have created the golden age of abundant fertility and plenty renewed by Vespasian and Domitian, the imperial world remained for many a sickening place, marked by, as the elite provincial Philo puts it, "many great evils . . . famine, war, ravaging, devastation of estates, loss of property, abductions, fears of enslavement and death" (*Legat.* 16–17, 110). Or as Tacitus's British chief, Calgacus describes Roman colonizing activity: "Robbers of the world, now that earth fails their all-devastating hands, they probe even the sea; if their enemy have wealth, they have greed; if he be poor, they are ambitious; neither east nor west has glutted them . . . to plunder, butcher, steal these things they misname empire; they make a desolation and they call it peace" (*Agr.* 31). In the face of rhetoric about the emperor as the good shepherd exposed by daily life to be not so, John's construction of Jesus the good shepherd as healer and supplier of food claims a contrastive and contestive—and superior—reality marked by *actually* caring for the sheep, protecting them, not running away, providing healing and food, not stealing life from them. Of course, Jesus must continue to deliver healing and nutrition for the Gospel's audience to remain believe-able.

But second, not only is there contest, contrast, and challenge, there is also imitation, replication, mimicry, reinscribing. The Gospel's construction of

Jesus as the good shepherd reinscribes a number of features of this ideal king or emperor. Recalling Dio Chrysostom's discussion of kingly/shepherdly features, Jesus too has divine origin. He comes from God and his kingdom, his empire, that is, his *basileia* is not from this world but from God, a statement of origin rather than the sphere in which it operates (1:1–3; 5:29, 39; 13:1–3). He too exhibits piety as the agent of divine purposes (5:19–30). He too cares for his subjects (10:11; 15:9). He too effects healing (4:46–54; 5:5–9) and supplies food (6:1–14). He too has moral character and self-control (10:17–18). He too has authority over people with followers and friends (1:35–51). He too honors God (8:49). He too is capable in the manly tasks of rhetoric and deeds of power (5:1–15, 19–30). He too is praised by people (7:12 40–41a). He too exhibits justice/ righteousness and courage (5:30; 18:5–14). He too forms one people (10:16). John's Jesus is a very masculine and imperial good shepherd; contest and imitation coexist.

Third, Dio Chrysostom's list of imperial or good shepherdly characteristics includes military prowess and success. Perhaps this is a significant point of difference with Jesus in John 10 where military success is not mentioned. And, of course, in 18:36 Jesus indicates that the refusal to employ violence is a mark of his followers and his *basileia*/empire. Yet commentators note in their discussions of chapter 10, that the good shepherd's willingness to die for the sheep—mentioned at least five times (10:11, 15, 17, 18 [2x])—has no parallel in the Hebrew Bible or Jewish traditions.[37]

An interesting intertext exists, however, with these imperial ruling/shepherd traditions. An emperor who is required to perform his masculinity and courage by means of military domination and thereby show his ability to protect his flock must be willing to lay down his life for the sheep/his people in battle. There is some modifying of the expectation for military dominance. The *Letter of Aristeas* (192–93) advises that military actions "are useless in bringing anything to a lasting conclusion." And John Moles argues that one of Dio Chrysostom's goals in his *Fourth Oration on Kingship* is, without completely denying military accomplishments, to temper Trajan's military aspirations fashioned, to a significant degree, by his desire to emulate Alexander, by redirecting Trajan to pursue a virtuous character.[38] Nevertheless, Jerome Neyrey has documented the extensive Hellenistic, Roman, and Jewish expressions of what he calls a noble and voluntary death tradition whereby rulers and soldiers courageously, honorably, and manfully choose to die for the benefit of others, their city, their nation, in warfare.[39] Akin to this tradition, though without a battle context, Jesus too lays down his life for his sheep in his execution by the Roman governor (10:11, 15, 17–18). Of course, John goes one step further. John's Jesus does not stay dead. He is super shepherd, with power to take his life up again (10:18). Hostile bad shepherds cannot keep him dead; he is not only a good shepherd, he is the superior, the best shepherd.

A fourth dimension in John's construction of Jesus as good shepherd needs attention in the light of these imperial intertexts. John's good shepherd has "other sheep that do not belong to this fold. I must bring them also and they will listen to my voice. So there will be one flock, one shepherd" (10:16). Some commentators note that this reference to "other sheep not of this fold," like the reference to laying down his life, is unknown to Jewish tradition;[40] others see the motif drawing from the reference in Ezek. 34:11–16 to God bringing sheep from the nations, hence the basis for interpretations concerning the inclusion of Diaspora Jews, and/or more commonly and likely, of Gentiles.[41] Regardless, bringing in other sheep to obey this shepherd's voice and form one flock under one shepherd's rule is very imperial rhetoric. It denotes the subordination of nations to one manly ruler; it signifies the expansive dominance of one ruler; it does not allow for dissent, or even difference; it marks the formation of one people. The catalogue of domination over the nations in Augustus's *Res Gestae* comes to mind (3, 12–13, 25–33),[42] as does the visual display of the subjugated nations presented in the approaches to the Sebasteion at Aphrodisias.[43] Dominance and subjugation are the accomplishments of good and bad shepherds.

To conclude, I have proposed setting John's good shepherd rhetoric in relation to political and imperial intertexts concerning rulers as good shepherds. I have also argued that we read both John 10 and these intertexts along an axis not of narrow religious rhetoric but rhetoric of power, societal rule, and visions of societal structure. I have argued that John 10 sets Jesus in intertextual relationship with not only the Jerusalem-based, Rome-allied alliance of Pharisees, *Ioudaioi*, and chief priests (Ezekiel 34) but also with political-philosophical intertexts concerning Greek and Roman shepherd-rulers who enact and sanction hierarchical societal structures and practices that benefit themselves and destroy others. The John 10 construction of Jesus the good shepherd offers both opposition to and assimilation with imperial good-shepherd claims, including significant intertextuality concerning claims of laying down one's life and adding other sheep to his fold.

I conclude that John 10's rhetoric evokes, resists, and reinscribes rhetoric of imperial rule, even as it promotes not the good shepherd but the best, the all-powerful super shepherd, ruler of one people and able to overcome the worst that any other imperial power can impose—even death itself. A very imperial good shepherd indeed.

NOTES

1. Warren Carter, "Jesus the Good Shepherd: An Intertextual Approach to Ezekiel 34 and John 10," in *Biblical Interpretations in Early Christian Gospels:*

Vol. 4 *The Gospel of John*, ed. Thomas R. Hatina, LNTS (London: Bloomsbury/T&T Clark, forthcoming, 2020).

2. Carter, "Jesus the Good Shepherd."

3. For representative examples, see Raymond E. Brown, *The Gospel According to John I–XII*, AB 29 (Garden City, NY: Doubleday, 1966), 383–400; Ernst Haenchen, *John*, Hermeneia (Philadelphia: Fortress, 1984), 2.43–52; Gail O'Day, "The Gospel of John," in *The New Interpreter's Bible*, ed. Leander Keck, vol. 9 (Nashville: Abingdon, 1995), 665–73; Craig S. Keener, *The Gospel of John: A Commentary*, 2 vols. (Peabody, MA: Hendrickson, 2003), 1:794–820.

4. Francis J. Moloney, *The Gospel of John*, SP 4 (Collegeville, MN: Liturgical Press, 1998), 303.

5. Elaborated in Carter, "Jesus the Good Shepherd," section II.

6. G. Lenski, *Power and Privilege: A Theory of Social Stratification* (Chapel Hill: University of North Carolina Press, 1984), 219–48.

7. Translations are from LCL editions.

8. Elaborated in Carter, "Jesus the Good Shepherd," section IV.

9. Carter, "Jesus the Good Shepherd," sections V–VI.

10. Warren Carter, *John and Empire: Initial Explorations* (New York: T&T Clark, 2008).

11. Christopher W Skinner, "John's Gospel and the Roman Imperial Context," in *Jesus is Lord Caesar is Not: Evaluating Empire in New Testament Studies*, ed. Scot McKnight and Joseph B. Modica (Downers Grove: IVP, 2013), 122–25.

12. For the record, I catalogue eleven objections that scholars have to this hypothesis (*John and* Empire, 7–11, 22–45), and misses the point that whatever one thinks about the synagogue expulsion theory, Jewish groups also constantly negotiated Roman power as I demonstrate with four examples. I do not claim John was written in Ephesus, only that it was most likely read there (*John and Empire*, ix). The book employs nine chapters covering some 250 pages to discuss the Gospel's use of figures from the past, the Gospel's genre, its plot, Christology, soteriology and eschatology, theology, ecclesiology, the passion, and Jesus's resurrection-ascension!

13. Francis J. Moloney, "Review Article," *Pacifica* 22 (2009): 90–95.

14. Carter, "Synagogues, Jesus-Believers, and Rome's Empire: Bridges and Boundaries," in *John and Empire*, 19–50.

15. For example, Joseph (Gen. 37:2; Philo, *Joseph* 2–3); Moses (Exod. 3:1; Num. 27:15–23, with Joshua; Isa. 63:11; Philo, *Moses* 1.60 shepherd as kingship); David the shepherd-king (2 Sam. 5:2; 1 Chron. 11:2; Ezek. 34:23); prophets like (second) Zechariah (Zech. 11:4–14; 13:7–9, a shepherd that dies). Psalm of Solomon 17:40 uses the image for the king who is the "Lord Messiah." Condemnations of bad shepherds/leaders include Isa. 56:11 (no understanding; pursue own gain); Jer. 22:22 (kings who have not listened to or obeyed God; wickedness); 23:1–4 (scattered the sheep, not attending to them); 25:34–38 (faithless kings); 50:6–7 (lead astray; forgotten the sheep; not protected them). For similar lists, see the commentaries and Nicholas Cachia, *The Image of the Good Shepherd as a Source for the Spirituality of the Ministerial Priesthood* (Rome: Editrice Pontificia Universita Gregoriana, 1997), 37–71; Jennifer Awes Freeman, "The Good Shepherd and the Enthroned Ruler: A Reconsideration of Imperial Iconography in the Early Church," in *The Art of Empire:*

Christian Art In Its Imperial Context, ed. Lee M. Jefferson and Robin M. Jensen (Minneapolis: Fortress, 2015), 159–95, esp. 174–76.

16. Valentine Muller, "The Prehistory of the 'Good Shepherd,'" *JNES* 3 (1944): 87–90; Cachia, *Image of the Good Shepherd*, 29–34; Freeman, "The Good Shepherd," 166–69.

17. Erwin Goodenough ("The Political Philosophy of Hellenistic Kingship," in *YCR* 1 [New Haven: Yale University Press, 1928], 55–102, esp. 84) notes the "good ruler as shepherd" image in Archytas of Tarentum (c. 400–350 B.C.E.; p. 60) and his contemporary Ecphantus. Jack Vancil, *The Symbolism of the Shepherd in Biblical, Intertestamental, and New Testament Material* (PhD diss., Dropsie University, 1975), 99–127; Freeman, "The Good Shepherd," 169–74.

18. Oswyn Murray, "Philodemus on the Good King according to Homer," *JRelS* 55 (1965): 161–82, esp. 174.

19. Oswyn Murray, "Philosophy and Monarchy in the Hellenistic World," in *Jewish Perspectives on Hellenistic Rulers*, ed. Tessa Rajak, Sarah Pearce, James Aitken, and Jennifer Dines (Berkley: University of California Press, 2007), 13–28, esp. 23.

20. M. M. Austin, "Hellenistic Kings, War, and Economy," *CQ* 36 (1986): 450–66, esp. 459–66.

21. Austin, "Hellenistic Kings, War, and Economy," 459.

22. Frank William Walbank, "Monarchy and Monarchic Ideas," in *The Hellenistic World* (vol. VII, Part 1 of *The Cambridge Ancient History*, 2nd ed., Cambridge: Cambridge University Press, 1984), 62–100, esp. 81–99.

23. Walbank, "Monarchy and Monarchic Ideas," 78.

24. Walbank, "Monarchy and Monarchic Ideas," 100. For example, Maximus of Tyre (second century C.E.; *Or.* 6.7) observes that Cyrus ruled Persia as a shepherd by protecting and nurturing his flock with military victories over the Medes and the Babylonians, but his successor Cambyses and Xerxes "turned from good shepherds into wicked wolves, ravaging the flock."

25. Elsewhere Philo (*Agr.* 29) declares a good ruler to be a good shepherd while a bad ruler is a cattle-rearer.

26. Colleen M. Conway, *Behold the Man: Jesus and Greco-Roman Masculinity* (Oxford: Oxford University Press, 2008), 39–49 (Augustus); Deirdre Good, *Jesus the Meek King* (Harrisburg, PA: Trinity Press International, 1999), 39–60; Walbank, "Monarchy and Monarchic Ideas"; Austin, "Hellenistic Kings."

27. In his fourth discourse on kingship, Chrysostom uses the format of a dialogue between Alexander and Diogenes and an implied interplay between Persia and Parthia to critique the Emperor Trajan's expansionist proclivities in Parthia by arguing that the essence of a good ruler or shepherd is found in divine origins (*Disc.* 4.21) and character virtues like self-control and care for the sheep rather than militarism. Quoting Homer, he speaks against the excessive use of expansionist military power. Kings and rulers who recklessly sacrifice their armies—like Xerxes and Darius—are butchers of the sheep not shepherds (4.43–45). Chrysostom claims that Zeus, "King of Kings," deposes violent and unjust kings and admires the caring king (*Disc* 2.77). John Moles, "The Date and Purpose of the Fourth Kingship Oration of Dio Chrysostom," *ClAnt* 2 (1983): 251–78.

28. Rudolf Bultmann, *The Gospel of John: A Commentary*, trans. G. R Beasley-Murray, R. W. N. Hoare, and J. K. Riches (Philadelphia: Westminster Press, 1971), 367.

29. See the lack of discussion of these traditions in Johannes Beutler and Robert Fortna, eds., *The Shepherd Discourse of John 10 and Its Context*, SNTSMS 67 (Cambridge: Cambridge University Press, 1991). Notice the restricting singular "context" in the title. One article engages something of a slightly wider context as "background" but not the material engaged here: John D. Turner, "The History of Religions Background of John 10," in Beutler and Fortna, *Shepherd Discourse*, 33–52.

30. Peter Garnsey, *Food and Society in Classical Antiquity* (Cambridge: Cambridge University Press, 1999), ix. This discussion is elaborated in Carter, "Jesus the Good Shepherd," section III.

31. Carter, "Jesus the Good Shepherd," 48–60.

32. Steven Friesen, "Poverty in Pauline Studies: Beyond the So-called New Consensus," *JSNT* 26 (2004): 323–61; Bruce Longenecker, *Remember the Poor: Paul, Poverty, and the Greco-Roman World* (Grand Rapids: Eerdmans, 2010), 36–59.

33. Jerry Toner, *Popular Culture in Ancient Rome* (Cambridge: Polity Press, 2009), 58–91.

34. Bruce Frier, "Roman Demography," in *Life, Death, and Entertainment in the Roman Empire*, ed. David Potter and David Mattingly (Ann Arbor: University of Michigan Press, 1999), 87–88, average life expectancy at birth was twenty-one to twenty-two years; at age ten about thirty-five further years. Also Ann Hanson, "The Roman Family," in Potter and Mattingly, *Life, Death*, 19–66.

35. Emperor Augustus (Philo, *Legat.* 145); Nero and Vespasian (Josephus, *J.W.* 2.264; 3.3; 4.406), Nerva and Trajan (Tacitus, *Agr.* 3.1–2), Aristides refers to Rome's healing presence in a previously sick world (*Or.* 97). Vespasian is associated with several literal healings: blind man, lame man, a man with a withered hand in Tacitus, *Hist.* 4.81, Suetonius, *Vesp.* 7, and Dio Cassius, 65.8.1.

36. Warren Carter, "'The Blind, Lame, and Paralyzed' (John 5:3): John's Gospel, Disability Studies, and Postcolonial Perspectives," in *Disability Studies and Biblical Literature*, ed. Candida R. Moss and Jeremy Schipper (New York: Palgrave MacMillan, 2011), 128–50.

37. Brown, *John*, 1.398; Moloney, *Gospel of John*, 304; C. K. Barrett, "The Old Testament in the Fourth Gospel," *JTS* 48 (1947): 155–69, esp. 163–64.

38. Moles, "Date and Purpose," 272–76.

39. Jerome Neyrey, "The 'Noble Shepherd' in John 10: Cultural and Rhetorical Background," *JBL* 120 (2001): 267–91. Judas Maccabeus, for example, demonstrates this good shepherd ideal in declaring, "It is better for us to die in battle than to see the misfortunes of our nation and of the sanctuary" (1 Macc. 3:9; 9:14–22).

40. Moloney, *Gospel of John*, 305.

41. Brown, *John*, 396–97; Keener, *Gospel of John*, 1:818–20.

42. Brian Bosworth, "Augustus, *Res Gestae*, and Hellenistic Theories of Apotheosis," *JRS* 89 (1999): 1–18.

43. R. R. R. Smith "The Imperial Reliefs from the Sebasteion at Aphrodisias," *JRelS* 77 (1987): 88–138; Smith, "*Sacra Gentium*: The *Ethne* from the Sebasteion at Aphrodisias," *JRelS* 78 (1988): 50–77.

Chapter 7

Persuasion through Allusion

Evocations of "Shepherd(s)" and Their Rhetorical Impact in John 10

Catrin H. Williams

The shepherd discourse of John 10 lays bare one of the perennial problems in the discussion of John's reception of the Jewish Scriptures: the discourse is widely held to be saturated with scriptural resonances of shepherd imagery, and yet it contains no direct citations, not a single reference to "what is written in Scripture," and no overt markers to an authoritative source like Moses or the prophets. Furthermore, the rich metaphorical deposit of sheep and shepherds in the Jewish Scriptures complicates the task of identifying clear allusions to specific texts, not least because John's Gospel generally seems to favor allusive and often multilayered scriptural references. Since John also shows preference for composite quotations—where two or more scriptural passages are fused together to form a single quotation[1]—the same principle is probably at work in what can be termed its composite allusions, in that the allusion in question does not necessarily have to be pinned down to a single scriptural antecedent but may have been drawn from multiple sources.

In John 10, as in other discourses underpinned by Jesus's metaphorical "I am" pronouncements, the basic contours of its imagery can be comprehended by readers and hearers if they draw on their broad Mediterranean cultural inheritance, or even through knowledge of pastoral practices in rural settings. However, if scriptural overtones furnishing deeper layers of christological meaning can also be detected in John 10, how do these overtones "work" within the shepherd discourse, and to what extent are the Gospel's original audiences meant to tap into and hear these allusive modes of scriptural reference? Another complicating factor is the figurative and polyvalent character of several potential scriptural references in John 10, and this involves bringing together two complex and highly enigmatic fields of enquiry relating to "metaphor" and "allusion." How are *pastoral images* and *scriptural traditions* intertwined within the discourse, and does the interaction between them play any part in driving the discourse forward?

In an attempt to address these questions, this chapter will examine the ways in which John's presentation of Jesus as "shepherd" draws, to varying degrees, on an intricate network of Jewish scriptural associations. By coupling the discourse's core images with certain scriptural evocations, both the images and the evocations are markedly reconfigured and transformed as Jesus's speech develops. This intertextual strategy, I will argue, dovetails with the rhetorical aims of John 10: as persuasive speech, the discourse seeks to draw its audiences into a distinctively Johannine understanding of Jesus as shepherd. Particular attention will be given to the pattern and rhetorical dynamics of scriptural allusions within the structure of the discourse, in order to examine how the composite—and (at least initially) indeterminate—character of shepherd imagery in John 10 is designed to function as an effective rhetorical tool.

THE RHETORIC OF ELUSIVENESS AND ALLUSIVENESS

I begin this part of the investigation by highlighting how ancient rhetorical categories can provide a valuable lens for interpreting the ways in which the Jewish Scriptures contribute to the shaping of John 10 as persuasive discourse. Much of the relevant work on this subject, especially in Johannine scholarship, has so far centered on how John's explicit quotations and overt references to scriptural figures and events "contribute to the rhetoric of the Gospel [and] its characterization of Jesus."[2]

But what about the more allusive modes of scriptural reference embedded within the narrative? To assess the role of scriptural allusions within John's rhetorical strategies, that is, in the making of persuasive speech, I draw on explorations of the power of "elusiveness" in Graeco-Roman rhetoric. Frank Thielman, in a 1991 essay on John's style, examined the significance of "obscurity" (*asapheia, obscuritas*) for the rhetorical expression of religious themes,[3] noting the use of double meanings for the purpose of emphasis and, as the *Rhetorica ad Herennium* suggests, to enable the reader to pause and take stock (4.53.67). More recently, the rhetorical function of elusiveness and indeterminacy to promote audience participation has been examined by Kathy Reiko Maxwell, in her study of how Luke-Acts conceives its audiences as fellow-workers "hearing between the lines,"[4] while Michael Whitenton investigates the contribution of rhetorical techniques to what he calls "inference generation" in the characterization of Jesus in the Gospel of Mark,[5] and, even more recently, with reference to audience-orientated and rhetorically sensitive constructions of the characterization of Nicodemus in the Gospel of John.[6]

Both Maxwell and Whitenton demonstrate that, according to ancient theorists, authors should deliberately withhold certain information in order to encourage their audiences to fill the gaps and draw conclusions for themselves as an argument is being advanced. In his treatise *On Style* (*Libro de Elocutione*), Demetrius cites Theophrastus (Frag. 696; third century B.C.E.), noting that the "essentials of persuasiveness" are that one "should not elaborate on everything in punctilious detail" but should omit some points so that an audience can work out the meaning.[7] In this way, listeners are enlisted as "witnesses" offering "testimonies" to information otherwise withheld (*On Style* 222). The rhetorical value of hinting at arguments rather than stating everything explicitly is also highlighted by Quintilian; audiences will be "led to seek out the secret which they would not believe if they heard it openly stated, and to believe in that which they have found out for themselves" (*Inst.* 9.2.71). Among the cluster of rhetorical figures identified as encouraging audiences to search for deeper levels of meaning are the following: intentionally ambiguous arguments (*emphasis* and irony); open-ended comparisons (such as metaphors, riddles, and parables); and subtle allusions which, with varying degrees of volume, were used to help people make connections with existing "cultural script."[8] Thus, "Audience members are . . . prompted to infer comparisons between the allusive script and the character(s) or scene in the story prompted by the allusive language."[9]

Highlighting the persuasive force of elusiveness, including the rhetorical effect of techniques like metaphors and allusions, alerts one also to the importance of a number of other related factors. First, due attention must be given to the oral-aural environment from which many ancient texts emerged,[10] since the rhetorical techniques described by ancient theorists like Quintilian were in fact closely linked to the function of texts as textually inscribed "sound maps" emphasizing "the persuasive power of the spoken word."[11] While contemporary intertextual studies tend to focus on the literary relationship between written compositions, it is increasingly being recognized that texts like the Gospel of John were produced in a cultural milieu in which the dynamics between textuality and orality were a significant factor in the composition and reception of texts. Given, therefore, the relatively low literacy rates in the first-century Mediterranean world, texts were primarily—though not exclusively—read aloud for the benefit of *listening* audiences. This is not to deny that authors like John display close familiarity with scriptural texts that circulated in written form, but the likely impact of settings in which those texts were recited and "heard" by audiences should not be overlooked.

Secondly, it also needs to be taken into account that an author's intention, as far as engagement with the Jewish Scriptures is concerned, can differ from the communicative effect of that engagement on ancient audiences, particularly in a performative setting. Such considerations remind us that allusions, more often than not, are deliberate on the part of the author and that audiences are expected to be able to catch them.[12] Even so, the decipherment of an allusion may not always happen, or may not even be necessary for interpreting at least the surface meaning of a text, particularly if the audience's profile is marked by cultural diversity. In view of the varying degrees of allusiveness in John's scriptural references, how many echoes would need to be heard and recognized for its earliest audiences to be kept on the Johannine track? For audience members of Jewish origin who were "orally," if not "visually," literate in the Jewish Scriptures,[13] scriptural texts would be activated by a broad range of allusive references embedded within the narrative. However, since the Gospel's originally anticipated audiences were, in all likelihood, not limited to those of Jewish heritage but included Gentiles, there would have been a wide spectrum of familiarity with Israel's Scriptures, ranging from high levels of scriptural competence to more limited knowledge of Israel's core stories.[14]

For the envisaged first audiences of John's Gospel, a variety of interpretations of the shepherd discourse would have been open to them, depending on the cultural encyclopedia to which they were already exposed.[15] For those familiar with, even steeped in, the Jewish Scriptures, distinctive scriptural themes and motifs linked to shepherds and sheep would be actively evoked through the process of deciphering allusions intended by the author. For others, it would be possible to grasp the flow and essence of Jesus's discourse even if the deeper levels of (scriptural) significance attached to its imagery remained hidden from them, at least without the benefit of guidance from more scripturally literate audience members. What must also be noted, in the light of the various factors I have already highlighted, is the dynamic nature of the shepherd discourse in John 10 and its sense of progressive development. The notion of sequential disclosure is often emphasized in connection with its figurative language of sheep and shepherds, though not, curiously, in relation to the gradual unfolding of embedded scriptural references as part of that process. Commentaries, in particular, tend to offer a "global" account of possible scriptural intertexts in John 10; that is, they investigate its likely scriptural resources with reference to the discourse in its entirety, rather than examining what may be activated, at which particular point, within the text. My own investigation, in what follows, will seek to identify the likely sequence and levels of scriptural activation that occur, rather, at specific points within the shepherd discourse.

THE SHEPHERD AND HIS SHEEP: THE "FIGURE OF SPEECH" (JOHN 10:1-6)

The cluster of images that make up the opening section of John 10 (vv. 1–5) is not difficult to comprehend on the surface level. John focuses on the key elements associated with all such pastoral scenes: sheep, shepherd, and a sheepfold. The introduction of the gate and its gatekeeper becomes necessary in order to highlight the theme of proper access to the sheepfold (vv. 1–3a), whereas thieves, bandits, and strangers are included as negative foils in relation to a second theme: the legitimate shepherd enjoys a close relationship with his sheep (vv. 3b–5). All other elements, as accompanying description, are clearly subsumed under these two central themes.

It is only with Jesus's first "I am" pronouncement, in v. 7, that the metaphorical activation and explication of the imagery overtly takes place: "Very truly, I tell you, I am the gate for the sheep."[16] And yet, the labeling of the discourse's initial section as a "figure of speech" (v. 6: *paroimia*), precisely because up until this point it lacks explicit identification of its images, invites audiences to interpret the opening figurative description as obscure speech requiring interpretation.[17] Audiences are prompted, already at this early point in the discourse, to search their cultural encyclopedia(s)—scriptural or otherwise—for possible referents that will fill the gaps between what has and has not been said.[18] Noteworthy in this respect is Demetrius's comment about symbolic expressions (*ta symbola*) being like "brevity of speech," since one is left "to infer a great deal from a short statement" (*On Style,* 243). And in the case of wide-ranging images like shepherds and sheep, all kinds of possibilities could be initiated, depending on one's "interpretative filter."[19]

Whatever the exact filter, the *paroimia* in vv. 1–5 would certainly evoke images of leadership in view of the widespread connection between shepherds and rulers/kings in a variety of ancient sources.[20] But which associations would have been triggered for scripturally informed audiences by this configuration of images? What would they bring to the table in an attempt to decipher this figure of speech and, in particular, to what kind of comparison with known scriptural images would they subject the shepherd, the central character of the *paroimia*?[21]

In response to such questions, though usually with "blanket" reference to the whole discourse, most commentators—as I noted earlier—offer an outline in encyclopedic fashion of the many possible contenders for the role and/or designation of shepherd in Jewish Scripture and tradition. Some draw attention to Moses (Exod. 3:1; see Philo, *Mos.* 1.60–64) and Joshua (Num. 27:17–23), but the first figure usually to be mentioned is David, with attention given to the transition from his early life as a shepherd (1 Sam. 16:11,

19; 17:40) to his figurative designation as the ruler shepherding the people of Israel (2 Sam. 5:2; 7:7–8; 1 Chron. 11:2; Ps. 78:70–72). The discussion in commentaries then soon shifts to the wealth of examples of shepherd imagery in the Psalms and in prophetic traditions to express the relationship between God and his people. This scriptural-metaphorical network includes figurative images of God leading his people like sheep through the wilderness (Ps. 78:52; see 80:1), delivering them to safety (78:53), providing them with pasture (79:13; 95:7; see 74:1; 100:3), even gathering the lambs in his arms (Isa. 40:11; see Ps. 28:9; Jer. 23:3; 31:10; Mic. 2:12–13).[22] Such images are also frequently contrasted with the behavior of previously appointed "shepherds" who, different from God, have not cared for God's sheep but have been responsible for scattering and even destroying them (e.g., Jer. 23:1–2; see 1 Kings 22:17; Mic. 2:1–11; Zech. 11:15–17). The prominence and consistency of shepherd-sheep imagery in the Hebrew Bible thus makes it likely that the "figure of speech" or *paroimia,* in John 10:1–5, has the capacity to evoke a rich network of possible scriptural associations.

One particular scriptural passage that does bring together many, if not all, of these motifs is the prophetic scenario depicted in Ezekiel 34. It opens with an extended indictment of the unfaithful "shepherds of Israel" who cared for no one other than for themselves (34:2–4), thus causing the scattering of their sheep "because there was no shepherd" (34:5–6, 8). God removes them from their positions (34:10), announcing that he will himself assume the role of shepherd to his people, gathering and feeding them with abundant food (34:11–16). He will then appoint his servant David to serve as their one shepherd (34:23–24; see 37:24), even though the sheep in fact still belong to God (34:31: "You are my sheep, the sheep of my pasture, and I am your God, says the Lord God" [NRSV]).

Without having to proceed any further, then, than the *paroimia* as set out in vv. 1–5, some striking thematic resemblances can be detected between the opening of John's shepherd discourse and the repeated references in Ezekiel to God's leading and caring of his flock. It therefore comes as no surprise that this prophetic passage is widely regarded as *the* primary scriptural frame of reference for the imagery in John 10.[23] This does not rule out the composite character of possible scriptural evocations in the *paroimia,* particularly as the only precise scriptural analogue to the description of the sheep trustfully "hearing the voice" of their own shepherd (v. 3) is to be found not in Ezekiel but in Ps. 95:7 (94:7 LXX: "Because he is our God and we are people of his pasture and sheep of his hand! Today if you hear his voice, do not harden your hearts").[24]

What tips the balance, though, in favor of Ezekiel 34 as the central intertext for John's shepherd imagery is the narrative comment which follows in v. 6: "Jesus used this figure of speech *with them,* but *they* did not understand what he was saying *to them*." The seamless shift from John 9 to John 10—with no change in narrative setting, and no new audience—suggests that the bridge-like remark in v. 6 serves to direct audiences back to the previous scene and deduce that the referent in question ("them") is the Pharisees.[25] In other words, it sets up the sheep-shepherd *paroimia* as an implied critique of the Pharisees' actions (9:39–41) in mistreating the healed blind man, in rejecting Jesus, and now in failing to understand his speech. This negative assessment of the Jewish authorities could prompt the scriptural activation of other allusive layers linked directly to Ezekiel 34,[26] particularly its dominant contrast between bad shepherds (Jewish rulers and leaders) and the good shepherd (God).

WHO IS THE SHEPHERD? THE ROLE OF (RHETORICAL) INDETERMINACY (JOHN 10:7–18)

Regardless of whether individual scriptural verses, or even specific texts, would be recalled by an audience upon engaging with the imagery of the *paroimia* (vv. 1–5), its deeper significance would remain unclear at this point in the discourse. Even if the shepherd imagery triggers the evocation of Ezekiel 34 above all other possible intertextual associations, the fact that both God and David are here assigned the role of "shepherd" sustains the open-ended character of John's images in any attempt at precise comparisons. No markers are given to enable audiences to draw decisive conclusions at this stage about the identity of the shepherd at a second level of interpretation.

All the same the *paroimia*, as it stands, would certainly evoke images of God as shepherd, supported by the accompanying motifs of the shepherd guiding and leading the sheep that hear his voice. This interpretative stance could easily continue with Jesus's self-identification as "the gate" (vv. 7–10), as it leaves open the following possibility: if Jesus is the gate providing access to life-sustaining pastures, then God must be the shepherd guiding the sheep.[27] It is when Jesus identifies *himself* as "the good shepherd" (v. 11) that matters become more complex. It not only raises the question of how Jesus can be both gate and shepherd, but creates confusion for readers/hearers who have already selected the image of God as shepherd as their interpretative filter. What is highlighted by John's fluid application of the pastoral imagery—including any engagement with likely scriptural resources—is the close connection between "the gate" and "the shepherd": Jesus's explication of his salvific role as "the gate," who enables the sheep to find pasture and "abundant life" (vv. 9–10), mirrors the repeated emphasis in Ezekiel 34 upon the pasture and deliverance that God provides as shepherd (vv. 10, 12, 13, 14, 22, 31).

The sense of indeterminacy continues in John's discourse, certainly when it comes to pinning down the referents and implications of its scriptural evocations, even though the metaphorical presentation of Jesus as "the good shepherd" progressively undergoes greater precision in v. 10 through v. 18. The lack of care displayed by the hired hand (vv. 11–13) again recalls Ezekiel's depiction of faithless shepherds who are more preoccupied with their own welfare than with that of their flock (34:2–6), but, as many interpreters have rightly noted, there is no scriptural precedent for a shepherd giving his life for the sheep (10:5, 17–18). The Jewish Scriptures may supply images of shepherds whose lives are in danger (see 1 Sam. 17:34–37), but there are no more than vague scriptural hints that this imagery prepares for the idea that a shepherd's "goodness" is understood in terms of his voluntary death for his own sheep.[28]

Gradually, nevertheless, a scripturally literate audience would be prompted to fill or close the "gaps of indeterminacy" in the discourse by listening carefully to the signals offered within the text.[29] Where John's presentation of Jesus bears closest resemblance to scriptural images of God as shepherd is in the articulation of *why* Jesus willingly lays down his life. Different from the fleeting responsibilities of a hired hand, "the good shepherd" behaves as he does because the sheep *belong* to him (10:12, 14, 15, 16; see 10:3–4, 27). And it is at this point that the discourse moves progressively toward spelling out the implications of depicting Jesus as the shepherd who owns his sheep; it is a relationship based on trust and mutual knowledge (10:14, 16), as manifested in the shepherd's protection and deliverance of "his own" (10:11, 15). Above all other distinguishing features, therefore, it is the notion of a relationship centered on ownership that links Jesus as "shepherd" most closely to the scriptural presentation of God as shepherd.[30] Repeatedly in Ezekiel 34, God speaks of "my sheep" (34:6, 8, 10, 11, 12, 15, 17, 19, 22, 31) and states that all previous shepherds have been selected by God to carry out this role solely on his behalf. He, and he alone, owns the sheep. Scripturally informed audiences of John's Gospel could, on this basis, draw the conclusion that Jesus's claim to deliver his *own* sheep is tantamount to him assuming a function that is otherwise attributed to God alone, thereby associating himself with God in the closest possible terms.

An important clue as to how this reconfiguration "works" within the discourse can be gleaned from Jesus's assertion that this shepherd-sheep relationship is modeled upon that between the Father and himself (10:15). It is a bond based on love (10:17) and on obedience to the Father's command (10:18). The emphasis on "one shepherd" (*heis poimēn*) in v. 16 also spells out both the uniqueness of Jesus and his unifying role: he will bring in "other sheep" from other flocks. It is also the most striking and accessible example of scriptural evocation in the whole of Jesus's speech, because this concentration on a single shepherd forms a close verbal parallel to God's eschatological announcement in Ezekiel 34 that he will appoint "my servant David" as "one shepherd" to care for God's own sheep (34:23 LXX: "And I will raise up over them one shepherd [*poimena hena*], and he shall shepherd them, my servant David, and he shall be their shepherd"; see Ezek. 37:24 LXX: "And my servant, David, shall be ruler in their midst, and they shall all have one shepherd [*poimēn heis*]"). The scriptural derivation of the designation "one shepherd" is further bolstered by resemblances between Jesus as the gatherer of different flocks and God's promise that scattered sheep, from various groups, will be brought together under the rule of the expected Davidic shepherd (Ezek. 34:22–23; 37:24), a theme developed in later Jewish tradition with reference to the *messianic* shepherd (Pss. Sol. 17:40–41).

From a rhetorical perspective, several indeterminate elements from earlier parts of Jesus's discourse are now clarified for audiences familiar with the Jewish Scriptures, even though the elements in question are undeniably given a new focus: Jesus is the good shepherd because he fulfills the designated role of God's servant, his long-awaited Messiah-shepherd, with the focus remaining firmly on Jesus's care for his sheep rather than on his ruling kingship.[31] Having said that, it is still left somewhat open-ended, even for those with good knowledge of the Jewish scriptural resources, as to how Jesus can lay claim to God's own prerogative of *owning* the sheep. Even as the discourse draws to its conclusion (v. 18), there is still some oscillation between the various images, and it appears that their possible connotations are left to stand side by side. And this is because as far as scriptural promises are concerned, the question still remains unanswered: how can Jesus, in his capacity as "messianic" shepherd, fulfill roles traditionally assigned to God as shepherd?

RHETORIC AND RESOLUTION (JOHN 10:24–30)

The shepherd discourse may end on a somewhat elusive note (10:18), but its indeterminacy gradually gives way to clarity and resolution in the next narrative scene (10:19–33). It may be separated chronologically from Jesus's discourse because of the shift to a different festival (10:22), even though there is no change in terms of Jesus's dialogue partners ("the Jews") or location (the temple). The shepherd imagery also returns in Jesus's speech, prompted by the call of "the Jews" who had gathered around him, "How long will you keep us in suspense? If you are the Messiah, tell us plainly (*parrēsia*)" (10:24). This quest for a definitive answer regarding Jesus's identity is, in all likelihood, to be understood as motivated by Jesus's earlier self-identification as shepherd. If so, his Jewish interlocutors act as narrative carriers of the interpretative filter whereby Jesus's earlier claims (10:7–18) are perceived to fall within *messianic* (rather than divine) categories.[32] That Jesus seeks to clarify the christological implications of his claim to be the "good shepherd" is confirmed by his response to them, "I have told you, and you do not believe" (10:25). He may not have directly asserted his messiahship to the Jewish leaders, but he now offers an implicitly positive response to the messianic understanding of his role as shepherd.

What follows in vv. 26–29 amounts to a (re)statement on Jesus's part for the purpose of clarification, with various earlier figurative threads now being drawn together: the reason why the Jewish leaders do not believe is because they do not belong to Jesus's sheep and do not hear his voice (10:26–27; see 10:5, 6). The life that Jesus gives to his sheep is *eternal* life (10:28; see 10:9–10), and he is able to do so because he works in unity with God: "The Father and I are one" (10:30).[33] It is precisely at this point in the encounter that the Jewish interlocutors identify a shift to a different filter: Jesus is claiming oneness with God and asserting that he has been *given* the sheep whose rightful owner, according to their scripturally informed estimation, can only be God himself.[34]

Undoubtedly, from the perspective of Jesus's conversation partners *within* the text, there is no longer any obscurity: his claims are tantamount to blasphemy. For John's audiences, however, the rhetorical force of this follow-up encounter (10:19–33) is the disclosure that Jesus's identity as "one shepherd" (*heis poimēn*) cannot be contained within the Davidic-messianic terms envisaged in certain strands of Jewish Scripture and tradition. Because of Jesus's unique relationship with God and the unity between them (10:30: "The Father and I are one [*hen*]"), the Messiah-as-shepherd category is ultimately reshaped—not in isolation from, but precisely on the basis of, those scriptural testimonies which portray God as the one who owns and cares for his sheep. John brings together both categories—Messiah as shepherd and God as shepherd—through the notion of the divine "oneness" (*hen*) of the Son and the Father,[35] thereby interpreting the prophecies of Ezekiel (especially 34:23 and 37:24) as facilitating the christological blending of the two "shepherds" into "one."

CONCLUSION

In the end, of course, it is the *shaping* of the Johannine discourse itself that dictates how the Jewish Scriptures can inform its presentation of Jesus. This is not to deny the importance of the scriptural matrix that underpins John 10, and which furnishes the discourse with multiple layers of depth. And yet, John's christological interpretation of Jesus as shepherd is brought to the surface not through direct scriptural citations and unmissable allusions to specific texts, but in and through Jesus's interaction with those who question him about his identity. Only toward the end of John 10, when Jesus overtly quotes a psalm text in support of his oneness with the Father, is "Scripture" unmistakably given its own authoritative platform (10:34–36). Jesus's appeal to the wording of Ps. 82:6 in John 10:34 ("Is it not written in your Law, 'I said, you are gods'") provides decisive scriptural warrant for his identity as the unique Son of God who has been sent by the Father to speak and work on his behalf. But for those among John's audience who cannot draw on a rich deposit of Jewish scriptural texts for the elucidation of shepherds—messianic or divine—the gradual unveiling of the discourse's core imagery serves as an indispensable rhetorical tool to draw them, step by step, into what it actually means, for John, to call Jesus "the good shepherd."

NOTES

1. See Catrin H. Williams, "Composite Citations in the Gospel of John," in *Composite Citations in Antiquity: Volume Two: New Testament Uses*, ed. Sean A. Adams and Seth M. Ehorn, LNTS 593 (London: Bloomsbury/T&T Clark, 2018), 94–127.

2. Alicia D. Myers, *Characterizing Jesus: A Rhetorical Analysis on the Fourth Gospel's Use of Scripture in its Presentation of Jesus*, LNTS 458 (London: Bloomsbury/T&T Clark, 2012), 2.

3. Frank Thielman, "The Style of the Fourth Gospel and Ancient Literary Critical Concepts of Religious Discourse," in *Persuasive Artistry: Studies in New Testament Rhetoric in Honor of George A. Kennedy*, ed. Duane F. Watson, JSNTSup 50 (Sheffield: JSOT Press, 1991), 175–77, 178–81.

4. Kathy Reiko Maxwell, *Hearing Between the Lines: The Audience as Fellow-Workers in Luke-Acts and Its Literary Milieu*, LNTS 425 (London: Bloomsbury/T&T Clark, 2010), esp. 27–76.

5. Michael R. Whitenton, *Hearing Kyriotic Sonship: A Cognitive and Rhetorical Approach to the Characterization of Mark's Jesus*, BibS 148 (Leiden: Brill, 2017).

6. Michael R. Whitenton, *Configuring Nicodemus: An Interdisciplinary Approach to Complex Characterization*, LNTS 549 (London: Bloomsbury/T&T Clark, 2019), esp. 95–103, 119–36.

7. Unless otherwise noted, non-biblical Greek and Latin texts are cited by their LCL translations.

8. Maxwell, *Hearing Between the Lines*, 74–76; Whitenton, *Hearing Kyriotic Sonship*, 77–82.

9. See Whitenton, *Hearing Kyriotic Sonship*, 80.

10. See, for example, Catrin H. Williams, "How Scripture 'Speaks': Insights from the Study of Ancient Media Culture," in *Methodology in the Use of the Old Testament in the New: Context and Criteria*, ed. David Allen and Steve Smith, LNTS 579 (London: Bloomsbury/T&T Clark, 2019), 53–69.

11. Holly E. Hearon, "The Implications of Orality for Studies of the Biblical Text," in *Performing the Gospel: Orality, Memory, and Mark: Essays Dedicated to Werner Kelber*, ed. Richard A. Horsley, Jonathan A. Draper, and John Miles Foley (Minneapolis: Fortress, 2006), 3–4.

12. For the view that one must define scriptural allusions as references "intended to be heard," see especially Ruben Zimmermann, "Jesus im Bild Gottes: Anspielungen auf das Alte Testament im Johannesevangelium am Beispiel der Hirtenbildfelder in Joh 10," in *Kontexte des Johannesevangeliums: Das vierte Evangelium in religions—und traditionsgeschichtlicher Perspektive*, ed. Jörg Frey and Udo Schnelle, WUNT 175 (Tübingen: Mohr Siebeck, 2004), 96, 111.

13. See further Dale C. Allison, "The Old Testament in the New Testament," in *The New Cambridge History of the Bible: From the Beginnings to 600*, ed. James Carleton Paget and Joachim Schaper (Cambridge: Cambridge University Press, 2013), 497.

14. See especially Craig R. Koester, *Symbolism in the Fourth Gospel: Meaning. Mystery, Community*, 2nd ed. (Minneapolis: Fortress, 2003), 18–24.

15. For a recent survey of "shepherd" associations (literal and figurative) in the ancient world, see R. Alan Culpepper, "The Ethics of the Shepherd," in *Biblical Ethics and Application: Purview, Validity, and Relevance of Biblical Texts in Ethical Discourse*, ed. Ruben Zimmermann and Stephan Joubert, WUNT 384 (Tübingen: Mohr Siebeck, 2017), 142–50. See also Koester, *Symbolism in the Fourth Gospel*, 16–18, 109–16, 262–63.

16. Jan G. van der Watt, *Family of the King: Dynamics of Metaphor in the Gospel according to John*, BibS 47 (Leiden: Brill, 2000), 59, 62.

17. Tom Thatcher thus defines John 10:1–18 as a typical riddling session: riddle (10:1–5), confusion (10:6), new answer (10:7–18), confusion (10:19–21). See Tom Thatcher, *The Riddles of Jesus in John: A Study in Tradition and Folklore*, SBLMS 53 (Atlanta: SBL Press, 2000), 252.

18. For the definition of *paroimia*, at least as applied in John 10:6, as "a symbolic saying which requires interpretation," see Adele Reinhartz, *The Word in the World: The Cosmological Tale in the Fourth Gospel*, SBLMS 45 (Atlanta: Scholars Press, 1992), 51.

19. Van der Watt, *Family of the King*, 57 n. 148. Harold W. Attridge, moreover, proposes a "cubist" approach to John's symbolism: it can be viewed from different angles of vision, which "increases the complexity of the symbolic system" and at the same time seeks to "penetrate to the 'essence' of what is symbolized" ("The Cubist Principle in Johannine Imagery: John and the Reading of Images in Contemporary Platonism," in *Imagery in the Gospel of John: Terms, Forms, Themes, and Theology of Johannine Figurative Language*, ed. Jörg Frey, Jan G. van der Watt, and Ruben Zimmermann, WUNT 200 [Tübingen: Mohr Siebeck, 2006], 47).

20. Attention is frequently paid in this respect to Homer's identification of Agamemnon as "shepherd of his people" (*poimēna laōn*) in the *Iliad* (2.243). See Myers, *Characterizing Jesus*, 120 n. 110; Marianne Meye Thompson, *John: A Commentary*, NTL (Louisville: Westminster John Knox, 2015), 225 n. 272. For other

examples see, for example, Aristotle, *Eth. nic.* 8.11.1; Aeschylus, *Ag.* 795; Plato, *Rep.* 343a–b. See also Philo, *Legat.* 44, where it is stated that the emperor is like a shepherd and protector of a flock.

21. The comparative or *synkritic* implications of "allusions" are clearly articulated by Whitenton, *Hearing* Kyriotic *Sonship*, 80.

22. See also Gen. 48:15; 49:24; Ps. 23.

23. For example, Gary T. Manning Jr., *Echoes of a Prophet: The Use of Ezekiel in the Gospel of John and the Literature of the Second Temple Period*, JSNTSup 270 (London: T&T Clark, 2004), 111–19, though with particular reference to John 10:10–16; Andrew T. Lincoln, *The Gospel According to St John*, BNTC (London: Continuum, 2005), 292–93; Jean Zumstein, *L'Évangile selon Saint Jean (1–12)*, CNT IVa (Genève: Labor et Fides, 2014), 338; Thompson, *John*, 226–27; Brian Neil Peterson, *John's Use of Ezekiel: Understanding the Unique Perspective of the Fourth Gospel* (Minneapolis: Fortress, 2015), 142–50.

24. Manning, *Echoes of a Prophet*, 104–5, suggests that the primary scriptural background to the notion of the sheep hearing the shepherd's voice (v. 3) is Num. 27:20 LXX, although the verbal parallels are more precise in the case of Ps. 94:7 LXX. All translations of biblical Greek are from NETS (for the LXX) and NRSV (for the NT).

25. See Thompson, *John*, 220–21. Jo-Ann Brant, *John*, PCNT (Grand Rapids: Baker Academic, 2011), 159, notes in this regard that the discourse ends where the conflict began, with some among "the Jews" remarking: "These are not the words of one who has a demon. Can a demon open the eyes of the blind?" (10:21; see 9:1–12).

26. For the view that Ezekiel 34 (also) offers "a rationale for the context and placement of John 10 in the Gospel as a whole," drawing attention to plot-line similarities between John 8–11 and Ezekiel 33–37, see Mary Katherine Deeley, "Ezekiel's Shepherd and John's Jesus: A Case Study in the Appropriation of Biblical Texts," in *Early Christian Interpretation of the Scriptures of Israel: Investigations and Proposals*, ed. Craig A. Evans and James A. Sanders, JSNTSup 148 (Sheffield: Sheffield Academic, 1997), 252–64.

27. The "gate" imagery could also evoke scriptural pronouncements of salvation, given that Ps. 118:20–21 (117:20–21 LXX) speaks of the righteous, albeit with no connection to a figurative shepherd and sheep, entering salvation through "the gate of the Lord." Consequently, this could be taken as a reference to Jesus as God's agent. See Andrew C. Brunson, *Psalm 118 in the Gospel of John: An Intertextual Study on the New Exodus Pattern in the Theology of John*, WUNT 2/158 (Tübingen: Mohr Siebeck, 2003), 317–50.

28. See Lincoln, *John*, 296. Note, however, Margaret Daly-Denton, *David in the Fourth Gospel: The Johannine Reception of the Psalms*, AGJU 47 (Leiden: Brill, 2000), 308–9, who proposes that Davidic hues could be heard at this point, since the shepherd-king is frequently depicted as risking his own life for others (see 1 Sam. 19:5; 17:38–39, 45; 2 Sam. 21:17), including when he offered himself ("shepherd") in place of his people ("sheep") when they were being killed (2 Sam 24:17 LXX). See also Culpepper, "The Ethics of the Shepherd," 159.

29. On the strategy of closing "gaps of indeterminacy" in performative contexts, see, for example, John Miles Foley, *Immanent Art: From Structure to Meaning in Traditional Oral Epic* (Bloomington: Indiana University Press, 1991), 42–44.

30. This is accentuated by Zimmermann, "Jesus im Bild Gottes," 106–8; Manning, *Echoes of a Prophet*, 114–15.

31. See further Culpepper, "The Ethics of the Shepherd," 156–57. The royal connotations of the scriptural image of Jesus as shepherd only become evident if John 10 is linked to the emphasis on kingship in the wider Johannine context. See also Reinhartz, *The Word in the World*, 110–12.

32. As noted by Koester, *Symbolism in the Fourth Gospel*, 115: "From the crowd's perspective, a human being could be the Messiah or God, but not both."

33. See Thompson, *John*, 229.

34. See Zimmermann, "Jesus im Bild Gottes," 110–12. He also makes the important point (p. 113) that the notion of John 10 containing deliberate allusions to Jewish scriptural traditions is made more likely—and indeed confirmed—as a result of the *reaction* of Jesus's interlocutors (John 10:31, 33).

35. See further Lori Baron, "The Shema in John's Gospel and Jewish Restoration Eschatology," in *John and Judaism: A Contested Relationship in Context*, ed. R. Alan Culpepper and Paul N. Anderson, RBS 87 (Atlanta: SBL Press, 2017), 167, proposes that the "oneness" motif in John 10:30 also evokes another related scriptural tradition (Deut. 6:4) to form "the Johannine Shema."

Chapter 8

Discerning Characters
Parrēsia, Paroimia, *and Jesus's Rhetoric in John 10:1–21*

Alicia D. Myers

In John 10 Jesus gives what is often called the "Good Shepherd Discourse." Although one of his most well-known speeches, this chapter is also the subject of frequent debate because Jesus combines figurative images to describe himself, his opponents, his followers, and even God in this, his final speech during the Feast of Tabernacles (9:39–10:21). In 10:1–6, Jesus implicitly describes himself as a shepherd, before changing the image to a "door" in 10:7–10. In 10:11–18, he returns to the shepherd image, this time explicitly claiming the role of the "good" or "noble shepherd" (*ho poimēn ho kalos*) who gathers all his sheep together, "lays down his life," and "takes it again" at his Father's (i.e., God's) command. The rapid succession of images in these verses encourages some scholars to divide John 10 into redacted units joined together at some later date.[1] Robert Kysar, however, suggests that there is a coherent substructure of imagery, even if the shifts surprise and confuse those encountering them.[2] Indeed, this could be part of their intended effect.

This chapter will follow Kysar's lead in reading John 10 in its final form. Rather than interpreting the meanings of the images Jesus uses, however, I will focus on the sudden switch in Jesus's type of speech in 10:1–21. In 10:6, the narrator describes Jesus's speech as *paroimia* ("figurative") in contrast to the *parrēsia* ("boldness") with which he spoke in earlier Tabernacles scenes (7:14–26; see 8:20, 45–58). Such a switch is surprising because *parrēsia* was often considered virtuous speech in the ancient Mediterranean world, which friends and good citizens employed to guide others toward truth. *Paroimia*, however, could be considered secretive or insulting, characteristics many of us do not often associate with Jesus. Moreover, in John's Gospel, Jesus claims to have used *parrēsia* throughout his ministry. In John 18:20, he defends himself before the high priest saying, "With *parrēsia* I have spoken to the world. I always (*pantote*) taught in a synagogue and in the temple, where all the Jews gather together, and in secret (*kryptō*) I spoke nothing!"³ Given Jesus's "secret" (*kyrptō*) trip to Tabernacles in 7:10 *and* his use of *paroimia* in John 10, we may well wonder about the truthfulness of such a defense!⁴

In what follows, I will utilize elements of classical rhetorical analysis to understand better the techniques of *parrēsia* and *paroimia*, as well as take cues from New Rhetoric to reflect on the ethics of Jesus's speech. Noting the recipients of Jesus's *paroimia* in John 10, as well as the bold manner in which he uses them, I will argue that Jesus's words are truthful and bold (at least from the Gospel's perspective) while simultaneously unsettling. They indict the Pharisees from John 9:38–41, but they do so in ways that reach beyond the characters in the story to challenge the audience listening to or reading the Gospel as a whole.⁵ Jesus's words warn the Gospel audience against becoming overconfident in their own abilities to discern God's work and messengers, lest they find themselves in the role of bandits and thieves, rather than shepherds or sheep.

PARRĒSIA AND *PAROIMIA* IN THE GRECO-ROMAN WORLD

The art of rhetoric in the ancient Mediterranean world was built on the assumption that effective communication took skill and practice. In order to persuade audiences to see things your way (which was also hopefully a "truthful" way) rhetoricians cultivated skills in speech: techniques that helped them frame an argument by highlighting logic, emotion, or character; colorful figures that played on the rhythmic elements of language and the pleasing sounds of repetition or rhyming schemes; as well as gestures and tones for delivery.

What lies underneath these complex systems and rhetorical practices is another assumption: how one speaks is an indication of one's character or identity. Quintilian (ca. 35–100 C.E.) comments on the pervasiveness of this view: "Speech," he explains, "is very commonly an index of character, and reveals the secrets of the heart. There is good ground for the Greek saying that a man speaks as he lives" (*Inst.* 11.1.30; cf. Seneca, *Ep.* 114.1).⁶ Plutarch writes with similar conviction in his biography of Alexander the Great: "A slight thing like a phrase or a jest often makes greater revelation of character than battles where thousands fall" (*Alex.* 1.2). Jesus, too, gives his own version of this saying in Luke 6:45, "The good person out of the good treasure of the heart produces good things, and the evil person out of evil produces evil things; for out of the fullness of the heart, the mouth speaks" (see also Matt. 12:34).

Understanding Jesus's speech in the Gospel of John, therefore, whether *parrēsia* or *paroimia*, is hardly a trivial matter: the content of his character is at stake. This fact is made even more profound since Jesus says he only speaks as God, his Father, commands (John 5:16–18; 8:20). Jesus's speech is the revelation of God's character because, in John's Gospel, Jesus is the Logos (Word) of God become flesh (1:14–18).

The Virtues of *Parrēsia*

According to George Parsenios, *parrēsia* is generally considered a positive type of speech in the ancient Mediterranean world.[7] It is "open," or "frank," speech that tells the truth even when the truth hurts. *Parrēsia* is the type of speech one uses with family members and genuine friends who share love for one another by only seeking the others' good (Seneca, *Ep.* 3.2–3). In fact, for Plutarch (ca. 45–125 C.E.) *parrēsia* is a perfect litmus test for deciphering true friends from chameleon-like flatters. He writes, "The flatterer's object is to please in everything he does, whereas the true friend always does what is right, and so often gives pleasure, often pain, not wishing the latter, but not shunning it either, if he deems it best" (*Adul. amic.* 11.52). A friend does not recoil from speaking with *parrēsia*, regardless of the potential outcome (even if that outcome could be rejection or violence!) because they truly desire good for the other over protection or reward for themselves.[8] When Jesus speaks "with *parrēsia*" either to crowds, to the world, or to his disciples in the Gospel of John, therefore, he acts as a true friend, even when he is executed as a result.[9]

Parsenios adds, however, that such speech was not *only* reserved for private friendships, but also was a mark of an *ideal citizen*. He explains that men[10] who spoke boldly, in *public* settings, were considered "friends" of their cities because they spoke truth even before their foes. He writes,

> *Parrēsia* was a political virtue in the city-states of ancient Greece, especially Athens. Whether sitting on public juries to decide the fate of an individual neighbor, or gathered in the public assembly to decide their fate collectively, Athenian citizens were asked to speak their minds with no filter and with no fear of punishment or reprisal. The good of the city depended on frank and open discussion.[11]

Centuries later, the Roman Empire still considered *parrēsia* a civic virtue even as it underwent its own transition from Republic to Empire, thus diminishing the role of civic speech by citizens. Epictetus (ca. 55–135 C.E.), for example, writes that it is "cruel to leave uncorrected" young noblemen who would benefit from frank speech, even if it is cutting. Not to correct them not only leaves the young men warped but endangers those whom they will lead once they are grown (*Disc.* 3.1; see Dio, *Or.* 32, 5). Indeed, to refrain from well-timed and truthful *parrēsia* was cowardly and selfish. It was as bad as masking "vainglorious posturing" and "insolent presumption" in the guise of *parrēsia* (Plutarch, *Pomp.* 60.4).[12] When interpreting Jesus's speech in John 10, therefore, we must ask why he speaks as he does: Is it for the sake of himself or for the good of others? And we must determine the truthfulness of what he says, even when those words are cloaked in *paroimia*.

The Purposes of *Paroimia*

A *paroimia* is an allegorical proverb, metaphor, or figurative language. *Paroimiai* do not convey "openly" in terms of "plainness" or "clarity," and in this way, can be secretive and sarcastic, delivering veiled insults or threats. Yet, they can also be used to communicate hard-to-hear truths as in more typical *parrēsia*. Emphasizing the latter, Uta Poplutz is among the many scholars who highlight the use of the Greek word "*paroimia*" to translate the Hebrew *mashal* (proverb) in the LXX.[13] As short, pithy, and memorable sayings, proverbs challenge their hearers and encourage them to respond rightly by following wisdom. Rather than obfuscating truth, therefore, proverbs capture it in easy-to-recall forms. In fact, in the LXX Proverbs is titled "The *Paroimiai* of Solomon, son of David, who Ruled in Israel" and it contains *paroimiai* that emphasize the importance of *parrēsia* such as in 10:10: "The one winking with his eyes gathers guile for men, but the one reproving with boldness (*parrēsia*) makes peace" (see 1:20). In this context, therefore, *paroimia* is the content of a friend's (or parent's) bold and truthful speech.

Focusing on the definition of *paroimia* outside the biblical canon, Jo-Ann Brant highlights Quintilian's description in his *Institutes on Oratory*.[14] Quintilian classifies *paroimiai* under his larger discussion of examples, which are a type of "technical proof" in argumentation (5.11). This category also includes *parabolē*, a term commonly used of Jesus's sayings the Synoptic Gospels, as another technique that creates a comparison with allegorical or typological associations (e.g., Mark 4:1–20). According to Quintilian, a *paroimia* is "a sort of abbreviated fable understood allegorically," often in the form of collected sayings from well-known figures. Rhetoricians integrated *paroimiai* into their speeches for support and to evoke emotional responses (*Inst.* 5.11.21). Demetrius of Phaleron (ca. 350–280 B.C.E.) notes the usefulness of *paroimiai* because they allow a speaker to communicate without suffering immediate rejection. Offering an example from the tyrant Dionysius of Corinth, he writes:

If Dionysius had expressed his meaning directly, saying that he would ravage the Locrian land, he would have shown at once irritation and less dignity. In the phrase actually used the speaker has shrouded his words, as it were, in allegory. Any darkly-hinting expression is more terror-striking, and its import is variously conjectured by different hearers. On the other hand, things that are clear and plain are apt to be despised, just like men when stripped of their garments. (*On Style*, 2.100)

Although Demetrius's example is from a negative figure (a tyrant is always self-serving and never caring for the good of others) his description of the usefulness of allegories is relevant for positive contexts as well. *Paroimiai* help a speaker to communicate with some freedom, whether by veiling threats or instructing in the ways of wisdom, when such words are difficult to hear. Moreover, Demetrius's comments suggest that a *paroimia* could cause a greater emotional response as audiences grappled with interpreting the images. The words could not simply be taken in, but needed interpretation.

Returning to Quintilian's definition, Brant suggests that Jesus uses a *paroimia* in John 10 to "veil offensive or hurtful speech" directed against the Pharisees (*Inst.* 8.6.57).[15] Not only does the *paroimia* enable Jesus to speak more freely, delaying his rejection until after the Pharisees hear his entire speech in 9:38–10:18, but it also incorporates well-known images to evoke an emotional response and require intentional interpretation. Jesus's speech in John 10, then, even when colored by *paroimia*, is "bold" (*parrēsia*) because it is truthful, at least from the Gospel's perspective. In fact, that the end of Jesus's speech results in division at 10:19–21, instead of outright rejection as it does in 10:31–39, indicates the usefulness of his *paroimia*: Jesus's rejection is delayed and some in the crowd are persuaded by him (see 10:40–42).

Summary

The above overview of *parrēsia* and *paroimia* in the ancient Mediterranean world shows that both types of speech can have positive and negative qualities, depending on the motivations of their use. A good friend, or good citizen, thinks about what is best for others whom they love. This person will speak truth boldly and publicly, with *parrēsia*, offering praise and rebuke when warranted, regardless of the potential and actual consequences they face. Parsenios notes that people who spoke frankly were often targets of retribution in the ancient world, particularly when the populace became unaccustomed to hearing boldly proclaimed truths.[16] For this same reason, therefore, *paroimiai* could be useful to the truthful speaker to create analogies, rather than straightforward statements, and thus avoid immediate rejection while also having greater emotional impact. With this background established, it is time to examine John 10 in more detail.

CONTRASTING MOTIVATIONS: TYPES OF *PARRĒSIA* IN JOHN 7–10

In order to understand Jesus's speech in John 10, we must recognize it as the culmination of scenes occurring during Tabernacles, which began in 7:1. This section of the Gospel is linked by a number of themes along with its consistent Tabernacles setting.[17] One of these themes is *parrēsia*: although Jesus has already established himself as a giver of speeches in the Gospel (see John 3–6), it is not until John 7 that Jesus's ways of speaking and behaving are explicitly tied to *parrēsia*.

In John 7:3–4, Jesus's brothers challenge him saying, "Leave here and go to Judea so that your disciples also may see the works you are doing; for no one who wants to be in public (*parrēsia*) acts in secret (*kryptō*). If you do these things, show yourself to the world." Although we may wonder at the brothers' words (Jesus has, after all, just fed a crowd of 5,000 in Galilee in John 6!) Parsenios argues that they are calling Jesus a coward.[18] He is performing signs and teaching publicly in Galilee, but his brothers accuse him of hiding from the Judean religious leadership by remaining in the north rather than travelling to Jerusalem. Indeed, Jesus's Galilean feeding in John 6 was set during Passover, a festival for which Jesus previously travelled to Jerusalem in John 2. For his brothers, Jesus's geographical location is a sign of fear and they challenge him to travel to Jerusalem for Tabernacles rather than staying in the safety of Galilee. Jesus, however, rebukes his brothers by saying: "I am not going to this festival, for my time has not yet been fulfilled" (7:8). Jesus's response resonates with his earlier comments to his mother about the importance of his hour in John 2, and also foreshadows his final trip to Jerusalem for Passover in John 12. According to the Gospel, Jesus stayed in Galilee not out of fear, but out of obedience to God. His brothers, who "were not believing in him," are unable to recognize this fact (7:5).

Jesus's behavior in 7:10–24, however, seems to upend his conviction. Rather than remaining in Galilee, Jesus seems to give in to his brothers' nagging and then does precisely what they accused him of when he travels to Jerusalem for Tabernacles "in secret" (*kryptō*)! Once he is in Jerusalem, we hear no more of his brothers, but we do learn that Jesus is speaking with *parrēsia*, even to the astonishment of the frightened crowds listening to him. The crowd secretly wonders where Jesus is in 7:11–12, but "no one was speaking with *parrēsia* about him [Jesus] because of the fear of the Jews" (7:13). In contrast to the crowds' fear, Jesus arrives and begins to teach, even bringing up the Sabbath day healing from 5:1–18 that initially earned him the ire of the religious leaders and debating Mosaic Law in 7:14–24. So bold are Jesus's words that the crowd responds with shock, "This is the man whom they are seeking to kill, right? And look! he is speaking with *parrēsia* and no one is responding to him! It's not that the leaders truly know that this man is the Christ, is it?" (7:25–26). Eventually, Jesus's boldness ends with an attempt to stone him in 8:58, but he disappears presumably because it was not his "time" (7:6–8, 30; 8:20). Creating an inclusio with 7:1–9, the narrator says that Jesus "was secreted" (*ekrybē*) out of the temple, using a passive verb that implies divine involvement secured his escape from the crowd (8:59). This combination of "secrecy" and "boldness" in John 7–8 creates tension and even more confusion: Is Jesus contradicting himself by lying to his brothers? Does he actually want to be in public (*parrēsia*) or not?

From the perspective of the Gospel, the answer lies in Jesus's motivation: Jesus speaks and acts with *parrēsia*, but not for the sake of his own glory. Contrary to what his brothers think, it is not something he wants for himself (7:3–4). As Jesus shows throughout the Gospel, and especially in scenes situated in Jerusalem, he is not interested in that sort of false *parrēsia*. In 2:23–25, for example, Jesus gathers "believers" through the signs he performs in Jerusalem during Passover, but he does not reciprocate this belief with "trust." According to the narrator, Jesus "did not have a need for someone to testify about humanity, for he knew what was in humanity." In other words, Jesus already knows that humans, and the glory they bestow, are fickle. During his second trip to Jerusalem in John 5, therefore, Jesus does not retreat or mollify the hostile religious leaders with his words; instead, he boldly offers his own judgment:

> I do not receive glory from people, but I know that you do not have the love of God in you. I have come in the name of my Father, and you do not receive me. If another should come in his own name, you would receive that one. How are you able to believe when you are receiving glory from one another and you are not seeking glory from the one who alone is God? (5:41–44)

According to Jesus, the religious leaders are distracted by the pursuit of human glory. They love, and are loyal to, *that* glory rather than to God: they desire public attention *and* approval. As a result, they are made insecure by God's messenger before them instead of comforted by his presence. Jesus unsettles their (and our) systems of value and power. Human glory is capricious and leaves these leaders in a perilous and fearful place (11:45–53).[19]

In John 7–10, the Gospel continues its extended comparison between Jesus and the religious leaders started in John 5. Jesus travels to Jerusalem to speak again, even though the religious leaders are supposedly still seeking him after John 5. He travels "in secret" in order to undermine his brothers' interpretation of his actions, and he speaks boldly once he arrives: he brings up his Sabbath day healing from 5:1–18 and interprets the Torah in 7:14–24. If the people did not remember Jesus from his previous trip to Jerusalem, he makes sure they do now! Picking up on the theme of judgment from John 5, Jesus finishes in 7:24 with a maxim, commanding the crowd: "Stop judging by appearances, but judge with just judgment!" As the Tabernacles episode continues, the religious leaders repeatedly fail to abide by this command.

In 7:45–52 the chief priests and Pharisees call the crowd listening to Jesus "accursed" because they "do not know the Law." This condemnation, however, falls back on these religious leaders not only because Nicodemus cites the Law's provision that one must be tried before they are convicted of a crime, but also because it is their responsibility to teach the crowds the Law; the crowd's failures (if they are failures) are only a result of their own. In addition, the religious leaders also participate in the rejection of Jesus in 8:12–59 and then misjudge the man born blind in John 9.

After being questioned by his disciples, Jesus pronounces the man blind from birth (and his parents) innocent before guiding the man toward his healing in 9:1–5. This same man is declared as a sinner by the religious leaders after, like Jesus, he offers bold words. In the final of three interrogation episodes, the man tells the religious leaders:

> In this is a wonder! You do not know where he [Jesus] is from, but he opened my eyes! We know that God does not listen to sinners, but he does listen to the one who worships him and obeys his will. Never since the world began has it been heard that anyone opened the eyes of a person born blind. If this man were not from God, he could do nothing. (9:31–33, NRSV)

The man's wonderment contrasts his own understanding, his "opened eyes," with the blindness of the religious leaders. Perhaps unsurprisingly, these leaders are not persuaded. Instead, they render a faulty judgment that confirms their blindness: "You were born entirely in sins, and you are trying to teach us?!" and "cast him out outside" (9:34). It is outside that Jesus finds the man and welcomes him into his fold (9:35–38).

From the perspective of the Gospel, therefore, these religious leaders have tragically failed the Jewish people in John 7–9. In contrast, Jesus offers just judgment, truth, freedom, life, and a place of belonging. In John 10, Jesus's teaching culminates with *paroimiai* that reinforce this contrast. Karoline Lewis emphasizes the connection between John 9 and John 10 when interpreting Jesus's shepherd discourse.[20] She highlights the fact that Jesus is not speaking to a general crowd in 10:1–21, but rather, to the Pharisees who reacted to his welcoming of the healed man in 9:35–38. These Pharisees are implicated, at least in name, in the expulsion of that same healed man in 9:34. After the healed man worships him, Jesus proclaims:

> "I came into this world for judgement; so that the ones not seeing might see and the ones seeing might become blind." The ones from the Pharisees, being with

him, heard and said to him, "We are not blind, are we?" Jesus said to them, "If you were blind, you would not continue having sin. But now you say, 'We see,' your sin remains. Amen, amen I say to you, the one not entering through the gate into the sheepfold but climbing in another way, that one is a thief and bandit." (9:38–10:1)

Jesus continues speaking straight through 10:5, only interrupted in v. 6 by the narrator's interpreting interjection: "Jesus spoke this *paroimia* to them, but these ones did not know the things which he was saying to them."[21]

The Pharisees' inability to understand, then, is the reason Jesus continues in 10:7–18 with more *paroimiai*: first, one which pictures him as the "gate" (*thyra*) by which a rightful shepherd enters (vv. 7–10a); a second, that describes him as the "good" or "noble" shepherd who "came so that [the sheep] might have life and have it abundantly" (vv. 10b–16), and a third, that portrays him as Son and God as Father (vv. 17–18). In these allegories, those who are in Jesus's care are the "sheep" and those who oppose him are "thieves" and "bandits" who destroy. The allegorical language is not, on its own, difficult to understand. Indeed, the chapters by Catrin Williams and Warren Carter in this collection ably demonstrate the pervasiveness of shepherding allegories in Jewish literature and in the larger Greco-Roman world. What is difficult for the Pharisees is recognizing their own, negative, place in Jesus's *paroimiai*. They are stuck in a state of confusion: "We are not blind, are we?" (9:40). It is not that the Pharisees are mystified by a shepherd *paroimia*, rather they cannot see themselves as possible thieves and bandits.

As Brant suggests, Jesus's *paroimia* enables him to reprimand the Pharisees to whom he speaks without condemning them directly.[22] Nevertheless, reading John 10 as the continuation of John 9, we recall that Jesus *did* condemn them directly in 9:41 concluding, "If you were blind you would not continue having sin, but now that you are saying, 'We see,' your sin remains." Such words are even harsher given Jesus's comments on sin from the Tabernacles scenes as a whole. In John 8:21, Jesus tells the Pharisees, "I am departing and you will seek me, but you will die in your sins." He repeats this comment in 8:24 to a crowd now described as "the Jews": "I said that you will die in your sins, for if you do not believe that I am he, you will die in your sins." Jesus is certainly not afraid of offending his audience; instead, he is invested in communicating to them truthfully even when the truth he offers is unpleasant. As Brant explains, "The *paroimia* [of John 10] becomes a trap: Jesus's opponents are baffled by Jesus' obliqueness and prove themselves blind to his meaning."[23] Just as their casting out of the healed man in 9:34 demonstrated their inability to act as "good" shepherds, their continued confusion about Jesus (even in spite of being "with" him) proves not only their "blindness" but also the veracity of Jesus's judgment in contrast to their own (8:14–20; 9:3–5). Instead of hiding this truth, Jesus's *paroimia* makes it quite plain to the

Gospel audience. Such a move also (and even perhaps primarily) challenges the Gospel audience to "judge with just judgment" not only Jesus's identity as God's Son and Christ but also their own as sheep, shepherds, or even bandits.

DISCERNING CHARACTER: REFLECTING ON THE ETHICS OF JESUS'S *PAROIMIA*

The final step in this chapter is to reflect on the ethics of Jesus's communication. From the perspective of the Gospel, Jesus is speaking and behaving in ways that reveal and reaffirm God's glory rather than his own. That Jesus is unwilling to placate the Pharisees, other religious leaders, crowds, or even the Roman governor reinforces his focus on God's will alone, even when it results in harsh condemnation and his own rejection. Thus, even with these words, Jesus is not exhibiting hatred, but rather love because he is telling the truth for the sake of others. This, the Gospel argues, is part of the way Jesus shows God's love for the world (3:16).

Focusing on John 10, it is significant that Jesus directs his *paroimia* at the Pharisees, thereby taking aim at the powerful rather than the weak. These Pharisees have real power in the Gospel of John, regardless of the actual power they may have had in the historical world of first-century Palestine. Their disapproval of Jesus sparks fear among the crowd in 7:13, and their distrust of him results in the sending of soldiers for his arrest in 7:32. They do not interfere to prevent the attempt to stone Jesus in 8:58, and their power to expel people from fellowship intimidates parents from defending their son even before the Pharisees cut off this innocent man from the community (9:12, 34). When Jesus pictures these Pharisees as thieves and bandits who destroy, his words are indeed difficult, but they are also consistent with the presentation of the Pharisees in the surrounding context. Regardless of their own beliefs, they have not protected anyone like a "good shepherd" should; instead, they have thrown at least one sheep to the wolves. Jesus's persistence in explaining this reality to them is a show of love that indicates hope for change, rather than a reveling in their confusion.

A wise audience will not fixate on the troubles of the Pharisees in John 10, however, nor will they universalize such a presentation to apply to "all Pharisees," or worse all Jews, everywhere. Instead, they will remember that all main characters in the Gospel are Jewish, including Jesus, his disciples, and most (but not all!) of his opponents, just as the earliest Johannine community was.[24] For this reason, the Gospel audience should hear Jesus speaking to them with *paroimia* and *parrēsia* here and throughout.

The final references to *paroimiai* occur in John 13–17, when Jesus teaches the disciples for the final time. Throughout this intimate exchange, he repeatedly refers back to John 7–10, applying words previously spoken to the

Pharisees and the Jews to his disciples. In 13:33, he says: "Little children, still a little I am with you. You will see me, *and just as I said to the Jews*, 'Where I am going, you are not able to come,' *also now I am saying to you*." Jesus's departure is the motivation for his giving the disciples the command to "love one another just as I loved you" (13:34). He returns again and again to this command, assuring his disciples that he *is* leaving and they cannot now follow (13:36–14:7, 28; 16:5, 16–33). In his last iteration of this teaching, Jesus uses the *paroimia* of a woman giving birth to describe the pain the disciples will experience at his departure as well as the joy that will accompany his return (16:20–22). Like the Pharisees before them, the disciples are confused by this rather straightforward allegory. They cannot understand themselves as a woman in labor, perhaps unsurprisingly so since earlier in the Gospel birth imagery describes the Father and Jesus's own work (1:12–13; 3:1–10; 7:37–39). Worse than the Pharisees in John 10, however, the disciples mistake Jesus's *paroimia* for *parrēsia*, which Brant argues is an attempt to prevent Jesus's departure.[25] The disciples' confusion is confirmed when they flee after Jesus is arrested in John 18, and cower together in fear even after hearing about Jesus's resurrection from Mary in John 20. The Pharisees are certainly not the only ones who misinterpret Jesus's words.

In fact, as part of the Gospel narrative Jesus's *paroimiai* are not for the religious leaders or disciples in the past. Rather, these sayings are spoken to those listening and reading the story *now*. To reflect on the ethics of Jesus's communication, therefore, we should read John 10 in its larger context of John 7–10, the Gospel as a whole, as well as in past traditions and our current contexts. Past interpretations of the Gospel of John have too quickly joined in the condemnation of the Pharisees and other religious leaders in the narrative, with the result that many have universalized this characterization to extend to contemporary Jewish leaders and believers. This troubling history overlooks the *paroimia* of John 16, the failures of Jesus's own disciples, as well as Jesus's enduring love that mirrors God's consistent love for the whole world (3:16–18). Indeed, it is love, and not condemnation, that motivates the entire Gospel story. Jesus's boldness is, certainly, hard to hear, but it becomes unethical when we apply it only to "others" rather than to ourselves. We might be sheep and shepherds at times, but we can change quickly to the roles of thieves, bandits, and fearful disciples waiting for Jesus's return whenever we claim to "see" instead of relying on God's assistance in supplying our sight.

NOTES

1. For example, Kim E. Dewey, "*Paroimiai* in the Gospel of John," *Sem* 17 (1980): 81–99; Ulrich Busse, "Open Questions on John 10," in *The Shepherd Discourse of John 10 and Its Context*, ed. Johannes Beutler and Robert T. Fortna,

SNTSMS 67 (Cambridge: Cambridge University Press, 1991), 6–17; Urban C. von Wahlde, *The Gospel and Letters of John. Vol. 2: Commentary on the Gospel of John*, ECC (Grand Rapids: Eerdmans, 2010), 457–62.

2. Kysar, "Johannine Metaphor—Meaning and Function: A Literary Case Study of John 10:1–18," *Sem* 53 (1991), 86–90. See also Raymond E. Brown, *The Gospel according to John*, AB 29 (Garden City, NY: Doubleday, 1966), 388–90; Karoline M. Lewis, *Rereading the "Shepherd Discourse": Restoring the Integrity of John 9:39–10:21*, StBibLit 113 (New York: Peter Lang, 2008), 129–45.

3. Unless otherwise noted, all translations from the NT are my own.

4. For example, Jerome H. Neyrey, *The Gospel of John in Cultural and Rhetorical Perspective* (Grand Rapids: Eerdmans, 2009), 280–81; Adele Reinhartz, "The Lyin' King? Deception and Christology in the Gospel of John," in *Johannine Ethics: The Moral World of the Gospel and Epistles of John*, ed. Sherri Brown and Christopher W. Skinner (Minneapolis: Fortress, 2017), 132–33.

5. As I will note in the conclusion, John's Gospel has a long history of anti-Jewish interpretation that should remind readers against universalizing its presentations of Jewish religious leaders. R. Alan Culpepper and Paul N. Anderson, eds., *John and Judaism: A Contested Relationship in Context*, RBS 87 (Atlanta: SBL Press, 2017); Paula Fredrickson and Adele Reinhartz, eds., *Jesus, Judaism, and Christian Anti-Judaism: Reading the New Testament after the Holocaust* (Louisville: Westminster John Knox, 2002).

6. Unless otherwise noted, translates from ancient Greek and Latin works are from the Loeb Classical Library.

7. George L. Parsenios, "Confounding Foes and Counseling Friends: *Parrēsia* in the Fourth Gospel and Greco-Roman Philosophy," in *The Prologue of John*, ed. Jan G. van der Watt, R. Alan Culpepper, and Udo Schnelle, WUNT 359 (Tübingen: Mohr Siebeck, 2016), 251–72.

8. In contrast to a friend, a flatterer has too much self-love. Plutarch characterizes Alcibiades, the fourth-century B.C.E. Athenian general, as a flatterer and tyrant. Because Alcibiades "loves to be first" in all things, he is willing to do *whatever it takes* to put himself on top, even if it means the betraying Athens (*Alc.* 19–25, 34–35). See also the condemnation of Diotrephes in 3 John 9–10.

9. On friendship in John, see Martin M. Culy, *Echoes of Friendship in the Gospel of John*, NTM 30 (Sheffield: Sheffield Phoenix, 2010).

10. The assumption for these ancient writings is that the speakers are freed or free-born men, citizens, and mostly of the elite classes. Women, children, and slaves were considered "feminine" or "effeminate" and, therefore, were not welcome in the public sphere but were either to be protected from it (wives, children) or simply dismissed by it (slaves). Maud W. Gleason, *Making Men: Sophists and Self-Presentation in Ancient Rome* (Princeton: Princeton University Press, 2008).

11. Parsenios, "Confounding Foes," 251.

12. Parsenios, "Confounding Foes," 256–57.

13. Uta Poplutz, "Paroimia und Parabolē. Gleichniskonzepte bei Johannes und Markus," in *Imagery in the Gospel of John: Terms, Forms, Themes, and Theology of Johannine Figurative Language*, ed. Jörg Frey, Jan G van der Watt, and Ruben

Zimmermann, WUNT 200 (Tübingen: Mohr Siebeck, 2006), 105. See also Dewey, "*Paroimia*," 82; Christopher W. Skinner, "'The Good Shepherd Lays down His Life for the Sheep' (John 10:11, 15, 17): Questioning the Limits of a Johannine Metaphor," *CBQ* 80 (2018): 99–100. Susan E. Hylen ("The Shepherd's Risk: Thinking Metaphorically with John's Gospel," *BibInt* 24 [2016]: 388–89) uses the more general term "metaphor" to describe Jesus's shepherd imagery throughout John 10.

14. Jo-Ann A. Brant, *John*, PCNT (Grand Rapids: Baker Academic, 2011), 160.

15. Brant, *John*, 160–61.

16. Parsenios, "Confounding Foes," 261–66.

17. Two themes unique to this section include accusations of Jesus's demonic possession (7:20; 8:48, 52; 10:20) and attempts to stone him (8:58; 10:31, 39). Brown (*Gospel*, 389) argues that 10:1–21 is a transitional passage that brings together Tabernacles themes with those appropriate to the Feast of Dedication, which is the setting for 10:22–39.

18. Parsenios, "Confounding Foes," 254.

19. Although scholars usually interpret the phrase "fear of the Jews" (7:13; 19:38; 20:19) as an objective genitive meaning that one is *fearing the Jews*, it could also be read as a subjective genitive, meaning *the fearfulness the Jews experience*. In John, the Jewish leadership is expressly fearful of Rome and its ability to destroy Jerusalem and the temple. It is this fear that leads them to condemn Jesus.

20. Lewis, *Rereading*, 131.

21. Although 10:6 uses a singular form of *paroimia*, the shepherd image is not the only use of allegorical language in John 9–10. Jesus uses the *paroimia* of blindness and sight in 9:39–41, which was a common metaphor for understanding in the ancient world (Chad Hartsock, *Sight and Blindness in Luke-Acts: The Use of Physical Features in Characterization*, BibS 94 [Leiden: Brill, 2008]).

22. Brant, *John*, 160–61.

23. Brant, *John*, 161.

24. Most scholars argue for a Jewish milieu for the Gospel because of its use of Scripture, including the festival calendar. This interpretation is rooted in the work of Raymond E. Brown, *The Community of the Beloved Disciple* (New York: Paulist Press, 1979) and J. Louis Martyn, *The History and Theology of the Fourth Gospel*, 3rd ed., NTL (Louisville: Westminster John Knox, 2003).

25. Brant, *John*, 224.

Part 3

JOHN 20

NARRATIVE, SOCIOCULTURAL, INTERTEXTUAL, AND RHETORICAL READINGS

Chapter 9

Narrative-Critical Interpretation of John 20

Craig R. Koester

The story of Jesus's resurrection in John 20 is a dramatic narrative that demonstrates how seeing does not guarantee believing. In it an erroneous inference prompted by an open tomb leads to a quest for answers that generates a series of clues and case of mistaken identity. There are points where grief and fear seem to dominate, but these are interspersed with humorous moments of incomprehension that give way to new insights. Tension builds as characters in the story struggle to make sense of what they observe, even as narrative cues enable readers to discern aspects of meaning that are hidden from the characters themselves; and all the while the dynamics of the story press toward final resolution. Studies in narrative criticism provide ways of approaching this story that are valuable for interpretation. After introducing these methods, we will turn to John 20 itself, showing how a narrative-critical approach contributes to a generative and yet disciplined way of interpreting the text.

NARRATIVE-CRITICAL METHOD AND JOHN 20

Narrative criticism recognizes that the reader plays an active role in the formation of meaning. The words on the page evoke associations in the mind of the reader, and readers must sort and combine these associations into meaningful patterns. The text provides some details while leaving much unsaid, and readers must fill in the gaps with associations they bring from other contexts. Narrative critics often use the category of the "implied reader" to discipline their own interpretation of the text. Whereas an "actual reader" could be any person from antiquity to the present, who actually reads the text, the "implied reader" is a purely literary construct that is formed by bringing together what the text presupposes that a reader might know.[1]

Here we assume that the implied reader knows Greek, the language of John's Gospel. For the many actual readers who do not know Greek, a word like *"mnēmeion"* would not evoke any meaningful associations. The Gospel, however, presupposes readers for whom that word would evoke images of a chamber hewn in rock where the dead were placed—something that in English is called a "tomb." At the same time, the implied reader does not know Semitic languages, since the text assumes that the word *"rabbouni"* must be translated "teacher" for the reader to find it meaningful (John 20:16). We also assume that the implied reader can recall everything that has happened in the Gospel prior to this point, and in this sense, the implied reader is an ideal reader. For example, such a reader is assumed to know all the places that the characters in the resurrection story have appeared in previous chapters and what they have said or done. This reader can also recall prior scenes in which a *mnēmeion* or tomb is mentioned and is therefore in a position to imagine meaningful connections between the tomb scenes.

The narrator shapes the perspective of the reader by selectively providing information and occasionally commenting on the story.[2] In John 20 the narrator speaks in the third person, giving details about the setting, the movement of the characters, what they see, and how they interact. Most of the time the narrator speaks as an observer, describing what someone witnessing the scene would see and hear. At points, however, the narrator is omniscient and able to reveal the unspoken thoughts of the characters: the Beloved Disciple believes, though he does not say so, and neither he nor Peter understands the Scripture (20:8–9); Mary Magdalene thinks that Jesus is the gardener, although she does not actually say so (20:15), and the disciples meet behind closed doors because they fear the Jewish authorities (20:19). Finally, the narrator addresses readers in the second person, disclosing that the reason the narrative was written was that the readers themselves might believe (20:30–31).

The plot has to do with the sequence of events within the narrative. John 20 unfolds in two pairs of scenes, the first two set at Jesus's tomb on Easter morning (20:1–10, 11–18) and the last two in the room where the disciples gather (20:19–23, 24–29). A comment by the narrator concludes the chapter (20:30–31). As in many plotlines, John 20 begins with an issue and then moves through complicating circumstances until finally reaching some resolution. Here readers are taken from Mary Magdalene's initial incomprehension at the sight of the open tomb to Thomas's final recognition of the risen Jesus as his Lord and God. Within each scene the characters' insights develop and advance the plot, yet each time the story appears to reach a climax, there is a step back because of some indication that there is more to come. Even after Thomas's climactic confession, comments by Jesus indicate that the horizon of the story extends beyond the narrative, as he speaks of those who have not seen as Thomas did and yet come to believe.[3]

Characters in John's Gospel are portrayed in ways that range from simple to complex, and from static to dynamic.[4] Although interpreters have sometimes construed the characters as mainly positive or negative in their manner of relating to Jesus, it is important to recognize that they often exhibit traits that work in tension with each other, and in some cases their responses are ambiguous. In John 20 there are individuals like Mary Magdalene, Peter, the Beloved Disciple, and Thomas, as well as the group of disciples, who collectively function as a single character, responding in unison to what transpires. Tracing the developments among the characters will provide an important interpretive perspective on the narrative as a whole.

SCENE 1: JESUS'S FOLLOWERS AT THE OPEN TOMB (20:1–10)

Mary Magdalene's Interpretation of the Open Tomb (20:1–2)

Mary Magdalene's discovery of the open tomb and her report to Peter and the Beloved Disciple (20:1–2) form the introduction to the two scenes that follow. In John's narrative Mary has appeared only one other time, standing near the cross when Jesus entrusts his mother to the care of the Beloved Disciple (19:25–27). Readers can assume that Mary knows both the reality of Jesus's death and the location of his tomb, which is near the place of crucifixion (19:41–42). The temporal setting is that a day and two nights have passed since Jesus's death. Readers know that he was dead and entombed prior to the beginning of the Sabbath (19:31–33, 42), and Mary now comes on the morning after the Sabbath (20:1).[5]

Mary "sees that the stone has been removed from the tomb" (20:1). The specific mention of seeing introduces the key device in the plot. In each scene people see something pertaining to Jesus, and the question is how they will interpret and respond to what they see. Here Mary interprets the removal of the stone as evidence of body snatching. The narrator does not explain why Mary interprets what she sees in this way, leaving readers to fill in the gap. For example, ancient readers might find Mary's explanation plausible because thieves sometimes opened tombs when searching for valuables. Moreover, in an ancient cultural context, removing a body was a kind of hate crime, designed to show vengeance or intimidate the family and friends of the deceased.[6] But regardless of what information actual readers might supply in order to make sense of Mary's interpretation, a crucial point has been made at the narrative level: Mary has voiced what readers are to assume is the logical response to an open tomb. Her initial interpretation is *not* that Jesus has risen from the dead. Rather, if there is to be faith in the resurrection, it will need to emerge despite her plausible alternative explanation.

The ideal or implied reader is positioned to see intimations of resurrection that are not as yet apparent to Mary. The narrator says that "the stone had been removed from the tomb" (20:1). The Greek words for "remove" (*airō*), "stone" (*lithos*), and "tomb" (*mnēmeion*) were all used earlier in the Gospel, when Jesus approached the tomb of Lazarus and said, "Remove the stone" and "they removed the stone" (11:38–41).[7] In that earlier scene the removal of the stone was the prelude to Jesus summoning Lazarus, who had died, to come out of the tomb alive (11:43–44). By using the same language for Jesus's tomb, the narrator provides a clue that it again functions as a prelude to resurrection—this time involving Jesus, who in the Lazarus episode was called "the resurrection and the life" (11:25).

The implied readers might also infer that there is more to the story than Mary recognizes, since they are told that she came to the tomb "while it was still dark" (20:1). The reference to darkness (*skotia*) can be taken as simple elaboration of how early it was when Mary arrived, but the Gospel has also used darkness in symbolic ways. Depending on the context, darkness and light can be correlated with death and life, unbelief and belief, ignorance and knowledge, or evil and God.[8] The positive role played by Mary Magdalene at the narrative level screens out the most negative connotations of darkness, since her bond with Jesus is clear, but the darkness in the setting could be correlated with her inability to "see"—that is, "recognize"—that Jesus is not dead but alive at this point. The dawning of that realization will occur only later.

Peter and the Beloved Disciple (20:3–10)

Simon Peter responds to Mary's report by going to the tomb. As a character, Simon Peter is complex.[9] He has been depicted as both faithful and disloyal, insightful and uncomprehending. He was one of the first to follow Jesus (1:42–44), and when others fell away, Peter was faithful and showed insight when saying, "Lord, to whom shall we go? You have the words of eternal life. We have come to believe and have come to know that you are the Holy One of God" (6:68–69). Peter tried to act faithfully when refusing to let Jesus wash his feet out of respect for his teacher (13:6–11), then by declaring he would be loyal until death (13:36–38), and finally by trying to defend Jesus with a sword at the arrest (18:10–11). At each point, however, his actions demonstrated his inability to understand Jesus's purposes. Then, after following Jesus to the high priest's house, Peter proved to be disloyal when denying

Jesus three times (18:15–27). Given the complex characterization, readers cannot fully anticipate what Peter will do now and must wait to see how he responds at the tomb.

The Beloved Disciple has been a more consistent character.[10] He has been trustworthy, able to develop insight, and has not demonstrated actual misunderstanding at any point. At the last supper, this disciple is said to be especially loved by Jesus and is next to Jesus (13:23). He does not know the identity of the betrayer, but he asks Jesus about it and Jesus discloses it to him (13:25–26). The Beloved Disciple is probably the "other disciple" (*allos mathētēs*), who went to the high priest's house along with Peter but did not deny Jesus (18:15–16). He is the one male disciple who is present at the crucifixion, where he is entrusted with the care of Jesus's mother (19:25–27), and he may therefore be one attesting that blood and water flowed from the side of the crucified Jesus (19:35). By calling this figure the "other disciple" (*allos mathētēs*) and the one whom Jesus loved in 20:2, the narrator positions readers to anticipate that his actions here will be consistent with traits depicted earlier.

The plot moves rapidly in three steps around the theme of seeing. First, the Beloved Disciple arrives, looks into the tomb, and sees the linen grave cloths (*othonia*) inside (20:3–5). This advances the plot, since Mary saw only that the stone had been removed. Readers know that the body of Jesus had been wrapped in linen grave cloths for entombment (19:40). Therefore, seeing only the cloths and not the body creates incongruity with Mary's interpretation because it seems odd to take away the body while leaving the grave cloths behind.

Second, Peter goes into the tomb and sees not only the grave cloths but the face cloth (*soudarion*) rolled up in a place by itself (20:6–7). The added details heighten the incongruity, since readers are presumably to assume that a grave robber would not roll up the face cloth in this manner. At the narrative level, the implied or ideal reader would know that the last time a face cloth was mentioned was when the once-dead Lazarus came out of the tomb alive, still wearing the linen bands and his face cloth (11:44a), yet Jesus commanded the bystanders, "Unbind him, and let him go" (11:44b). The implication is that one who is risen no longer needs the linen bands or face cloth.

Third, the action climaxes when the Beloved Disciple enters the tomb and "saw and believed" (20:8). Initially this seems to be the moment of recognition toward which the plot is moving, but the narrator turns the moment into an anticlimax with the puzzling comment, "For as yet they did not understand the Scripture that he must rise from the dead" (20:9). The word "for" (*gar*) is typically used when explaining the reason for something. Yet it seems odd to say that the reason the Beloved Disciple believes is that he does not understand the connection between Scripture and Jesus's resurrection. Given the peculiarity, one might conclude that the Beloved Disciple "believed" that Mary was correct and that the body had indeed been stolen, which would also fit the concluding comment that these two disciples then "returned to their homes" without saying anything (20:10). Their silence could be read as tacit agreement with Mary's message. Nevertheless, the repeated references to the grave cloths and face cloth, along with similarities to the risen Lazarus's grave cloths being removed, give the opposite impression. No grave robber would leave the linen bands behind or neatly roll up the face cloth.

To make sense of this apparent anticlimax from a narrative perspective, we can initially consider the characters. The Beloved Disciple is said to believe, whereas nothing is said about Peter believing. Portraying different responses would fit the differences in character portrayal overall. By coming to the tomb Peter shows loyalty to Jesus, yet his ability to believe or understand is limited, which would fit what is said about Peter elsewhere. The Beloved Disciple differs in that he has been consistently trustworthy and capable of increasing insight, as seems to be the case here. If anyone could "believe" that seeing the grave cloths showed that death had been overcome, it would be this disciple, since he is never mistaken elsewhere. His response also anticipates the blessing Jesus will pronounce on those who "have not seen and yet have come to believe" (20:29), since he may see the grave cloths, yet he believes without actually seeing the risen Jesus.

Next we can ask why the narrator comments that neither of the disciples could as yet understand what Scripture said about Jesus's resurrection. The Fourth Gospel does not make understanding Scripture into a prerequisite for faith. Instead, the assumption is that faith can lead to a deeper understanding of Scripture. For example, when recounting Jesus's cleansing of the temple and triumphal approach to Jerusalem on a donkey, the narrator remarked that the disciples correlated those events with Scripture after Jesus rose from the dead (2:22; 12:16).[11] The narrator follows that approach in 20:9–10 by indicating that Jesus's resurrection did not simply confirm what the disciples already understood from Scripture. Instead, their understanding of Scripture will develop retrospectively, as they read the older texts in new ways in light of the resurrection.

SCENE 2: JESUS AND MARY MAGDALENE (20:11–18)

Mary Magdalene now resumes a central role in the narrative. In some respects, this scene is parallel to the previous one. Here again the action moves forward in three steps, reaching a climax in Mary's initial recognition of Jesus, which is followed by comments that show the limits of her understanding. The most important difference between scenes 1 and 2 is in their endings, since the disciples leave the tomb without saying anything, whereas Mary is directed to go and tell others about the message she receives from Jesus, and she does so. That movement from the disciples' silence to Mary Magdalene's witness is a major advance in the narrative.

Step 1 continues the theme of seeing. Previously Mary had seen only that the stone had been removed from the entrance to the tomb. Now she looks into the tomb, and instead of grave cloths sees two angels in white (20:11–12). References to angels (*angeloi*) earlier in the Gospel assume that readers will know that they are messengers of God (1:51; 12:29). They ask Mary, "Woman, why are you weeping?" and without missing a beat Mary says, "They have taken away my Lord, and I do not know where they have laid him" (20:13). Then, before they can reply, she turns around.

This encounter can be appreciated as an instance of Johannine humor.[12] Humor often revolves around incongruity. The writer sets up a situation in which readers expect things to go one way, only to have them take a very surprising turn. Typically, some aspect of an encounter begins on an impressive or elevated level, then humor emerges when things abruptly tumble down from the sublime to the mundane as a character completely misses the point.

For readers to see Mary Magdalene's encounter with the angels as humorous, they would need to approach it with certain expectations. A common pattern is that the heavenly messenger suddenly appears and has an imposing appearance, so that a person responds with fear. The angel then quells the fear and delivers a message with weighty implications.[13] In Mary's case the narrator sets up the story in the typical way, for the angels are suddenly present in what has been an empty tomb, and their brilliant white appearance seems impressive enough. But rather than showing fear, Mary is completely unfazed and speaks to them just as she spoke to the disciples, telling them about body snatching. Just at the point where readers would expect the angels to deliver a weighty message, Mary turns away, so that the heavenly messengers are left speechless in the tomb. Through such humor, readers are shown that seeing is certainly not believing, since not even an encounter with divine messengers shakes Mary's conviction that the dead remain dead. For there to be recognition that Jesus is alive, something of another order is needed.

Step 2 is that upon turning around Mary sees the risen Jesus himself, yet this actually heightens the narrative tension, since she does not recognize who he is (20:14). Jesus repeats what the angels said, "Why are you weeping," and then he adds, "Whom are you seeking?" (*tina zēteis*, 20:15). The added question fits the Gospel's characterization of Jesus, since it recalls how Jesus asked those who first followed him, "What do you seek?" (*ti zēteite*, 1:38). Yet Mary continues to interpret what she sees from the perspective of ordinary experience. Since the tomb was located in a garden, the narrator discloses that she assumes that the one she meets is the gardener (19:41; 20:15), and she speaks to the risen Jesus in the same way she spoke to the disciples and the angels, construing what she has seen as evidence of body snatching.

At this point readers might try to close the gaps in the narrative by trying to explain why Mary has *not recognized* the risen Jesus, perhaps speculating that his appearance might have changed or that Mary was simply overwhelmed by grief. But the momentum of the story presses for resolution in a different way, inviting readers to ask what it would take for Mary *to recognize* the risen Jesus. She has seen the open tomb, she has seen angels, and now she has seen the risen Jesus himself, but there has been no change in her perspective. At each juncture she construes the situation in light of common experience, interpreting it as a case of body snatching.

Step 3 brings the narrative tension to partial resolution when Jesus says, "Mary," and she responds by calling him "*rabbouni*," which the narrator explains means "teacher" (20:16). The catalyst for recognition is that Jesus calls Mary by name. Readers are positioned to recall that Jesus previously identified himself as the good shepherd, who "calls his own sheep by name," and "the sheep follow him because they know his voice" (10:3–4; see 10:16, 27). That pattern informs Mary's encounter with the risen Jesus. Notably, what she hears alters the way she interprets what she sees. Calling Jesus "*rabbouni*" locates Mary's moment of recognition within established forms of relationship, since Jesus's followers called him "rabbi" (1:38, 49; 4:31; 9:2; 11:8) or "teacher" (11:28; 13:13–14) during his ministry. At the same time, her initial recognition is limited. She can see that the risen Jesus is the person she knew before, but she has not yet recognized that the nature of their relationship is changing.

Jesus signals the change by saying, "Do not hold on to me, because I have not yet ascended to the Father" (20:17a). The problem is apparently not that there is something inherently wrong about touching the risen Jesus, since Jesus will soon invite Thomas to do so (20:27). Instead, the issue is that her gesture implies a desire to "hold on" to things as they have been, with Jesus in the role of teacher and rabbi, but after Jesus has returned to the Father that will change. Therefore, instead of holding on to the teacher, Jesus directs Mary to return to the disciples in a new role as the one bringing them the message. She does so, in contrast to the two disciples in the previous scene, who apparently return home without saying anything. The implication is that the proclamation of the resurrection is not based primarily on inferences from an empty tomb; it occurs in response to the risen Jesus himself.

Jesus's words to Mary also set the direction for further plot resolution. He says, "I am ascending to my Father and your Father, to my God and to your God" (20:17). Throughout the Gospel Jesus has referred to God as his Father, but through his resurrection and ascension he indicates that his followers too will relate to God as Father. For the implied reader, Jesus's words recall earlier passages where God's role as Father was linked to giving life (5:21; 6:57) and showing love (14:23; 16:27; 17:23), and especially to God begetting or generating within people the faith that is true life through the agency of the Spirit (1:12–13; 3:3–5, 16). Thomas will develop this aspect of the plot by recognizing that in the risen Jesus he encounters the one he can call "my God" (20:29).

SCENE 3: JESUS AND THE DISCIPLES (20:19–23)

The disciples who hear Mary Magdalene's testimony are the focus in the next scene (20:18, 19). They function as a single collective character, responding to Jesus as a group. Previously the disciples have been portrayed in a moderately complex way, comparable to Peter. In their actions they have generally been loyal to Jesus, believing in him (2:11) and accompanying him (2:2, 12; 6:21; 13:5; 11:54; 18:1). Yet they repeatedly misunderstand Jesus (4:27–38; 11:7–15; 16:17, 29), they are "scattered" at the time of his arrest (16:31–32), and their most important insights come after the resurrection, not before it (2:22; 12:16).[14]

It is striking that Mary conveys the message of Jesus's resurrection to the disciples, but nothing is said about their response, and the setting of this new scene in 20:19 has details that suggest instability, which presses for resolution. In temporal terms, scene 3 is the counterpart to scene 1. Where Mary came to the tomb "early (*prōi*) on the first day of the week," the disciples gather "late" (*opsias*) or in the "evening of that day, the first day of the week" (20:1, 19). Both scenes are set in between night and day, which seems appropriate for moments in between incomprehension and recognition. Where Mary saw the tomb had been opened, the disciples gathered behind doors that are shut—and the reason is "fear of the Jews" (20:19). Previously the narrator ascribed such fear to people who were themselves Jewish but were afraid to speak openly of Jesus or profess faith in him because of their fear of "the Jews" in positions of authority (7:13; 19:38; see 9:22). Whenever the narrator mentions such fear, it is a barrier to open profession of faith, and the issue is how that barrier can be overcome.

The catalyst for change is that Jesus comes to the disciples and says, "Peace be with you" (20:19). In previous parts of the narrative, Jesus overcame his disciples' fear by means of his presence and words (6:19–21), and he persisted in teaching and conveying love to them despite their incomprehension (4:31–38; 13:1, 34–35). The narrative in John 20 underscores Jesus's faithfulness by prompting readers to see how the promises Jesus made to the disciples during the last supper are now kept after his resurrection. At the Last Supper, Jesus told the disciples, "Peace I leave with you;

my peace I give to you. . . . Do not let your hearts be troubled, and do not let them be afraid" (14:27). Accordingly, when the risen Jesus meets the disciples, who are afraid, he gives the greeting "Peace" not just once but twice (20:19, 21).

Readers might expect the narrator to say that in response the disciples "believed," but the narrative says that after Jesus showed them his hands and his side, the disciples "rejoiced" (20:20). That detail again recalls Jesus's words at the Last Supper, when he repeatedly said he was going to the Father and yet would come again to the disciples, so they would see him and "rejoice" (14:28; 16:16–24). The joy that Jesus promised is now given as he comes to them through resurrection (20:20). What may seem incongruous at the narrative level is that Jesus made the promises at the Last Supper in anticipation of going to the Father before coming again to the disciples (14:28; 16:17). When speaking to Mary Magdalene by the empty tomb, Jesus said that he had "not yet ascended to the Father" but was apparently in the process of doing so (20:17). So one might wonder whether Jesus returned to the Father in between his encounters with Mary Magdalene in John 20:17 and the disciples in 20:19–20.

The Fourth Gospel differs from Luke 24:50–53 and Acts 1:1–11, which give descriptions of Jesus's ascension. In John's narrative, the idea is that readers will know that Jesus's return to the Father has been completed when the Spirit is given to his followers. Again, the essential perspective is informed by Jesus's words at the Last Supper. There he promised that along with peace and joy, the disciples would receive the Holy Spirit or Advocate (*paraklētos*) after he returned to the Father. He said that "if I do not go away, the Advocate will not come to you; but if I go, I will send him to you" (16:7; see 14:16–17, 25–29; 15:26). This happens on Easter evening when Jesus breathes the Holy Spirit into the disciples (20:22). By giving the disciples Spirit, Jesus indicates that his return to the Father is complete.

Receiving the Spirit is then linked to the disciples' commission to continue the work of Jesus by forgiving and retaining sins (20:23). In some respects, readers might find this aspect of the story to be peculiar. In the Synoptic Gospels Jesus is shown forgiving sins during his ministry, but this has not specifically said about Jesus in John's Gospel.[15] From a narrative perspective, however, Jesus is the Lamb of God, who died to "take away the sin of the world" (1:29), and during his ministry he did hold people to account for their sin, specifically their sin of unbelief and the actions or sins that flowed from it (8:24; 9:41). Moreover, at the Last Supper Jesus told the disciples that the Spirit or Advocate they would receive would prove the world wrong about sin, righteousness, and judgment (16:7–11). So again, the plot advances by showing how the words Jesus spoke at the Last Supper are realized through his resurrection and gift of the Spirit.

SCENE 4: JESUS AND THOMAS (20:24–29)

Attention now turns from the disciples collectively to Thomas as an individual.[16] The first part of the scene creates a transition in which the narrator notes that Thomas was not with the other disciples when Jesus came. When they tell him, "We have seen the Lord," he replies that he will not believe unless he sees and touches the wounds in Jesus's hands and side (20:24–25). The implied reader would know that Thomas first appeared in the narrative after Jesus announced that he was going to Judea to raise Lazarus, who was dead, even though opponents in that area had previously tried to stone him; and Jesus's stated intent was that the disciples "may believe" (11:7–15).

Thomas, however, responded, "Come, let us also go that we may die with him" (11:16). Since no voice tones are indicated by the narrative, readers might imagine Thomas speaking with bravado in the face of danger or with exasperation at Jesus's suicidal plan. But in either case, it seemed clear that Thomas was convinced that the outcome would not be new life for Lazarus but death for Jesus and those who followed him. If readers assume that Thomas accompanied Jesus to Judea, as he said he would, then the implication is that seeing the raising of Lazarus did not prepare Thomas to believe the disciples' report about the resurrection of Jesus. Ironically, for Thomas seeing has previously *not* guaranteed believing.

The story continues a week after Jesus's resurrection, when the setting replicates that of Easter evening: the disciples are again behind closed doors when Jesus comes to them and says, "Peace be with you" (20:26). Jesus tells Thomas to touch his hands and side, as he had insisted on doing, adding, "Do not doubt but believe"; or we might translate it, "Do not be unbelieving (*apistos*) but believing (*pistos*)" (20:27).

The narrator does not indicate whether Thomas did or did not put his finger into Jesus's wounds but moves instead to Thomas's verbal response, "My Lord and my God" (20:28). The words signal an abrupt shift from unbelief to belief, and also mark a narrative climax. Readers have known since the opening lines of the Gospel that Jesus is the Word, who was with God and was God (1:1, 14). No character in the story, however, has addressed Jesus as God, so when Thomas finally does so, his elevated confession of faith at the end of the story corresponds to the insight that readers have had since its beginning.

In retrospect, readers can also trace the way the portrayal of Thomas as a character leads up to his climactic statement. Thomas's experience of the resurrection occurs within a context that is shaped by what he has already heard from and about Jesus. The first element is that at the last supper Thomas is told what it means to see God in the person of Jesus. In that scene Jesus was speaking of his departure from this world, when Thomas interjected, "Lord we do not know where you are going; how can we know the way?" (14:5). After identifying himself as the way, truth, and life, Jesus said, "If you know me, you will know my Father also. From now on you do know him and have seen him" (14:7). The second element is that the disciples told Thomas, "We have seen the Lord" (20:25).

The climactic moment comes when Thomas interprets what he sees in light of the words he has already heard. The disciples had told Thomas, "We have seen the Lord," (20:25), and Thomas now makes their words his own by calling Jesus, "My Lord" (20:28). Similarly, Jesus had told Thomas that those who see who he is will see who God is (14:7), and Thomas now makes those words his own by calling Jesus, "My God" (20:28). What Thomas sees in the encounter with the risen Jesus is interpreted through the lens of the testimony he had previously heard from the disciples and from Jesus.

Jesus then draws together the major narrative threads of the resurrection scenes when he tells Thomas, "Have you believed because you have seen me? Blessed are those who have not seen and yet have come to believe" (20:29). The portrayal of Thomas shows that seeing does not guarantee believing. If readers can assume that he accompanied Jesus for the raising of Lazarus, then seeing that resurrection did not create any readiness to believe in Jesus's resurrection. Moreover, what decisively shaped Thomas's perspective were the words he had previously received. Seeing alone did not yield his confession. Rather, the encounter with Jesus enabled Thomas to make his own the words he had already received from Jesus and the other disciples.

The implication is that those who "have not seen" actually have what is essential "to believe," namely, the testimony that they are being given (20:29). That point is made explicit when the narrator addresses the readers directly, telling them, "Jesus did many other signs in the presence of his disciples, which are not written in this book. But these are written so that you may come to believe that Jesus in the Messiah, the Son of God, and that through believing you may have life in his name" (20:30–31). The assumption is that the readers are like Thomas in that they are not part of the group that first saw the risen Jesus, and they are also like Thomas in that they have received testimony about Jesus through the Gospel itself. Therefore, when Jesus says, "Blessed are those who have not seen and yet come to believe" the readers are encouraged to receive the message of resurrection without making seeing and touching the risen Jesus a precondition for faith, as Thomas did. Readers have what is needed in the written text, which enables them to "see" Jesus through the narrative it offers them.

NOTES

1. R. Alan Culpepper, *Anatomy of the Fourth Gospel: A Study in Literary Design* (Philadelphia: Fortress, 1983), 203–27; Jeffrey Staley, *The Print's First Kiss: A Rhetorical Investigation of the Implied Reader in the Fourth Gospel*, SBLDS 82 (Atlanta: Scholars Press, 1988), 1–49.

2. On narration, see Culpepper, *Anatomy of the Fourth Gospel*, 13–49.

3. On the narrative shape of John 20, see Francis J. Moloney, *Glory Not Dishonor: Reading John 13–21* (Minneapolis: Fortress, 1998), 153–81.

4. For a survey of approaches to characterization in John, see Christopher W. Skinner, "Introduction: Characters and Characterization in the Gospel of John: Reflections on the *Status Quaestionis*," in *Characters and Characterization in the Gospel of John*, ed. Christopher W. Skinner, LNTS 461 (London: Bloomsbury/T&T Clark, 2013), xvii–xxxii; Steven A. Hunt, D. Francois Tolmie, and Ruben Zimmermann, "An Introduction to Character and Characterization in John and Related New Testament Literature," in *Character Studies in the Fourth Gospel: Narrative Approaches to Seventy Figures in John*, ed. Steven A. Hunt, D. Francois Tolmie, and Ruben Zimmermann (Grand Rapids: Eerdmans, 2016), 1–33.

5. On Mary Magdalene as a character, see Jaime Clark-Soles, "Mary Magdalene: Beginning at the End," in Hunt, Tolmie, and Zimmermann, *Character Studies in the Fourth Gospel*, 626–40; Cornelis Bennema, *Encountering Jesus: Character Studies in the Gospel of John*, 2nd ed. (Minneapolis: Fortress, 2009), 329–37.

6. A first-century inscription mandates legal prosecution for anyone who has "extracted the buried or has maliciously transferred them to other places in order to wrong them" (C. K. Barrett, *The New Testament Background: Selected Documents* [New York: Harper & Row, 1961], 15).

7. Author translation.

8. On light and darkness in John, see Craig R. Koester, *Symbolism in the Fourth Gospel: Meaning, Mystery, Community*, 2nd ed. (Minneapolis: Fortress, 2003), 141–68.

9. On Peter as a character, see Bennema, *Encountering Jesus*, 111–26; Michael Labahn, "Simon Peter: An Ambiguous Character and His Narrative Career," in Hunt, Tolmie, and Zimmermann, *Character Studies in the Fourth Gospel*, 151–67.

10. On the Beloved Disciple as character, see James L. Resseguie, "The Beloved Disciple: The Ideal Point of View," in Hunt, Tolmie, and Zimmermann, *Character Studies in the Fourth Gospel*, 537–49; Susan E. Hylen, *Imperfect Believers: Ambiguous Characters in the Gospel of John* (Louisville: Westminster John Knox, 2009), 92–109.

11. In the story of Jesus disrupting trade in the temple, the disciples are said to have "remembered" how the Scripture said, "Zeal for your house will consume me" (John 2:17; see Ps 69:9). Although this could be taken to mean that they remembered the Scripture with insight at the time of Jesus's action, it most probably refers to post-resurrection insight, since that is explicit a few verses later in John 2:22.

12. See Craig R. Koester, "Comedy, Humor, and the Gospel of John, in *Word, Theology, and Community in John*, ed. John Painter, R. Alan Culpepper, and Fernando F. Segovia (St. Louis: Chalice, 2002), 123–41.

13. Examples of stories in which people respond to angels with fear include Matt. 1:20–21; 28:1–7; Luke 1:12–13, 26–31; 2:9–12; see Judg. 6:21–23; Dan. 8:15–17; 10:5–14.

14. On the disciples as a collective character, see Hylen, "The Disciples."

15. For examples of Jesus offering forgiveness, see Matt. 9:2; Mark 2:5; Luke 5:20; 7:47. In John 8:10–11, Jesus does say he will not condemn the woman caught in adultery, but that passage was not part of the earliest text of the Gospel.

16. On Thomas as a character, see Thomas Popp, "Thomas: Question Marks and Exclamation Marks," in Hunt, Tolmie, and Zimmermann, *Character Studies in the Fourth Gospel*, 504–29.

Chapter 10

Reading Mary Magdalene with Stacey Abrams

Developing an Inclusive National Consciousness

Angela N. Parker

In the past mid-term elections of 2018, many viewers across the United States of America followed the gubernatorial race of Stacey Abrams in the state of Georgia. Even though Abrams inevitably lost her bid to Brian Kemp amid voter suppression allegations, Democratic leadership selected Abrams as the Democratic response speaker to the February 5, 2019, State of the Union address.[1] As a critically thinking African American woman who was born and raised in these United States of America, I greatly anticipated hearing Abrams's response to Donald Trump's State of the Union address. However, like other African American women, I was also slightly flummoxed that Bernie Sanders, the Independent Senator from Vermont, provided *another* Democratic response to the State of the Union, even after Abrams had provided the "official" response. Sanders's response raised the question of how African American women navigate the intersecting oppressions of patriarchy, sexism, racism, and classism in the midst of pursing high office.

As a womanist[2] biblical scholar, I do not see these interests as being too far afoot from how women in the narrative of early Christianity underwent the same pursuits of "office" within early Jesus communities. Thinking through the example of Stacey Abrams as a representative of a more inclusive national consciousness[3] in the United States, this chapter engages the idea of Mary Magdalene as a symbol of national consciousness in the Gospel of John. More specifically, I will interrogate commentators' negative interpretations of Mary Magdalene as a symbol of national consciousness. Moreover, I interrogate commentators' lack of identifying Mary Magdalene as a leader of early Jesus communities following the death and resurrection of Jesus.

Specifically, I will perform a womanist postcolonial reading of John 20:11–18 in an attempt to read Mary Magdalene with Stacey Abrams in order to promote an inclusive national consciousness. Proposing that readers of John's Gospel must approach this text as multilayered and multileveled, I argue that, for the Johannine author, Mary Magdalene does not merely represent a woman who announces Jesus's resurrection to the disciples, nor is she "just" a figure that promotes the ability of women to "preach," she also serves as a symbol of an inclusive national consciousness who embodies consequences for my understanding of the national culture in Israel even as she served as a leader in her own right. Accordingly, my womanist postcolonial reading will allow the identification of "multiplicity of meaning" in the biblical text thus providing an expanded understanding of Mary, not only for women preaching, but for a more nuanced view of women leading in the nation, women leading in ecclesial settings, and women reclaiming their time[4] both in the nation and in ecclesial settings.

I have structured this chapter as follows. First, I provide a brief summary of postcolonial studies. More specifically, I juxtapose the work of postcolonial work of Franz Fanon and Anne McClintock for an understanding of national consciousness and the use of women as national symbols. After this summary, I outline the historical situation in John's[5] Gospel that relates to postcolonial studies and allows for an understanding of Mary Magdalene as a symbol of national consciousness. Third, I provide a womanist postcolonial exegetical analysis of John 20:11–18. Finally, I offer concluding reflections which propose how the United States of America must reimagine African American women as symbols of an inclusive national consciousness through the work of Stacey Abrams.

INTEGRATING WOMANIST THOUGHT INTO ACADEMIC BIBLICAL STUDIES

The academic study of Bible has its own evils whether the purveyors of this particular system want to acknowledge it or not. As a junior scholar within the field of biblical studies, I argue that one of the systemic "evils" of academic biblical studies is its viewpoint of objective reality as a stance for biblical interpretation. For generations biblical scholars studied under the auspicious belief that "objective" inquiry was the prime way to do biblical scholarship. Renita Weems, for example, begins her seminal article on womanist hermeneutics by stating that scholarship is now beginning to assert the "inherent biases and limitation of the historical-critical method as an objective, scientific approach to the Bible."[6] Weems has already identified a particular systemic evil within the realm of academic biblical studies.

The issue of objectivity within interpretation is not the only systemic evil found within biblical interpretation. Once we couple the issue of objectivity with the issue of identity, I believe that actively engaging these issues may force biblical scholarship to construct methodologies that are relevant both within the halls of the academy, in the pulpits of churches, and on the sidewalks of society where lived experiences occur. Proposing that a turn to identity coupled with relationality can be one area that moves scholarship out of the conundrum within which we find ourselves, I argue that identity, specifically womanist identity, is important to my particular constructive process as it moves scholarship away from the objective, scientific approach to the biblical text.

One aspect of womanist identity that is important for my specific contribution to a womanist biblical hermeneutic is the subject of womanist relationality. As womanists engage the concept of relationality for Trinitarian theology,[7] I argue similar ideas scaffolding that scholarship are helpful for integrating womanist thought with the system of academic biblical studies as a methodology for womanist biblical interpretation. Karen Baker-Fletcher argues that the role of praxis in womanist theology is to bring together life experience, reason, Scripture, and tradition in order to name God and to construct an understanding of the mutuality and relationality of the Trinity. Baker-Fletcher is helpful for thinking through womanist identity, the triad of race, class, and gender, and how identity and oppressions impact biblical scholarship and the reading of the biblical text. For Baker-Fletcher only the "real-lived" experience of black women can begin the construction of womanist theology wherein right-relationship with God and with the world means integrating theory and practice.[8] Accordingly, for my particular womanist hermeneutic, reading the biblical text as a womanist means integrating the traditional, historical-critical practices of biblical scholarship with the "real-lived" experiences of black women (e.g., Stacey Abrams). What I am suggesting, therefore, is a mutual and relational reading of the biblical text between black women's lived experience, black women's reasoning, Scripture, and tradition in order to construct a womanist biblical methodology that impacts biblical scholarship.[9] Accordingly, my particular womanist hermeneutical strategy moves from what I identify as "traditional" biblical interpretation to "non-traditional" methodologies (i.e., a nuanced womanist hermeneutical reading strategy).

In order to add more theoretical grounding to the lived experience of black women's lives as we engage the biblical text, I argue that attention to critical social theory provides language around why the integration is important. In order to begin to focus on a combined womanist and postcolonial reading of John, I now turn to the theoretical work of Frantz Fanon and Anne McClintock in order to construct a nuanced reading strategy for national consciousness.

Thinking Through National Consciousness in Postcolonial and Feminist Theorists unto a Womanist Hermeneutical Strategy

In his work Frantz Fanon begins to theorize about the concept of "national consciousness" as follows:

> Instead of being the all-embracing crystallization of the innermost hopes of the whole people, instead of being the immediate and most obvious result of the mobilization of the people, will be in any case only an empty shell, a crude and fragile travesty of what it might have been.[10]

In essence, Fanon forces theorists to think about how a national consciousness *should* function in societies that have groups of people who have experienced colonization, racism, classism, and gender discrimination in their everyday lives. For Fanon, however, the idea of a national consciousness becomes a symbol of how the elite understand the stories and worldviews of a nation for a particular group of people. As I work toward the conclusion of this chapter, I will argue for a definition of national consciousness as an inclusive national consciousness culminating in a shared identity that embodies the stories and worldviews of all peoples in a nation, not just the privileged few. In biblical and theological parlance, scholars do not often use "national consciousness" in our exegetical work for biblical interpretation. Accordingly, I ask how biblical scholars can understand the concept of "national consciousness" for biblical interpretation.

I turn to the theoretical thinking of Fanon for an answer. Fanon describes the trials and tribulations that a nation undergoes in its struggle for independence from a colonial situation. While American consciousness remembers the struggles for independence against British colonialism, the American spirit cannot understand that same concept when applied to black and brown bodies struggling against colonial and imperial violence perpetrated upon black and brown bodies.

In his thinking about a national bourgeoisie, Fanon identifies a type of nationalism stemming from a return to mythic origins of the land which then leads to an ultra-nationalism, chauvinism, and racism within the nation.[11] I would argue that Fanon, even though writing in the context of Africans fighting against France, is helpful for thinking about the ultra-nationalism, chauvinism, and racism found in ideas circulating in recent years; for example, specifically, around the August 12, 2017, rally in Charlottesville, Virginia, where Heather Heyer was mowed down by James Alex Fields Jr., a person who espoused neo-Nazi and white supremacist beliefs. For the purposes of this chapter, I identify the term "ethnonationalism" as a way to understand what is happening in the United States of America. As a womanist biblical scholar engaging the Bible within the United States of America, part of what I am wrestling against is the spirit of ethnonationalism found across the country.

Another aspect of Fanon's thought that is helpful for my argument is his insistence that the bottom must construct a national consciousness.[12] Of course while thinking through the events of Charlottesville, one could argue that the bottom part of white male society is reconstructing a national consciousness of the United States with statements like, "The Jews will not replace us." However, even if these men are the "bottom" of the nation, there still is an element of white supremacy in their thinking. Accordingly, three issues are important from Fanon's thought as I ponder the concept of ultranationalism and construct a womanist hermeneutic for reading Mary Magdalene with Stacey Abrams. First, Fanon believes that members of the nation must struggle with problems that are not their own. While I am not a white male living in the United States, there is a problem that occurs when Heather Heyer is killed during the rally or even when a shooter steps foot into a California synagogue with the intent of killing Sabbath observers. A womanist contextualized hermeneutic must be a hermeneutic that engages and seeks liberation for all people, including white citizens of the United States.

Second, Fanon shapes his theoretical thinking through transformation of reality by praxis and the deployment of violence as part of the agenda for liberation. While I do not condone actual violence, I do envision symbolic violence against traditional readings of the Johannine text as central to a womanist contextualized hermeneutic. In this way, I will connect symbolic violence to the questioning of male sanctioned theories that Anne McClintock highlights in her work. As I engage and envision symbolic violence against ideological readings of Mary Magdalene, I extend the findings in the Gospel to the ways that womanists must do symbolic violence to aspects of the white ethnonationalism (and it connection to evangelical Christianity) that is arising in the United States of America.

While I do employ Fanon's work, I must admit that I do not use his theoretical framework uncritically. Fanon's language borders upon misogyny while, oftentimes, attempting to speak for women. In order to expand upon Fanon's thought regarding women and nationalism, I will briefly engage him with Anne McClintock and her view of feminist nationalism.

In her work, Anne McClintock develops a "situated psychoanalysis"[13] that effects a "decolonization of psychoanalysis and a psychoanalysis of colonialism"[14] by exploring the relationship between domesticity, desire, and female labor in Victorian England and its colonies. McClintock argues that the "the cult of industrial rationality and the cult of domesticity formed a crucial but concealed alliance"[15] that essentially erased women's labor from history. Because capitalism, race, gender, and sex were all interlocking issues that helped to create the concepts behind nationalism, McClintock advocates a fourfold feminist theory of nationalism that accomplishes the following: (1) investigates the gendered formation of sanctioned male theories; (2) brings into historical visibility women's active cultural and political participation in national formations; (3) brings nationalist institutions into critical relation with other social structures and institutions; and (4) pays attention to the structures of racial, ethnic, and class power that continue to bedevil privileged forms of feminism.[16] McClintock is important for a womanist contextualized hermeneutic because she adds a specific view of feminism to Fanon where he lacks gender, class, and capitalistic notions of what nationalism looks like for women.

Therefore, interweaving the work of Anne McClintock with the findings already espoused from the work of Frantz Fanon allows me to construct a reader response[17] strategy that takes into account the feminist ideas of nationalism and leadership with the effects of colonial racism on the black body as engaged in Fanon's work, in order to highlight my commitments to a hermeneutic that is relevant for womanist thought while also engaging with women from diverse cultures. I seek to identify the connections between these theorists in order to draft a hermeneutic that socially just reading of biblical passages.

What does this mean for my own constructed womanist hermeneutic as I read John 20:11–18? Specifically, I am reading the text and asking questions and attempting to do symbolic violence against the sanctioned male interpretations that scholars still teach in our seminaries today. I am reading the text and asking questions about nationalism and a national consciousness as found in the text and in today's world. Finally, I am asking questions about women and women's leadership both in the biblical text and today.

John 20:1–2, 11–18 from a Womanist Perspective

As I begin reading the text of John 20, I see what is retold in all of the Gospel narratives: some story of women going to the tomb. In the Gospel of John, the narrative only names Mary Magdalene and not the other women as identified in Matthew, Mark, and Luke. For the Johannine narrative, the story essentially proceeds as follows: Mary Magdalene is the first witness to the empty tomb (20:1). She arrives, sees the stone rolled away, and runs to tell the disciples (v. 2). Peter and the disciple whom Jesus loved run to the tomb (vv. 3–4). Peter and Mary come to the logical conclusion that someone has taken Jesus's body out of the tomb. The Beloved Disciple "sees and believes" (vv. 5–8). However, Mary's view changes based on which interpretations you read. According to most traditional interpretations of the Gospel of John, Mary Magdalene is at the tomb and speaks to (the about-to-ascend-to-his-Father)

Jesus, but according to traditional interpreters, she is not a true disciple and does not possess any apostolic authority.[18]

If, however, Mary Magdalene cannot claim "apostolic authority" in traditional interpreters' views,[19] that does not preclude her from having authority within the context of the Johannine community. Warren Carter assumes that the Johannine narrative probably originated in Ephesus with close ties to nearby city of Aphrodisias. In Asia Minor, there is epigraphic evidence that alludes to the acceptance of Roman imperial cult worship including in Ephesus and especially in Aphrodisias, which housed a statue of Emperor Nero being crowned as divine by female divinity who is referred to as the "Lady of Aphrodisias."[20] Archaeologists who discovered these ties also revealed that the statues of the Lady of Aphrodisias are similar to the statues of the goddess Venus/Aphrodite in Ephesus. This is particularly important because the Julian dynasty (of which Augustus and Nero are descendants) claim divine lineage to Venus. Since some scholars believe that the Johannine tradition was born in Ephesus, one can certainly opine that the traditions in Ephesus are also known by Aphrodisians since there was also a Jewish contingency in that city as well as in Ephesus.[21]

Moreover, even though the Roman imperial world was a hierarchal empire dominated by an emperor, his military force, and the elite class, the status quo could also recognize elite woman as high on the hierarchal ladder. Accordingly, not only does the identity of the emperor find itself manifested in the epigraphic evidence in Aphrodisias but one can also verify the identity of elite women such as the priestesses to Hera and the imperial cult located in Aphrodisias.[22] For instance, there are numerous inscriptions in Aphrodisias to a priestess named Tata who held the office of *stephanophorus*, "crownbearer" and underwrote the cost of religious festivals and public entertainments for the entire term of her office.[23] As a result of her benefaction, Tata was identified as a woman of honor and privilege. This benefaction also set Tata up as a "higher" classed citizen over someone who is a citizen of Aphrodisias but was not able to afford to underwrite such costs. In effect, the Roman imperial system had the capacity to imagine women as holding high office within the imperial system even if male commentators of the Gospel narratives cannot hold that imagination while reading the biblical texts.

Oftentimes scholars possess no imagination for realities other than what they already espouse. Many interpreters of the Johannine Gospel have no imagination for Mary Magdalene as authoritative in her own right.[24] Following Rudolf Bultmann,[25] Francis Moloney argues that Peter and the Beloved Disciple are the "foundational characters" in the narrative beginning at John 20:1–18.[26] Reading traditional commentators is striking to the point that there is no imagination that Mary Magdalene was an authoritative figure in her own right since traditional scholars essentially attempt to place any lack of belief found in the text onto either the "other disciple" or "Peter." Specifically, scholars argue that when the biblical text shifts from the plural to the singular at 20:2 where Mary Magdalene states, "They have taken the Lord and *we* do not know where they have laid him!"[27] Mary is trying to associate the disciples with her own lack of faith and knowledge. Feminist interpreter Anne Graham Brock, on the other hand, argues that the text most likely is an interpolation that flows from 20:1 to 20:11 suggesting that an earlier version of the narrative included the other women who were with her.[28] Brock's identification of the interpolation highlights the issue that later tradition would want the presence of two male disciples at the resurrection scene who can corroborate Mary Magdalene's story of the empty tomb since Jewish Law required two men as credible witnesses.[29]

The second interpretation that causes me to pause when reading traditional interpretations of Mary Magdalene is when scholars argue that the relationship between Mary Magdalene and Jesus has fundamentally changed when Jesus states *mē mou haptou* (translated as, "stop touching/taking hold of/clinging to me"). These scholars contend Mary Magdalene *only* understands Jesus as someone who best responds to "her present hopes and needs."[30] Moloney continues, "The fruits of Jesus' glorification means that the days of being associated with the *historical Jesus are over.*"[31] Such a statement is probably the most problematic statement related to the Mary Magdalene narrative because traditional scholarship separates Jesus from his Jewish roots unto a universal understanding. A universal understanding of Jesus then allows white supremacist ethnonational thought to occur in contemporary Christianity.

The work of Shawn Kelley is helpful to expound my point. Kelley's work *Racializing Jesus* evidences the problem that language centered on the Jesus of history and the glorified Jesus actually conveys. Arguing that nationalism arose in European scholarship and thinking through Hegelian philosophy, Kelley shows that the idea of an authentic, pure, uncontaminated culture rose up in scholarship. The prominence of pure ideas meant that ideas (and people) which Western thought considered alien, foreign, or corrupting had to be expelled. Specifically, the "pure" folk had to expel the racially "alien" (the Jew, the Oriental, the African, the non-European) from multiple areas of knowledge and the narrative of world history.[32]

Moreover, as nationalism arose in European academic thinking, the Hegelian logic of moving from lower consciousness to higher levels of consciousness began to take root in academic thought. Hegel espoused consciousness as developing geographically and racially, as the levels of consciousness are assigned to particular races and particular peoples. For Hegel, lower levels of consciousness demonstrate a real, albeit backward and despotic, culture, while Europeans, particularly Germans, are capable of higher levels of consciousness. It is the Germanic Europeans who possess the potential for authentic culture and for real freedom. Hegel develops a narrative of history that denies humanity to Africans and denies the consciousness of freedom to Jews and Orientals.

As we fast forward to the beginning of biblical scholarship, I agree with Kelley's delineation that Jesus (and the apostle Paul as well) become Aryan, German, or rational to fit the views of scholarship. As Hegelian philosophy took over the question of biblical scholarship, scholars had to disavow Jesus (and Paul) of their Jewish roots to make Christianity universal. As I read traditional scholarship's interpretation of Mary Magdalene's encounter with Jesus, I argue that scholars perpetuate the work of nationalist ideology with the strict dichotomy between the Jesus of history and the Jesus of glory.[33] Taking Jesus out of his Jewish nationalism and placing him in a strictly universal thought system becomes especially problematic in contemporary society when white evangelical Christianity[34] teaches and preaches a Jesus who is further separated from his Jewish roots while training its parish members to see all of "the Jews"[35] as Christ killers. Society has recently seen the increase in hatred and intention to kill Jewish people as a result of rising anti-Semitic thought.[36]

So then the next question becomes, "How do I place these thoughts in conversation with a womanist hermeneutical lens as I read Mary Magdalene with Stacey Abrams?" In order to begin to do that, I must continue interrogating the work of feminists who read Mary Magdalene but reach differing conclusions than traditional interpreters. One such scholar is the late Gail R. O'Day.[37] O'Day highlights a few hermeneutical observations about Mary Magdalene's narrative. First, O'Day states that Mary's story is the most detailed of the four stories about women at Jesus's tomb since we get Mary talking to Peter and the Beloved Disciple, and then Mary speaking to Jesus.[38] Moreover, O'Day notes that the only "recorded response" is in 20:8 wherein we learn that the "other disciple . . . saw and believed." While O'Day does not flesh out this recorded verse, others who have worked on this text become important conversation partners as we think through leadership and, specifically, women's leadership in the early Jesus movement.

In the second scene contained in 20:11–18, the reader finds Mary alone at the tomb, crying. She looks into the tomb and finds two angels/messengers in white sitting at the head and the foot of the place where Jesus has lain. When the angels question why she is weeping, Mary Magdalene responds that they have taken *ton kyrion mou* ("My Lord"). O'Day states that in previous conversation with Peter and the Beloved Disciple at 20:2, Mary responded with the phrase "the Lord" (*ton kyrion*). Contra traditional scholars, O'Day picks up on the personal nature of Mary calling Jesus "my Lord." O'Day states that

Mary is speaking out of her "personal" grief. As I read this "personal" grief, I am reminded of some black feminist's (e.g., Audre Lorde and the Combahee River Collective) rallying cry that "the personal is political."[39] I will expand upon this thought shortly as I connect to Stacey Abrams.

Moving further into the narrative of the story, the reader notes the wording of Mary Magdalene when she speaks to Jesus but assumes him to be a gardener. Mary says, "Sir, if you have carried him away, tell me where you have laid him, and I will take him away" or "I will raise him up" (20:15). Mary believes she has some control, will, or agency to carry away the body of Jesus. After Jesus speaks her name, Mary realizes the one whom she supposed was the gardener is her Lord.[40] While not wanting her to follow him in ascension (hence, the prohibition against "clinging" to Jesus), Jesus does, in fact, commission Mary Magdalene to announce the news of the resurrection to the brothers and sisters of the Lord. In essence, Jesus commissions Mary Magdalene's voice to the disciples.

Accordingly, O'Day (along with Brock) serves as more sympathetic reader to Mary Magdalene and her commissioning more so than traditional interpreters, thus I must ask what a particular womanist lens with attention to Frantz Fanon and Anne McClintock brings to this task. I would have to argue that the answer lies in O'Day's clarification that Mary Magdalene speaks out of her "personal" grief. Connecting personal grief to the Combahee River Collective's rallying cry that "the personal is political," I argue that a particular womanist reading of Mary Magdalene allows three points that all connect to the concept of "womanist voicing"[41] as a connection between Mary Magdalene and Stacey Abrams.

First, I highlight the voicing of personal grief. Not everyone has the privilege of voicing personal grief when others will listen to or even empathize with the personal grief. One can think through the deep wounded nature of black and brown mothers who have lost children to police violence, for example, which has not always yielded empathy for the voicing of that personal grief.

Second, I would argue that voicing personal grief while having a particular identity often precludes listeners without said particular identity from being empathic. Specifically, white men oftentimes cannot empathize with white women (as we have recently seen in the testimony of Christine Blasey Ford during the Brett Kavanagh hearings)[42] nor, oftentimes, can black men and white women empathize with African American women (as womanist thought has identified).[43] Thus, traditional and mainstream folks often exhibit difficult in understanding personal grief. Further, I wonder if Mary Magdalene's particular identity as a woman hindered traditional scholars from understanding her personal grief at seeing the empty tomb in the context of how women may experience emptiness in other areas of life.

Thinking through Fanon, McClintock, and womanist thought, I have to wonder whether traditional scholarship can even begin to speak to the emptiness that often occurs in women's and black women's bodily experiences. How can traditional male scholars speak to inherent emptiness or a presumption of incompetence when privileged positions often guarantee respect and acceptance of one's positions and arguments? Mary Magdalene and even Stacey Abrams face those presumptions in early Christianity and in the political arena. Mary Magdalene may have been presumed incompetent as a woman while Abrams experiences the triple incompetence presumption as a woman, as a black woman, and as a woman who has admitted to lower-class issues as a result of high student loans and medical bills.

Finally, I would argue that reading Mary Magdalene with Stacey Abrams through a womanist hermeneutical lens allows the voice of "counter narratives" to the dominant oppressive narratives. Specifically, scholars note that the major pillars of early Christianity may be James, Peter, Paul, and John. Feminist scholars have cogently argued that the list of pillars must include Mary Magdalene.[44] The Johannine narrative allows the idea of Mary as a pillar even though other writings, such as Paul's characterization of those appearing to Jesus in 1 Corinthians 15, do *not* recognize Mary Magdalene. Thinking through 1 Corinthians 15, we recall that Paul lists the people whom Jesus appeared to and then finally lists himself as one born "by miscarriage" or "born out of time" or "an aborted birth" (*tō ektrōmati*, v. 8). In Paul's own characterization of his apostolic lineage he only names the male disciples of Jesus even though the tradition does highlight the women disciples. Oral tradition would have placed Mary Magdalene in the line because all of the Gospels later state her going to the tomb. Essentially there are some portions of the biblical text that have attempted to marginalize Mary Magdalene from the lineage of Jesus and even away from who becomes leadership in the new Jesus movement. Essentially, part of the womanist task of reading Mary Magdalene means uplifting her counter narrative in such a way that marginalized stories have voice against oppressive "mainstream" narratives.

CONCLUDING THOUGHTS

On February 5, 2019, the Democratic leadership authorized Stacey Abrams's voice to respond to the State of the Union address.[45] However, what we see playing out in the biblical text continues to play out today in contemporary society. Even as traditional scholarship and power seeking men, both political and ecclesial (I am thinking of both Bernie Sanders and the Apostle Paul), construct narratives where they must have the last voice, this chapter argues that an inclusive national consciousness will give voice to all people in the nation. In a recent article against identity politics in politics, Francis Fukuyama states that groups have come to "believe that their identities—whether national, religious, ethnic, sexual, gender, or otherwise—are not receiving adequate recognition" thereby making policy making and collective action difficult in politics.[46] Stacey Abrams counters that Americans must "thoughtfully pursue an expanded, identity-conscious politics."[47] While not arguing specifically for an inclusive national consciousness, I believe that Abrams, coupled with my reading of Mary Magdalene with Abrams, is on the right track to get us to think about what an inclusive national consciousness that pays attention to all identities can offer to our ecclesial and political agendas for the greater good of church and society.

NOTES

1. Aki Soga, "Bernie Sanders Faces Progressive Backlash over State of the Union Response," *USA Today*, accessed May 25, 2019, https://www.usatoday.com/story/news/politics/2019/02/06/bernie-sanders-backlash-state-union-response/2790717002/.

2. As a term coined by Alice Walker, "womanism" may be defined as a type of thought pertaining to black women in order to set aside mainstream white feminists from feminists of color while also resisting anti-blackness within the feminist movement. By focusing specifically on black women, womanism aims for the transformation of society and liberation of all people in the black community. Some seminal texts include Jacquelyn Grant, *White Women's Christ, Black Women's Jesus: Feminist Christology and Womanist Response* (Atlanta: Scholars Press, 1989); Katie Cannon, *Black Womanist Ethics* (Atlanta: Scholars Press, 1988); Cannon, *Katie's Canon: Womanism and the Soul of the Black Community* (New York: Continuum, 1995); Cheryl Kirk-Duggan, *Exorcising Evil: Theodicy and African American Spirituals—A Womanist Perspective* (Maryknoll, NY: Orbis, 1993); Emilie Maureen Townes, *Womanist Justice, Womanist Hope* (Atlanta: Scholars Press, 1993); and Townes, *A Troubling in My Soul: Womanist Perspectives on Evil and Suffering* (Maryknoll, NY: Orbis, 1993).

3. I will define "national consciousness" shortly.

4. "Reclaiming my time" is a phrase that sparked social media hashtags after Rep. Maxine Waters (D-California) repeated the phrase consistently following Treasury Secretary Steven Mnuchin's continued roundabout answers during a House of Representatives hearing. "'Reclaiming My Time': Rep. Maxine Waters Interrupts Mnuchin's Roundabout Answer," *The Washington Post*, accessed May 25, 2019, https://www.washingtonpost.com/video/national/maxine-waters-reclaiming-my-time/2017/08/01/30fae7f4-76d4-11e7-8c17-533c52b2f014_video.html?utm_term=.e3a1233cbf57a.

5. When I state "John's Gospel," I follow scholarly consensus that one cannot actually prove that a literal author by the name of "John" wrote the Fourth Gospel of the NT canon.

6. See Renita Weems, "Womanist Reflections on Biblical Hermeneutics," in *Black Theology: A Documentary History*, ed. James H. Cone and Gayraud S. Wilmore (Maryknoll, NY: Orbis Books, 1993), 216–24.

7. See Karen Baker-Fletcher, *Dancing with God: The Trinity from a Womanist Perspective* (St. Louis: Chalice, 2006).

8. Baker-Fletcher, *Dancing with God*, 33.

9. Even though recent work on womanist biblical interpretation states that African American women have made minimal impact on biblical scholarship (see Nyasha Junior's *An Introduction to Womanist Biblical Interpretation* [Louisville: Westminster John Knox, 2015], 121), I argue that continued crossover between theology and biblical studies will make huge impact within both fields. There are a number of self-identified womanists who perform biblical interpretation and have made an impact on biblical scholarship within the past twenty-five years. I simply seek to add to this knowledge.

10. Frantz Fanon, *The Wretched of the Earth*, trans. Constance Farrington (New York: Grove Press, 1963), 148.

11. Fanon, *Wretched*, 156.

12. Fanon, *Wretched*, 203.

13. Anne McClintock, *Imperial Leather: Race, Gender and Sexuality in the Colonial Context* (New York: Routledge, 1995), 72.

14. McClintock, *Imperial Leather*, 74.

15. McClintock, *Imperial Leather*, 168.

16. McClintock, *Imperial Leather*, 357.

17. For excellent discussion on reader response criticism, see Wolfgang Iser, *The Act of Reading: A Theory of Aesthetic Response* (Baltimore: Johns Hopkins University Press, 1978), 37, 169, 214. Iser's theory serves the interests of my work because he stresses the idea of the reader's central role in determining meaning. Iser maintains that in the interaction between the reader and the text, "the role prescribed by the text will be stronger but the reader's own disposition will never disappear totally" (37). The reader's disposition will instead form the background and serve as a frame of reference for the act of understanding and comprehending the material of the text.

18. Raymond E. Brown implies that since the language of "apostle" is not within the purview of the Gospel of John, arguing for Mary Magdalene as an apostle appears to be a moot point. See "The Resurrection in John 20—A Series of Diverse Reactions," *Worship* 64 (1990): 194–206.

19. When I speak of traditional interpreters' views, I am often referring to a group of commentaries including, but not limited to, the following: G. R. Beasley-Murray, *John*, 2nd ed. WBC 36 (Nashville: Thomas Nelson, 1999); R. Alan Culpepper, *The Gospel and the Letters of John*, IBT (Nashville: Abingdon, 1998); Craig S. Keener, *The Gospel of John: A Commentary*, 2 vols. (Peabody, MA: Hendrickson, 2003).

20. Warren Carter makes the assumption that Ephesus is the city in which the Johannine tradition may have developed. See Warren Carter, *John and Empire: Initial Explorations* (New York: T&T Clark, 2008), ix. However, he also notes that Aphrodisias was approximately ninety miles east of Ephesus and shared elements of Jewish civic interaction that was similar to the happenings in Ephesus (34–36).

21. Carter, *John and Empire*, 34–36.

22. Ross Shepard Kraemer, *Her Share of the Blessings: Women's Religions among Pagans, Jews and Christians in the Greco-Roman World* (Oxford: Oxford University Press, 1992), 85.

23. Kraemer, *Share*, 84.

24. See Francis J. Moloney, *The Gospel of John*, SP 4 (Collegeville, MN: Liturgical Press, 1998), Kindle edition. See also Rudolf Bultmann, *The Gospel of John: A Commentary*, trans. G. R. Beasley-Murray, R. W. N. Hoare, and J. K. Riches (Philadelphia: Westminster Press, 1971), 685. Commentator Raymond E. Brown highlights Mary Magdalene's potential leadership role predominantly as a deliberate emphasis against Peter. See Brown, "Roles of Women in the Fourth Gospel," *TS* 36 (1975): 693.

25. See Bultmann, *Gospel of John*, 685.

26. Moloney, *John*, Loc. 14057. Coincidently, feminist commentator Ann Graham Brock does not believe the "other disciple" signifies the "Beloved Disciple" in John 20:2–10. See Brock, *Mary Magdalene, the First Apostle: The Struggle for Authority*, HTS 51 (Cambridge, MA: Harvard University Press, 2003), 56–57.

27. Emphasis added. All translations of the NT are my own unless otherwise noted.

28. Brock, *Mary Magdalene*, 57.

29. Brock, *Mary Magdalene*, 59. Brock cites James H. Charlesworth, *The Beloved Disciple: Whose Witness Validates the Gospel of John?* (Valley Forge, PA: Trinity Press International, 1995), 97–98.

30. Moloney, *John*, Loc. 13878.

31. Emphasis added. Moloney, *John*, Loc. 13881.

32. Shawn Kelley, *Racializing Jesus: Race, Ideology and the Formation of Modern Biblical Scholarship* (New York: Routledge, 2002), 47.

33. Let me remind the reader that this strict delineation between the Jesus of history and the Jesus of glory is the work of the traditional scholarship of historical criticism. See Raymond E. Brown, *The Gospel according to John*, AB 29–29a (Garden City, NY: Doubleday, 1966–1970).

34. For recent conversations of evangelical Christianity in the age of Trump, see the cogent essays in Miguel A. De La Torre's *Faith and Resistance in the Age of Trump* (Maryknoll, NY: Orbis Books, 2017). Specifically, the offerings of David P. Gushee's "Why Trump, and What Next? An (Ex-) Evangelical Response," 99–106; Santiago Slabodsky's "Jewish Resistances: Trumpism, Holocaustic Memories, and the Paradoxes of New Whiteness," 127–36; and Jim Wallis's "White Christian Complicity in Trump's Victory and Responsibility Now for Faith, Resistance, and Healing," 156–64 are excellent for discussions on the role of white evangelicalism, Jewish resistance, and issues plaguing minority, LGBTIQ+, and marginalized communities today.

35. The problem of anti-Semitic thought has been especially harmful in interpretations of the Gospel of John. The term "*hoi Ioudaioi*" appears over seventy times in the Gospel of John. Mostly translated as "the Jews," interpreters of the Gospel of John must always be alert to the hateful ways that anti-Semitism has entered into biblical interpretation. See Warren Carter, *John: Storyteller, Interpreter, Evangelist* (Grand Rapids: Baker Academic, 2006), 67–73.

36. Please see one of the most recent synagogue shootings committed by John Earnest. Shooter Earnest wrote a seven-page letter spelling out his core beliefs: that Jewish people are guilty in his view of faults ranging from killing Jesus to controlling the media, and therefore, are deserving to die. Earnest also believed that killing Jews would glorify God. Members of Earnest's denomination, Escondido Orthodox Presbyterian Church, were stunned that the manifesto spewed such hatred against Jews and racial minorities. Julie Zauzmer, "The Alleged Synagogue Shooter was a Churchgoer who Talked Christian Theology, Raising Tough Questions for Evangelical Pastors," *The Washington Post*, accessed May 26, 2019, https://www.washingtonpost.com/religion/2019/05/01/alleged-synagogue-shooter-was-churchgoer-who-articulated-christian-theology-prompting-tough-questions-evangelical-pastors/?utm_term=.a08a6944e58b.

37. See Gail R. O'Day, "John," in *Women's Bible Commentary: Twentieth Anniversary Edition*, ed. Carol A. Newsom, Sharon H. Ringe, and Jacqueline E. Lapsley (Louisville: Westminster John Knox, 2012), 517–30.

38. O'Day, "John," 527.

39. "The personal is political" became a rallying cry of early radical feminists and subsequent black feminists and womanists. For a delineation of feminisms and the beginning use of this rallying cry, see Rosemarie Tong and Tina Fernandes Botts's *Feminist Thought: A More Comprehensive Introduction* (New York: Routledge Taylor & Francis Group, 2018), 39.

40. The calling of Mary's name in 20:16 is reminiscent of the good shepherd's call in John 10:34. In that verse, "he calls his own sheep by name and leads them out. When he has brought out all his own, he goes ahead of them, and the sheep follow him because they know his voice." Scholar Reimund Bieringer notes an important difference, however. In 20:16–17, Jesus does not want Mary to follow him as he is ascending, therefore he prohibits her "clinging" ("Mary of Magdala and Jesus of Nazareth A Special Relationship in the Light of John 20:17," *PIBA* 30 [2007]: 1–14).

41. For a cogent discussion of "voice" and "testimony" connected to womanist interpretation and Mary Magdalene, see K. Evangeline Frye's "The Intersectional Significance of Voice and Testimony: Suggestions for a 21st Century Womanist Reclamation of Mary Magdalene," *JITC* 41 (2015): 19–38. While I do not agree with all of her argumentation, I find her use of voice helpful for contextualizing Mary Magdalene with Stacey Abrams.

42. Brett Kavanaugh serves as an Associate Justice of the Supreme Court of the United States. Christine Blasey Ford is a research psychologist who accused Justice Kavanaugh of sexually assaulting her when they were teenagers. The Senate Confirmation committee for Kavanaugh's appointment heard Dr. Blasey Ford's testimony in September 2018 but still confirmed Justice Kavanaugh to his lifetime appointment. See https://www.nytimes.com/2018/09/27/us/politics/brett-kavanaugh-confirmation-hearings.html. Accessed July 29, 2019.

43. For an early exploration into the inability of black men and white women to empathize with black women, see Gloria Hull, Patricia Bell Scott, and Barbara Smith, eds., *All the Women are White, All the Blacks Are Men, But Some of Us Are Brave* (Old Westbury, NY: Feminist Press, 1982).

44. See, for example, the work of Brock, *Mary Magdalene*; Karen King, "Canonization and Marginalization of Mary of Magdala," *Concilium* 3 (1998): 29–36; and Jane Schaberg, *The Resurrection of Mary Magdalene: Legends, Apocrypha, and the Christian Testament* (New York: Continuum, 2002).

45. "Abrams to Deliver Dems' State of the Union Response," https://www.ajc.com/news/state--regional-govt--politics/abrams-deliver-dems-state-the-union-response/2Oo3TTBaQB8OMaRNhBoc9L/ Accessed July 29, 2019.

46. See Stacey Y. Abrams et al., "E Pluribus Unum? The Fight Over Identity Politics," *Foreign Affairs* 98 (2019): 160–63.

47. Abrams et al., "E Pluribus Unum?" 163.

Chapter 11

Recognition and "Those Who Have Not Seen"

John's Reception of Synoptic Resurrection Narratives

Helen K. Bond

"Intertextuality" can work on many different levels. At its most basic form, it describes the way that a passage echoes or alludes to portions of another text, perhaps the great oracles of the prophet Isaiah or the powerful laments of the Psalms. By repeating vocabulary or other salient details, an author invites the audience to make connections between the earlier text and the newer one, to explore the patterns between the two works, and to arrive at a deeper appreciation of meaning. But "intertextuality" can also be used of an author's more thorough-going appropriation of earlier texts; here we might also want to use the language of *sources*, or to talk of a later writer's *reception* of prior written traditions. Sometimes authors might attempt to hide their use of sources, to produce works that are entirely complete in themselves and that do not lose anything if readers are unaware of their predecessors. At other times, however, their work might deliberately engage with an earlier text (or texts), rewriting and repackaging, amending and correcting, highlighting and drawing out themes, so that informed readers or hearers are encouraged to read the second text in the light of the first (and vice versa), and to reflect on the two documents together. Unpicking the precise relationship between a text and its predecessors is not always easy, especially when our texts are as ancient as the Christian Gospels, but sometimes a work leaves just enough clues for modern scholars to uncover a richer tapestry of meaning than might be obvious from the surface alone.

In many respects, John's Gospel is a treasure trove for students of intertextuality. Of primary importance are the Jewish Scriptures, which provide the building blocks from which John paints his distinctive portrait of Jesus.

Scripture is frequently quoted or alluded to; references to Jewish institutions, feasts, and patriarchs are common; and the narrative is permeated with biblical echoes, motifs, and themes. The Gospel opens with a clear allusion to Gen. 1:1 ("In the beginning . . .") and echoes of the creation story resonate through the all-important Prologue—light, life, becoming, and begetting (1:1–18). For John, the incarnation of the Word (the Logos, 1:14) is a new creation, and the rest of his work shows how Scripture not only points to but is fulfilled in Jesus. Far from rejecting the Jewish Scriptures, John reclaims them as a Christian text and shows how they are completed through Jesus.[1]

Although John 20 contains no direct quotations, it does include a number of scriptural echoes (as we shall see at several points below). My interest in this chapter, however, lies in a rather different direction. The chapter provides a particularly rich opportunity to examine our author's reception and appropriation of another group of texts: the Synoptic Gospels (Mark, Matthew, and Luke). In the following discussion, I shall ask where our author found material for the story of the empty tomb and the various resurrection appearances that make up this chapter, how he shaped that material so that it supported his own distinctive theological outlook, and—perhaps most importantly—how audiences might have responded to his finished text.

It is well to point out from the start that Johannine acquaintance with the Synoptic Gospels was out of scholarly favor for much of the twentieth century. The undeniable similarities between John and the other three Gospels in terms of their general structure, shared material, and even on occasion verbal agreements, were explained either by appeal to a complicated history of development in which Synoptic material became incorporated into John at a late stage or, more commonly, to shared oral tradition (a view which drew heavily on the insights of the form critics). According to this latter position, John knew not the Synoptic Gospels themselves, but some of the same traditions from which they also drew—often referred to as "Synoptic-like material" or "pre-Synoptic traditions." Over the last few decades, however, the view that John did in fact know the Synoptics (or at least Mark) has steadily grown in support, particularly in Europe where it always enjoyed a degree of popularity.[2] While it may be too early to talk of a new consensus, the scholarly mood has certainly changed, and the huge advantage of this position is that it substitutes known texts for hypothetical early traditions. John clearly did not draw on his precursors in the painstakingly scribal way that Matthew and Luke used Mark, but it is the latter two Gospels that are unusual here. Like most ancient authors, John uses his sources much more freely, adapting and editing them to fit with his rhetorical aims (as he does with the Scriptures).[3]

In an engaging and thought-provoking study, Richard Bauckham argues that John deliberately *complements* Mark's Gospel, adding extra material not included in the earlier work and avoiding repetitions.[4] John simply assumes, for example, that many of his audience already know the story of Jesus's baptism (alluded to at 1:32), that they are aware of the choosing of the Twelve (6:70), or the trial before Caiaphas (18:24, 28). This is not to reduce John to a mere supplement to Mark: Bauckham rightly notes that the Gospel has its own integrity and narrative logic, and that readers or hearers unfamiliar with Mark would still understand the story. Nor does it mean that John is always in agreement with the earlier text: he is quite happy to alter Mark's chronology (dramatically so in the temple incident of John 2:14–22//Mark 11:15–18) or to correct inaccuracies (e.g., the note that Jesus carried his own cross, John 19:17; compare Mark 15:21). Overall, however, John's purpose was not so much to *replace* Mark as to write a much more reflective gospel which built on the earlier narrative. By interpreting a handful of carefully selected "signs," John points to the way in which the "many other signs" (20:30) recorded elsewhere might now be understood. Thus, John's work situates itself both alongside earlier written gospel accounts and—crucially—as the hermeneutical key to understanding what precedes him.

Similar interests, I suggest, are at work in John 20. Mark's Gospel, of course, breaks off quite abruptly with the flight of the frightened women from the empty tomb in Mark 16:8, and so could not provide much of a basis for John's account. Instead, our author seems to have looked to the more complete narrative of Luke 24 which describes not only the empty tomb but a visit to the grave by Peter and an appearance to the disciples as a group. Although verbal parallels are rare, the two texts share a number of common features:

- Appearances of the risen Jesus are all in Jerusalem (or its environs)
- The risen Lord is not immediately recognized by his disciples (Luke 24:16// John 20:14–15)
- Scripture points to Jesus's resurrection (Luke 24:27, 46–47//John 20:9)
- Both accounts mention Jesus's return to the heavenly Father (Luke 24:51// John 20:17)
- Jesus invites one or more followers to look at and touch his hands and feet/ side (Luke 24:39–40//John 20:25, 27)
- The bestowal of the Spirit features in both (promised in Luke 24:49//John 20:22)
- The forgiveness of sin appears in both (Luke 24:47//John 20:23)
- Doubt appears in both (Luke 24:11, 25, 37, 41//John 20:25)

John's text may also show some influence from Matthew—specifically Matt. 28:9–10 where Jesus appears to the women who discovered the empty tomb, and also perhaps in the suggestion that the body had been taken away/stolen, which Matthew says was still current in his own day (Matt. 28:15)[5]—though John's knowledge of Matthew is far more debated within scholarly circles.[6]

By examining our author's use of these earlier texts we shall better understand how he crafts his own "life-giving" account (John 20:31).

As will now be familiar from the two previous chapters in this volume, John 20 exhibits a balanced structure which divides into two major sections, each opening with a time setting ("on the first day of the week," 20:1; "When it was evening on that day," 20:19). First, we have the story of Mary Magdalene at the tomb on Easter Sunday, which breaks to recount a visit by Peter and the Beloved Disciple and then resumes to tell of an appearance of the risen Jesus to Mary. Second, we have the appearance of Jesus to the disciples, first without Thomas, then with him. The chapter ends with what was probably the original conclusion to the Gospel (chapter 21 being an early addition).[7] In the context of John's Gospel as a whole, the chapter charts Jesus's return to the Father; the divine Word, which descended to "his own" (1:11, 14), now completes the upward journey which began with his exaltation on the cross and continues through resurrection and ascension until the Son is once again in his heavenly home. Along the way, a series of characters respond to the now risen Lord.

MARY MAGDALENE'S VISIT TO THE EMPTY TOMB (JOHN 20:1–2)

Like the Synoptics, John opens his account of Easter Sunday with the empty tomb.[8] A number of changes, however, heighten the drama of the episode. Unlike the other Gospels, which all feature a number of women at the tomb (three in Mark 16:1, two in Matt. 28:1, and an unspecified group in Luke 24:10), John focuses on only one—Mary Magdalene. This is a common technique of our author who typically pares down his cast list so that he can focus on Jesus's encounter with individuals or representative figures (such as Nicodemus in chapter 3, the Samaritan woman in chapter 4, or the unnamed High Priest in chapter 18). The technique adds tension to the story and spotlights attention on the various characters' reactions to Jesus. All extraneous details are omitted: John tells us nothing of Mary's background (she has previously appeared only in passing at the cross in 19:25), or the women taking note of the burial place, or the presence of the stone sealing its entrance.[9] All of these are simply assumed. The story progresses perfectly well without them, though readers familiar with the Synoptics can simply fill in the gaps. Even the time of day is more dramatic in John. While the other Gospels suggest, in various ways, that dawn was beginning to break, John specifies that it was "still dark" (20:1). Given our author's interest in light-dark symbolism elsewhere (e.g., in 1:4–5; 3:2, 20–21; 9:4–5; 12:35; 13:30), we are surely to see some significance here: Mary is quite literally "in the dark" and will not at first understand the significance of the tomb.[10]

Arriving at the graveside, Mary discovers that the stone has been removed and assumes that the body has been taken away. This follows quite naturally from the Johannine burial scene, which implies that Jesus's corpse was quickly placed in the new tomb in the nearby garden because of the approaching Day of Preparation, leaving open the possibility of its later removal (19:42). Mary runs off to find Simon Peter and the "other disciple," declaring that "they have taken the Lord out of the tomb, and we do not know where they have laid him."

Mary's expression, "we do not know," is often seen as a clue that John was indeed working with a source which included more than one woman. None of our extant Gospels, however, contain the phrase "we do not know" (*oidamen* in Greek), making it unlikely that John is simply repeating traditional material. More probably, Mary is cast here as a spokesperson for the Johannine Christians, who John elsewhere refers to in the third-person plural (1:14–16; 21:24; see also 1 John 1:1). They, like Mary, do not yet understand the significance of the tomb.

PETER AND THE BELOVED DISCIPLE VISIT THE TOMB (20:3–10)

The action now focuses on Peter and the "other disciple" (20:3–10). John's account seems to be largely based on Luke 24:12 where Peter, after hearing the women's report, ran to the tomb (apparently alone), saw the linen cloths (*othonia*), and went back home wondering what had happened.[11] There may also be some influence from Luke 24:24, where Cleopas and his companion on the Emmaus road tell the same story to the risen Jesus, now suggesting that a larger company of people went to the tomb ("some of those who were with us," *tines tōn syn hēmin*).

John's most dramatic departure from the Lukan text is of course the inclusion of the Beloved Disciple, the mysterious figure who appears only in this Gospel and only during Jesus's last visit to Jerusalem (13:23–26; 19:26–27, 35 and 21:20–13). Whatever the historical background to this character, he functions within the Johannine text as a literary device, as an idealized figure who sees and understands what others do not.[12] As usual, the Beloved Disciple appears alongside Peter. He outruns Peter, but holds back, allowing his companion to enter first (a structural device which will allow our author to highlight the Beloved Disciple's reaction). Peter enters the tomb and sees the linen cloths (*othonia*) lying where the body had been and the cloth that had covered Jesus's head (the *soudarion*) rolled up by itself. Like his Synoptic sources, John is probably keen to dispel any suggestion that the body of Jesus has been stolen by grave robbers—if that were so, the grave clothes would not have been lying in the tomb. (Similarly, Mary's earlier contrast between "they" who have removed the body and "we" who do not know where it is may be designed to subvert any suggestion that the disciples themselves removed the body.) Whatever has happened to Jesus is clearly very different to the resuscitation of Lazarus, who needed to have his bandages unbound (11:44);[13] and the careful placement of the grave-clothes supports the Johannine Jesus's claim that he has power both to lay down his life and to take it up again (10:18). The presence of the two male witnesses establishes beyond reasonable doubt that the tradition of the empty tomb is "true" (see Deut. 19:15; John 5:31; 8:17–18). The question is what the various characters will make of it.

Despite entering first and taking note of his surroundings, Peter has no further reaction. The focus of the scene is on the Beloved Disciple who, true to form, acts as the ideally perceptive follower. Not only does he "see" what Peter saw, but he also "believed"—presumably that Jesus had been raised from the dead. His belief was all the more exemplary given that, as our author points out, the disciples didn't yet "understand the Scripture, that he must rise from the dead" (John 20:9). There are a number of similarities here once more with the Lukan insistence that the risen Jesus taught his disciples how to interpret Scripture, both the two travelers on the way to Emmaus (Luke 24:25–27) and the remains of the Twelve (24:45–46). For John, however, the parenthetical comment goes deeper than this. Twice elsewhere our author makes a similar distinction between what could be known of Jesus during his earthly ministry and what could be known only later, after the resurrection. These two other passages frame the public ministry, one at the beginning (after the temple incident, 2:22) and the second after Jesus arrives in Jerusalem for the last time (12:14–16). What leads to this greater understanding is the coming of the Paraclete, the divine Spirit which will lead believers into a fuller appreciation of Jesus's significance (14:15–17, 25–26; 15:26–27; 16:5–15).[14] It is no wonder, then, that Peter did not perceive the significance of what he saw; while the Beloved Disciple models the ideal response to the empty tomb, Peter must, like the rest of the disciples, wait until he receives the Spirit truly to understand.

Like Peter in Luke 24:12, the disciples now return home. On a narrative level, we're not to ask why the Beloved Disciple doesn't share his belief with Peter (he is always extraneous to the action—even when he knows the identity of the betrayer in 13:21–30, for example, he does nothing to stop him), or why Mary doesn't go home too. John's focus is purely on the reactions of characters, and their response to the Easter events as the chapter proceeds.

Our author removes the male disciples so that Mary can once again take center stage.

MARY RECOGNIZES THE RISEN LORD (20:11–18)

As the next scene opens, Mary is found standing outside the tomb weeping. John gave no reason for her visit; following the lavish burial given to Jesus by Joseph of Arimathea and Nicodemus (John 19:38–42), there was no need for her to anoint the body as in Mark and Luke.[15] The impression is of a woman engulfed by grief ("weeping" occurs three times in this passage); presumably, like Mary of Bethany before her, Mary Magdalene goes to the tomb simply to be near the remains of her loved one and to mourn (John 11:31).

Although the ensuing episode describes the first appearance of the risen Jesus, it is best understood as a "recognition scene" (or *anagnorisis*; see Aristotle, *Poetics*, 1452a), a typical plot device found in tragic plays, comedies, and Hellenistic novels. The term refers to the moment of sudden insight when a character makes a critical discovery about another person's identity or significance. The classic "recognition scene" is the moment in Sophocles's *Oedipus Rex* when the hero learns of his true birth and realizes that he has married his mother, killed his father, and brought misfortune on Thebes. Here in John 20, our author's focus is similarly on the change in Mary, as she suddenly recognizes the true identity of the unknown figure before her (a change of understanding that is underscored by her double physical "turning," vv. 14, 16).[16] Readers familiar with Greek novels would have found a number of other common motifs in this scene—not least the search for the lover's body, the empty tomb and the suggestion that grave robbers have been at work, and the final reunion (often with a climactic recognition scene).[17]

The account begins much as it does in the Synoptics. Mary stoops to look into the sepulcher and sees two angels in white, reminiscent of Luke's two men in "dazzling clothes" who are clearly heavenly messengers (Luke 24:4; see also 2 Macc. 3:26 for another pair of angelic figures). There is no mention of the grave clothes now; instead the angels sit where the body of Jesus was laid, one at the head and the other at the feet (John 20:12). In many respects, the angels are redundant in John's story; they serve only to emphasize Mary's grief and to allow her to reiterate her concern over the missing body. Readers familiar with Exod. 25:17–22, however, might be put in mind here of the two golden cherubim that faced one another at either end of the mercy seat above the ark of the covenant. The seat was the place of God, where the invisible divine presence met to speak with Israel. Whether intended or not by John, such a reading fits well with the Fourth Gospel's stress on Jesus's divinity, and our author's insistence that Jesus is the fulfillment of Jewish institutions (the temple, the Paschal lamb, manna in the wilderness, and so on). At all events, the encounter with the angels lends an element of divine mystery to the unfolding scene.

Turning around, Mary sees Jesus, who echoes the question of the angels, "Woman, why are you weeping?" and adds a new query, "For whom are you looking?" (20:15). Like the disciples on the Emmaus road, Mary does not recognize Jesus. In many respects, the scene plays with the idea of misunderstanding, so common in this Gospel (e.g., 2:19–21; 3:3–6; 6:52; 18:36–37); rather than a metaphor, however, it is now Jesus himself who is misunderstood. Taking him to be the gardener, Mary asks Jesus to tell her what he has done with the body so that she might take it away. In response, Jesus addresses her not as "Woman" (the term used by the angels and Jesus himself in v. 13) but by her name, "Mary" (*Mariam* in Greek, v. 16). This is a powerful moment in the story, evoking not only Jesus's promise that the Good Shepherd knows his sheep and calls them by name (10:3), but more strikingly the words of God in Second Isaiah (a text that has provided rich resources for this author):[18] "Do not fear, for I have redeemed you; I have called you by name, you are mine" (Isa. 43:1). The Johannine Jesus speaks (as so often in this Gospel) with the voice of the God of Israel. If the Lukan disciples on the way to Emmaus recognized Jesus in the Eucharistic breaking of bread, it is through the spoken word of the all-knowing God that Mary recognizes the risen Lord. And just as Jesus promised in John 16:19–22, Mary's sorrow is turned into joy.

There are clues in the text, however, that suggest that full faith in the exalted Jesus is not yet possible. John 20 contains a number of links with the first chapter of the Gospel.[19] Jesus's question to Mary, for example, "For whom are you looking?" (*tina zēteis*) is reminiscent of his first words to the disciples in 1:38, "What are you looking for?" (*ti zēteite*). And Mary's recognition of Jesus as *rabbouni* (or "my teacher") echoes the responses of the first disciples to Jesus in 1:38, 49. It is in this connection that we need to understand Mary's attempt to hold onto Jesus (20:17). The verb here is a present imperative, suggesting that she is already holding onto him. The scene may have suggested itself to our author on the basis of Matt. 28:9–10, where, after seeing the risen Jesus, the women prostrate themselves at his feet and worship him. Or perhaps John had in mind the speaker in the Song of Sol. 3:1–10 who goes about the city desperately seeking the one she loves and holds onto him when she finds him. At all events, the motif of holding onto Jesus, coupled with the references back to the start of the story, strongly suggest that Mary here wants to hold onto the past and that she does not yet realize that a new, spiritual union with Jesus will only be possible once the risen Lord has fully ascended to the Father.

Jesus sends Mary to his disciples (see Matt. 28:10, where the phrase is similarly *hoi adelphoi mou*—literally, "my brothers"), saying: "I am ascending to my Father and your Father, to my God and your God" (20:11).[20] The reference to ascension in the present tense, which is presumably complete by the time that Jesus next appears (see below), seems at first glance to be out of step with the tradition of Acts that Jesus finally ascended to the Father after forty days (Acts 1:3). There is no evidence, however, that John knew Acts, and in any case Luke's interest in this later document is clearly to indicate when the appearances of the (now heavenly) Jesus stopped. The account of Jesus's ascension in Luke 24:51 gives the impression that it took place on Easter evening. For John, of course, ascension is one stage in the cosmic movement back to the heavenly home from whence he came; the cross, resurrection, and return to the Father all take place in rapid succession, though our author does not delineate the precise point at which Jesus's return to glory occurred.

Jesus's words also show Mary *why* he must be allowed to complete his heavenward journey. Only when the Son is once again united with the Father will disciples truly become children of God (1:11–12; 3:5; 14:18). The words used here echo the promise through Jeremiah that God would establish a new covenant: "I will be their God, and they shall be my people . . . for they shall all know me" (Jer. 31:33–34). More intimately, they also echo Ruth's devotion when she declares, "Your people shall be my people, and your God my God" (Ruth 1:16).[21] As a result of his mission, Jesus makes possible a new way to relate to God, as true children of the Father.

JESUS'S APPEARANCE TO THE DISCIPLES
(JOHN 20:19–29)

Both Matthew and Luke record an appearance of Jesus to the remaining disciples. While Matthew's account, however, seems to be little more than the promised Galilee appearance that is so noticeably absent in Mark (Matt. 28:16–20; see Mark 14:28; 16:7), Luke has a much fuller account which seems to be the basis for what we have in John (Luke 24:36–52).

Once again, John has transformed the relatively simple Lukan appearance story into a recognition scene, focusing this time on the assembled disciples. As in Luke, the action takes place in a room in Jerusalem, on the same night that the empty tomb was discovered; John repurposes the Lukan motif of fear (Luke 24:37) so that now the disciples are in a room with the doors tightly shut for "fear of the Jews" (see John 7:13; 9:22 and 19:38 earlier). Once again, Jesus mysteriously stands among the assembled disciples with the words "peace be with you" (*eirēnē hymin* in both cases) and shows the disciples his hands and feet, inviting them not only to look at him but also to touch him. There are echoes here, even in the Lukan version, with Eurycleia's recognition of the returned Odysseus when she sees an old scar on his foot as she washes it (Homer, *Od.* 19.393–466). In the Lukan version, however, the point is to show that Jesus is not a ghost (he eats a piece of fish and claims to have "flesh and bones," Luke 24:39). The point of John's reference to Jesus's wounds (here hands and side) is to make it clear that the same Jesus who died on the cross is now the risen Lord. Like Mary before them, the disciples suddenly recognize Jesus and are filled with joy.

While Luke has Jesus only promise "power from on high" at this point, reserving the story of the outpouring of the Spirit for Pentecost several weeks later (Luke 24:49; Acts 2:1–4), John will finish his account with the glorified Jesus breathing on his disciples and so endowing them with the promised Spirit/Paraclete (John 7:39; 16:7). That John sees this as a new creation is clear from his use of the same word that describes God breathing into Adam in Gen. 2:7 (*enophysēsen*). There are also echoes here of other biblical accounts of creation (see especially Wis. 15:11), the prophet's vision of the dry bones in Ezekiel 37, and the significance of the "garden" in the Mary Magdalene episode now becomes apparent (see Gen. 2:8). Thus, the ending of the Gospel picks up ideas once more from the beginning, as the creation motif here dovetails with the Johannine retelling of Genesis in the first part of the prologue (John 1:1–5). The narrative, like Jesus himself, has come full circle. Filled with the Spirit, the disciples now have authority over sin (see Matt. 16:19; 18:18), which for John involves failing to acknowledge God's revelation in Jesus (8:24; 9:39–41; 15:22, 24).

This might have been the end of John's Gospel, but our author has one more story to tell, again presented as a recognition scene. The theme of *doubt* appeared at several points in the Lukan narrative (Luke 24:11, 25, 37, 41; see also Matt. 28:17), but was never tackled head-on. John has removed the motif from the rest of his account, saving it all for this one scene, characteristically presenting a personal encounter between Jesus and a doubter, cast here as the figure of Thomas (who has appeared already in 11:16 and 14:5). The episode clearly has important apologetic value for John: Thomas raises the doubts that all intelligent followers will initially have, but his encounter with the risen Lord completely overwhelms him. Although invited to touch Jesus's wounds, there is no indication that he does so; his doubt is replaced by the engulfing Easter faith that John encourages all to share.

Here, at the end, Thomas utters the greatest christological confession of the Gospel: "My Lord and my God" (20:28). Although the narrator has repeatedly proclaimed Jesus's divinity (1:1, 18, see also 5:18; 10:33), this is the first time that a character in the story has affirmed it. Thomas's words evoke the Greek Scriptures where Lord (*kyrios*) and God (*theos*) are frequently used of the God of Israel; Psalm 35, for example, variously refers to

"My God and my Lord" or "O Lord, my God." Equally, the term had a wide currency as part of the stock of imperial titles. According to Suetonius, the Emperor Domitian (r. 81–96 C.E.) insisted on being addressed as "Our Lord and our God" (*dominus et deus noster*; *Dom.* 13). Whether or not John's audience knew this particular detail, the exorbitant claims of the imperial cult, especially when pressed into the service of a tyrant like Domitian, would have been only too familiar. In response, Jesus offers a benediction on those who have not seen and yet believe. The point is not to castigate Thomas or any of the others in this chapter who have believed on the basis of what they have seen, but to embrace a later generation of Christ-followers who were not themselves eyewitnesses. These people must believe on the basis of others' testimony, a group that includes not only John's intended audience but all who hear the Gospel in the future.

"MANY OTHER SIGNS" (JOHN 20:30–31)

With Thomas's confession and Jesus's blessing, John's work is complete and vv. 30–31 round off what was probably the original ending of the Gospel.[22] John draws on Greek literary commonplaces here, suggesting that he has had to be selective in his account (for similar endings, see 1 Macc. 9:22 and Lucian, *Demon.* 67). Our author does not tell us where these "many other signs" are to be found, but comparison with John 21:25, which seems to have been modeled on this earlier ending and which specifically mentions "books" (*biblia*), might well suggest that what John has in mind includes the Synoptic Gospels. If so—and it can be no more than a possibility—then our author may be deliberately alluding to other, well-known Gospels here. While they all have their place, John declares that only his retelling can truly inspire belief, and thus lead to eternal life.

FINAL REFLECTION

John retells Synoptic stories in his own distinctive way, drawing on themes and images from both the Jewish Scriptures and the Greco-Roman world of which he was part. Those who knew only John were faced with a coherent narrative which draws to a powerful close in chapter 20. Those familiar with Luke's Gospel (and perhaps Matthew), would hear a strikingly new telling of the Easter events, one that urged its audience to see a deeper meaning behind the appearances of the risen Lord, and situated older stories within a Johannine understanding of human salvation. Those familiar with Mark would find a welcome assurance that the story didn't end with the frightened women at the tomb, but with the completion of the Son's mission, the outpouring of the Spirit, and the possibility of a spiritual union with the risen Lord. Even in antiquity Mark's ending was felt to be unsatisfactory: not only did Matthew and Luke explicitly contradict the earlier Gospel's claim that that women failed to pass on the good news, but two conclusions were later added, one of which drew at least partly on John (Mark 16:9–10).[23] From the moment that the Fourth Gospel was disseminated, however, the other Gospels could never have been read in quite the same way again, and it's likely that John 20 (along with portions of Luke 24) already began to form a "mental conclusion" to Mark's Gospel in the minds of its hearers, well before the so-called longer ending was added. Through his distinctive reception of Synoptic material here, our author challenged his audience to "see" events through Johannine eyes, to embrace his distinctive articulation of the person of Jesus, and to experience life in Jesus's name.

NOTES

1. On John's use of Scripture, see Alicia D. Myers and Bruce G. Schuchard, eds., *Abiding Words: The Use of Scripture in the Gospel of John*, RBS 81 (Atlanta: SBL Press, 2015).

2. For an overview of John's relationship to the Synoptics, see D. Moody Smith, *John Among the Gospels: The Relationship in Twentieth Century Research* (Minneapolis: Fortress, 1992). Johannine knowledge of at least Mark was defended in the UK by Charles Kingsley Barrett, most notably in his commentary on John, and in Belgium by Frans Neirynck and Morits Sabbe, both members of the so-called Leuven school. See Neirynck, "John and the Synoptics," in Neirynck, *Evangelica: Gospel Studies—Etudes D'Evangile. Collected Essays* (Leuven: Leuven University Press, 1982), 365–400. More recently, see Andrew T. Lincoln, *The Gospel According to Saint John*, BNTC 4 (London: Continuum, 2005). For a fuller attempt to outline the ideas in this paragraph, see my essay on the "Gospel of John," in *From Paul to Josephus: Literary Receptions of Jesus in the First Century CE*, ed. Helen K. Bond. Vol. 1 of *The Reception of Jesus in the First Three Centuries*, ed. Chris Keith, Helen K. Bond, Christine Jacobi, and Jens Schröter (London: Bloomsbury Academic, 2019), 165–85. More generally, see Eve-Marie Becker, Helen K. Bond, and Catrin H. Williams, eds., *John's Transformation of Mark* (London: Bloomsbury/T&T Clark, 2020).

3. Richard Bauckham, "The Gospel of John and the Synoptic Problem," in *New Studies in the Synoptic Problem: Oxford Conference, April 2008. Essays in Honour of Christopher M. Tuckett*, ed. Paul Foster et al., BETL 239 (Leuven: Peeters, 2011), 657–88. On ancient literary practices, see (in the same volume) Robert A. Derrenbacker, Jr., "The 'External and Psychological Conditions under which the Synoptic Gospels were Written': Ancient Compositional Practices and the Synoptic Problem," 435–57 and F. Gerald Downing, "Writers' Use or Abuse of Written Sources," 523–48.

4. Richard Bauckham, "John for Readers of Mark," in *The Gospels for All Christians: Rethinking the Gospel Audiences*, ed. Richard Bauckham (Grand Rapids: Eerdmans, 1998), 147–71.

5. So also Frans Neirynck, "John and the Synoptics: the Empty Tomb Stories," *NTS* 30 (1984): 161–87. The article contains an overview of the background to John 20 proposed by a number of major twentieth-century commentators, including Brown, Bultmann, and Schnackenburg (all of whom acknowledge some parallel to the Synoptics here, though at a pre-textual or redactional level), 162–65. As Nierynck notes, however, "[T]hese Johannine sources are so Synoptic-like, so similar to the Synoptics, that Johannine dependence upon the Synoptic Gospels is just one step further," 165.

6. On John's use of Matthew, see James W. Barker, *John's Use of Matthew*, Emerging Scholars (Minneapolis: Fortress, 2015).

7. See Andrew T. Lincoln, "John 21," in Bond, *From Paul to Josephus*, 209–22.

8. The earliest accounts of Jesus's resurrection mention neither an empty tomb nor women: Paul's summary of inherited tradition in 1 Cor. 15:3–7 simply lists appearances of the risen Jesus, beginning with one to Peter and then to "the Twelve." Only with Mark do we hear that women returned to the burial place after the Sabbath to find the body gone (Mark 16:1–8).

9. Like John, Luke simply omits the stone (which is clearly noted by Mark 15:46, presumably in an attempt to show that the sealed tomb was inaccessible to both grave robbers and wild animals).

10. So also Raymond E. Brown, *The Gospel According to John*, AB 29a (Garden City, NY: Doubleday, 1966), 981; Lincoln, *Gospel*, 489.

11. Luke 24:12 is often printed in the margins of older Bibles, along with a number of other verses largely from Luke 22 and 24, known collectively as "Western non-interpolations." The great nineteenth-century text critic F. J. A. Hort regarded these verses as secondary interpolations because they are missing from a group of Western witnesses, the most significant of which is Codex Bezae. The theory was generally accepted until around about 1970, when the publication of better textual witnesses (specifically pap. 75) convinced most scholars that the verses were a genuine part of Luke's text. See the discussion in Bruce Metzger, *The Textual Commentary on the Greek New Testament: A Companion Volume to the United Bible Societies Greek New Testament*, 3rd ed. (London: United Bible Society, 1971), 191–92.

12. So Andrew T. Lincoln, "The Beloved Disciple as Eyewitness and the Fourth Gospel as Witness," *JSNT* 85 (2002): 3–26. As Lincoln notes, the disciple's anonymity encourages readers to identify with him, to share his perceptive witness, and therefore also his point of view.

13. The word "*soudarion*" is also found in the Lazarus story (John 11:44).

14. See Anthony LeDonne, "Memory, Commemoration and History in John 2:19–22," in *The Fourth Gospel in First-Century Media Culture*, ed. Anthony LeDonne and Tom Thatcher, LNTS 426 (London: Bloomsbury/T&T Clark, 2011), 133–54; also Michael Daise, "Quotations with 'Remembrance' Formulae in the Fourth Gospel," in Myers and Schuchard, *Abiding Words*, 75–91; and Jeffrey E. Brickle, "The Memory of the Beloved Disciple: A Poetics of Johannine Memory," in *Memory*

and Identity in Ancient Judaism and Early Christianity: A Conversation with Barry Schwartz, ed. Tom Thatcher, SemeiaSt 78 (Atlanta: SBL Press, 2014), 187–208, here 208.

15. In Matthew, the women go simply to look at the tomb, presumably because in this account the grave was guarded and access would have been impossible (Matt. 28:1).

16. On recognition scenes in John more broadly, see Kasper Bro Larsen, *Recognizing the Stranger: Recognition Scenes in the Gospel of John*, BibS 93 (Leiden: Brill, 2008).

17. See Lincoln, *Gospel*, 495–96. The scene has much in common, for example, with motifs from Chariton's *Chaereas and Callirhoe*.

18. See especially Catrin H. Williams, "Isaiah in John's Gospel," in *Isaiah in the New Testament*, ed. Steve Moyise and Maarten J. J. Menken (London: T&T Clark, 2005), 101–16.

19. For a fuller account than can be given here, see Mark W. G. Stibbe, *John* (Sheffield: Sheffield Academic, 1993), 198–99.

20. References to a promised appearance in Galilee have completely dropped out of John. Luke (who situates his appearance in Jerusalem) had already changed the tradition so that the words of the angels remind the women of what Jesus had told them while they were in Galilee (Luke 24:6); John is far less slavish to tradition.

21. This is a common refrain throughout the Jewish Scriptures, with roots in a number of exodus traditions, including Exod. 6:7; Lev. 26:12; Isa. 51:16; Jer. 32:38; Ezek. 11:20; 14:11; 36:28; 37:27; Hosea 1–2; and Zech. 13:9. Those who know the Scriptures will see that John is reframing a recognizable tradition here.

22. For similar views, see Chris Keith, "The Competitive Textualization of the Jesus Tradition in John 20:30–31 and 21:24–25," *CBQ* (2016): 321–37 (though I am less convinced of the competitive nature of the Johannine text). Those who detect an underlying "Signs (*Semeia*) Source" in John often regard this as its conclusion. For a good overview, see Tom Thatcher, "The Signs Gospel in Context," in *Jesus in Johannine Tradition*, ed. Robert T. Fortna and Tom Thatcher (Louisville: Westminster John Knox, 2001), 191–97. For an opposing view, see Frans Neirynck, "The Signs Source in the Fourth Gospel: A Critique of the Hypothesis," in *Evangelica II 1982–1991. Collected Essays*, ed. F. van Segbroeck, BETL 99 (Leuven: Leuven University Press, 1991), 651–78.

23. On later endings to Mark, see Anne Moore, "Longer Ending of Mark," in Bond, *From Paul to Josephus*, 187–95.

Chapter 12

Rhetorical Vividness in John 20
Making Jesus Present before the Eyes

Kasper Bro Larsen

> Do you see, dear friend, how he takes your soul along with him through these places and turns hearing into sight [*tēn akoēn opsin poiōn*]?
>
> —Pseudo-Longinus, *On the Sublime*
> 26.2 (author's translation)

THE READER AS SPECTATOR

People never forget a vivid storyteller from their childhood. Still today, when my mother hears the story of Jesus walking through the storm on Lake Tiberias in John 6, she is taken back to the wild sea by her hometown on the west coast of Jutland, Denmark. Her primary school teacher could make Bible stories come alive as if they were happening right outside the classroom door. Miss Hansen was a rhetorical natural. "Rhetorical," however, is an ambiguous adjective in contemporary English. Rhetoric is commonly understood as empty talk, words without action, or maybe even cynical propaganda. In the ancient Greco-Roman world, the situation was quite different. Though philosophers, like Plato, would occasionally criticize the misuse of rhetoric (Plato, *Gorgias*; *Phaedrus*), rhetoric was generally seen as a means of communicating the truth, not of obscuring it. Rhetoric was the art of eloquence and persuasion, a necessary tool for the orator (Greek: *rhētōr*) to make himself heard in the public assembly of the *polis* (city). It was the main theory of communication, not only for orators but also for writers of narrative.

The Gospel of John is a narrative from the ancient Greco-Roman world. According to the final verse of chapter 20, it is written with the purpose of persuading the readers to believe in Jesus as the Messiah and Son of God (20:31). As such it is a rhetorical narrative. In this chapter, I want to investigate how the anonymous author whom we call "John" used one particular feature of rhetoric, namely vividness, with special focus on John 20. Ancient rhetoricians and literary critics alike understood vividness of style to be one of the main virtues of storytelling and a crucial device in the toolbox of the skilled orator (e.g., Demetrius, *On Style* 208; Cicero, *De or.* 3.53, 3.202; Quintilian, *Inst.* 4.2.64). They called it *ekphrasis* (vivid description; Latin: *explicatio*) and *enargeia* (vividness; Latin: *evidentia*), often using the terms interchangeably, and they emphasized how vivid style could almost transport the audience into the story and turn the reader into a spectator present at the narrated events. Vividness contributed importantly to the persuasive effect of a given discourse as it induced consent by appealing to the audience's emotions.[1]

There are good reasons to highlight the use of *ekphrasis* and *enargeia* in a rhetorical critical analysis of the Gospel of John.[2] Although John himself did not use the terminology, he is, as we shall later see, certainly an author who invites his readers to become spectators so that they may sense the presence of Jesus. John wants to bridge the horizons of the readers and of Jesus, respectively, and to synchronize, as it were, the readers with Jesus: "You are in me, and I am in you" (14:20; see 15:4; 17:20–24).[3] This sense of presence relates to the two main questions that the Gospel of John attempts to answer. The first concerns the knowledge of God: How can humans know God when no one has ever seen God (1:18a; 5:37; 6:46)? John, of course, answers that one can see God by looking at Jesus: "Whoever has seen me has seen the Father" (14:9; see also 1:18b; 12:45; 14:6–10).

The second main question follows from this answer. Given that one can see God by looking at Jesus, what if one has not even seen Jesus? In other words: How does Jesus become present to the reader of the Gospel of John? This second question becomes more and more urgent as John's narrative approaches the end. It is, of course, conceptualized in John's peculiar understanding of eternal life as the believer's coexistence with Jesus, whether in the presence or in the future (e.g., 10:28; 17:3); but it becomes the main subject in the long farewell scene in chapters 13–17, where Jesus promises to extend his presence among the disciples by means of the Spirit-Paraclete (14:16, 26; 15:26; 16:7) and also describes his relation to "his own" as unbroken and organic like a vine and its branches (15:5). And in the final resurrection chapter (John 20), as we shall see, the continued vivid presence of Jesus among the Gospel's addressees becomes a rhetorical imperative. *Ekphrasis* and *enargeia* are important tools to establish that sense of presence.

THE VIRTUES OF VIVIDNESS

Before analyzing John's use of rhetorical vividness, let me describe the ancient understanding of the phenomenon in a little more detail. We will probably never know what kind of rhetorical training John underwent; but the simple facts that the Gospel was written with compositional skill and in reasonable Greek indicate that John's educational background exceeded the beginner's grammar level. There are no indications, however, that he had read the sophisticated rhetorical handbooks of, for example, Aristotle, Cicero, and Quintilian that reflected the elite level of rhetorical art. It is more possible that John was acquainted with elementary rhetorical training of the kind available to us in the *progymnasmata*, that is, textbooks containing elementary school exercises in prose composition and rhetoric. The *progymnasmata* were in wide use in the Roman Empire, and out of the roughly five different extant textbooks, all contain a separate chapter on how to teach and practice *ekphrasis*. It was a stock component of the curriculum.[4]

The oldest *progymnasmata* textbook, attributed to the teacher Aelius Theon from Alexandria and normally dated to the first or second century C.E., offers the following definition: "*Ekphrasis* is descriptive language, bringing what is portrayed vividly before the sight [*enargōs hyp' opsin*]" (*Prog.* 118.7–8).[5] Theon's definition, with its appeal to visualization ("before the sight"), reflects the common understanding of vividness among ancient teachers and rhetoricians. The Roman orator, Quintilian, for example, who published the most comprehensive account of rhetoric from antiquity (*Institutio oratoria*, ca. 95 C.E.), encouraged the good orator to create vivid effect by not only telling the story but showing it to the "mind's eye [*oculis mentis*]" (*Inst.* 8.3.62).[6] The orator should paint an image in words (*imago quodam modo verbis depingitur*; 8.3.63) and place the topic "before the eyes [*sub oculis*]" of the audience so that it would appear to be "a matter of seeing rather than of hearing [*ut cerni potius videantur quam audiri*]" (9.2.40; see also Cicero, *De or.* 3.202).[7] *Ekphrasis* and *enargeia*, in other words, could turn the subject of speech into something almost present and visible, whether the subject be persons (like Jesus in John's Gospel), events like wars and battles, places like cities or landscapes, and periods of time such as seasons and festivals (Theon, *Prog.* 118.8–9). *Ekphrasis* and *enargeia* were seldom understood as a genre but rather as a stylistic feature that could be used in all sorts of genres, for example, oratory, narrative, poetry, and history (Lucian, *How to Write History* 51); and it served to energize both shorter sentences (Theon, *Prog.* 118.9–14) and longer digressions such as Homer's famous description of the Shield of Achilles (*Il.* 18.478–608) and Virgil's equally meticulous word depiction of the Shield of Aeneas (*Aen.* 8.626–728).[8]

Fortunately for the purpose of our analysis, the ancient rhetoricians and literary theorists did not only applaud vivid style but also theorized about it and prescribed how the skilled communicator could best create vivid narratives and descriptions. Some of these authors mainly quoted a number of good literary examples of vividness for the aspiring orator to imitate (Theon, *Prog.* 118.9–119.27); but others tried to identify certain linguistic triggers of vividness such as the use of present tense, imitation of real discourse, simile or comparison, circumstantial detail, repetition, word choice appropriate to content, and suspense.[9] Below, I shall explain these triggers of vividness as I discuss how and why John made use of them.

Again, a rhetorical analysis of this kind does not depend on whether or not John was trained in, for example, the *progymnasmata* exercises. I am trying, rather, to read John from within the ancient atmosphere of communicative conventions. John wrote a narrative with the purpose of persuading in the context of a highly rhetorical culture, where a wide range of authors agreed fundamentally on the definition of *ekphrasis*, *enargeia*, and the linguistic features that triggered the visual imagination of the audience. In the analysis below, however, I restrict myself to mentioning only authors that were earlier than, contemporary with, or not very much later than John, who probably wrote in the decades around 100 C.E. What my analysis offers is a depiction of how an audience from the ancient Greco-Roman rhetorical culture may have appreciated John's visualization strategy of making Jesus present before the eyes.

SEEING THE WORD IN JOHN 1

In order to understand how rhetorical vividness stimulates the end of John's Gospel narrative in chapter 20 (I lean toward thinking that chapter 21 is an addition), it is useful to revert to the beginning in chapter 1. From an early point, the Gospel presents itself as communication of visual eyewitness experience. For example, in the Prologue about God's Word that became human in Jesus, the narrating voice says that "we have seen [*etheasametha*] his glory" (1:14). This vision of the divine is exactly what the Gospel attempts to share with the readers. John the Baptist serves as the first eyewitness: "And I myself have seen [*heōraka*] and have testified that this is the Son of God" (1:34). Later at the cross, the sight-and-testimony formula is repeated, apparently with reference to the Beloved Disciple: "He who saw [*ho heōrakōs*] this has testified so that you also may believe" (19:35; see 3:11; 20:30–31).[10] Whether or not the Gospel of John really contains historical eyewitness accounts, it purports to communicate visual experiences to the readers. According to the philosopher Plutarch, this ability to transfer eyewitness experience to the reader characterized the masters of vivid style, such as the classical historian Thucydides:

> Assuredly Thucydides is always striving for this vividness [*tēn enargeian*] in his writing, since it is his desire to make the reader a spectator [*theatēn poiēsai ton akroatēn*], as it were, and to produce vividly in the minds of those who

peruse his narrative the emotions of amazement and consternation which were experienced by those who beheld them. (Plutarch, *Glor. Ath.* 3 [347a]; see also Ps.-Longinus, *On the Sublime* 15.3)

John attempts to create a similar, vivid effect. In the opening chapter of his Gospel, he simulates ocular vision of Jesus in several of the ways described by ancient rhetoricians and literary critics. It happens in the Prologue (1:1–18) and in all the following scenes, that is, John the Baptist's testimony (1:19–28), his first encounter with Jesus (1:29–34), and the chain of calls to discipleship (1:35–51). First of all, John's style is characterized by frequent use of verbs in the dramatic present tense: "The next day [John the Baptist] sees Jesus coming toward him" (1:29); "Andrew first finds his brother Simon and says to him: . . ." (1:41); "Philip finds Nathanael and says to him: . . ." (1:45);[11] and so on. The dramatic present tense (or the sports commentator's present) transports events of the past into the present as if they were taking place in the reader's own time. In Pseudo-Longinus's treatise *On the Sublime* (first or second century C.E.), which applies rhetorical theory to the art of writing with energetic style, the author recommends using the dramatic present: "Again, if you introduce events in past time as happening at the present moment, the passage will be transformed from a narrative into a vivid [*enagōnion*] actuality" (25; see also *Rhet. Her.* 4.68 and Quintilian, *Inst.* 6.2.32; 9.2.41–44). Modern translations often polish away John's use of this feature by replacing verbs in the present tense with verbs in the past tense—maybe in an attempt to standardize John's style—but the Greek original speaks in the present again and again, not least when Jesus is talking, with the effect of situating Jesus in the presence of the readers (1:21, 36, 38, 39, 43, 46–48, 51).

Other triggers of vividness in John 1 are the mimetic elements, that is, imitation of real discourse. According to the orator Demetrius (ca. 300 B.C.E.), mimetic elements always add to vividness (*On Style* 219–20), whereas Quintilian, noting the bold use of imitation among his contemporaries, adds a note of caution that such vivid speech could distract a hearer (*Inst.* 9.2.42–43). In John 1:21, the Jerusalemite envoys interrogate John the Baptist in a quick exchange of words that imitates natural dialogue. Below is my translation:

And they asked him, "What then? Are you Elijah?"

He says, "I am not."
"Are you the prophet?"
He answered, "No."

Notice the ping-pong dialogue and how the narrator refrains from introducing the envoys' question ("Are you the prophet?"). The narrator rather withdraws for a short moment, as if not able to keep up with the action. As a consequence, the verbal exchange appears as natural dialogue or drama in the service of vividness (see Ps.-Longinus, *On the Sublime* 18–19, 26).[12]

Demetrius also thought that repetition could generate *enargeia*: "Consequently repetition is often more vivid than a single mention. . . . The same word is often put twice to increase the impact" (*On Style* 211–12; see also 213–15). In John 1, the abundant repetitive language of the Prologue in 1:1–18 is obvious, but the repetitions continue in 1:19–51, especially in relation to John the Baptist's eyewitness testimony. The Jerusalemite envoys' question regarding the identity of the Baptist appears in many forms: "Who are you?" (1:19), "What then? Are you Elijah?" (1:21), "Who are you? . . . What do you say about yourself?" (1:22). The Evangelist could easily have summarized this interrogation into, for example, one single question, but he chooses the repetitive, vivid style. The Baptist replies that he is not the Messiah, and the reply is also introduced by repetition: "He confessed and did not deny it, but confessed" (1:20). In fact, almost everything that the Baptist says in John 1, is stated at least twice: that Jesus existed before the Baptist (1:15, 30), that the Baptist is not the Messiah (1:20, 21, 22) and only baptizes with water (1:26, 31), that Jesus is the "the Lamb of God" (1:29, 36), and that the Baptist did not know him (1:31, 33) until he recognized him by the Spirit that descended on him (1:32, 33). In 1:32, the Baptist adds to the repetitions that the Spirit descended "like a dove," thus painting a visual image of the Dove-Spirit in the audience's imagination. According to Quintilian, comparisons or similes (sg.: *similitudo*) like this not only boost an argument but also place the issue before the eyes of the audience. His example, taken from the famous Roman orator and politician Cicero, is certainly not as lofty as the Johannine Dove-Spirit: "He fled from court like a man escaping from a fire without his clothes" (*Inst.* 8.3.81; see also 8.3.72–82; Aristotle, *Rhet.* 3.11.2–4).

John's most consistent trigger of vividness in chapter 1, however, is none of the above. It is rather his strikingly abundant visual vocabulary, which will also reappear as a constant in chapter 20. As we observed at the beginning of this section, John the Baptist was himself an eyewitness, but he also invites others to see: "See [*ide*], the Lamb of God who takes away the sin of the world!" (1:29; see also 1:36). And in the subsequent chain reaction of calls to discipleship, the refrain echoes: "Come and see!" (1:39), "Come and see!" (1:46). This call to see, however, is not only addressed to the characters in the story, but also directly to the readers, who are thus drawn into the story world. When Nathanael, the last disciple to receive his call in chapter 1, recognizes Jesus as the Son of God and Messiah on the basis of Jesus's supernatural knowledge, Jesus pronounces the final and climactic statement of the whole chapter (1:50–51). Notice in the quotation below how Jesus begins by addressing Nathanael in the second-person singular ("you," sg.), but then turns to the readers in the second-person plural ("you all," pl.)—something that does not easily show in an English translation but is remarkable in the original Greek:

> "Do you [sg.] believe because I told you that I saw you under the fig tree? You will see [*opsē*, sg.] greater things than these." And he says to him, "Very, very truly, I tell you all [pl.], you all will see [*opsesthe*, pl.] heaven opened and the angels of God ascending and descending upon the Son of Man." (1:50–51)

Jesus and Nathanael are presumably the only two characters present in this short scene, so the plural address in the latter part of the quotation comes as a surprise. The Evangelist makes Jesus turn toward the readers and breaks the fourth wall between the story world and the world of the audience. (A technique that the Netflix series *House of Cards* fully exploits by means of Frank Underwood's many asides.)[13] In antiquity, this technique was thought to create a vivid sense of presence. As Pseudo-Longinus says with regard to an example from the historian Herotodus: "All such passages with a direct personal address put the hearer in the presence of the action itself" (*On the Sublime* 26.2). Jesus thus promises Nathanael *and* the readers to "see heaven opened." It is the climax of John's opening chapter and a programmatic statement about the aim of the Gospel as a whole. In the course of the reading, the readers are included in a virtual visual encounter with Jesus. The Jesus saying in 1:50–51 excels in *ekphrasis* and *enargeia*: Dramatic present ("he says"), repetition and imitation of authentic Hebrew/Aramaic discourse ("very, very truly [*amēn amēn*]"), circumstantial detail ("the fig tree"), and visual verbs ("I saw," "You will see," "you all will see"). It certainly places Jesus "before the eyes."

RHETORICAL VIVIDNESS IN JOHN 20

Now, let us move to the final chapter of the Gospel, where the conflict between unbelief and belief that runs through the narrative is ultimately settled in favor of belief. Once-doubting Thomas exclaims by means of conclusion: "My Lord and my God!" (20:28). Apart from the final purpose statement in vv. 30–31, the chapter consists of a series of recognition scenes (sg., *anagnōrisis*), where the disciples in an instant moment realize that their crucified master has risen from the dead. These visual encounters prompt testimony ("go to my brothers and say to them: . . ." v. 17; see also vv. 2, 25) so that the message is spread in a manner comparable with the chain reactions described in 1:35–51. The main characters in the four scenes are (apart from Jesus): the first witnesses of the empty tomb (Mary Magdalene, Simon

Peter, and the Beloved Disciple, vv. 1–10); Mary Magdalene (vv. 11–18); the disciples without Thomas (vv. 19–25); and Thomas (vv. 26–29).[14]

John, of course, employs *ekphrastic* language in the whole Gospel, but the frequency of visual verbs is remarkably high in this short chapter (thirteen occurrences) just as it was in John 1 (seventeen occurrences).[15] And once again, the details of the story fuel the visual effect. According to Quintilian, instead of simply telling *that* something occurred in general lines, one should narrate *how* it happened in detail (*ex pluribus*, *Inst.* 8.3.66; *per partes*, 9.2.40). Though some ancient authors thought that one could overdose the amount of detail in a discourse, leaving nothing to the audience's own imagination (*Inst.* 8.3.64–65), many of them, at the same time, agreed that narrating with detail—and not least circumstantial detail, even fictitious—was one of the main virtues of the persuasive orator (*Rhet. Her.* 4.68; Demetrius, *On Style* 209–10; 217–18; Dionysius of Halicarnassus, *Lys.* 7.1–13; Quintilian, *Inst.* 8.3.63; 8.3.70; 9.2.40). Demetrius, for one, offers an example from one of Plato's dialogues. When the young Hippocrates was seeking Socrates's advice at night, Plato shows by means of circumstantial detail (blushing, daylight) how the young man reacted when confronted with his flirt with the sophists: "He was blushing, for there was already a first glimmer of daylight to reveal him" (*On Style*, 218; see Plato, *Prot.* 312a).

In John 20, vivid and lucid details are numerous. In the first scene, Mary comes to the tomb in the early morning "while it was still dark" and sees that the stone has been removed (v. 1). She runs to alarm Simon Peter and the Beloved Disciple, who race to the tomb, the latter outrunning the former (vv. 2–4). And Peter sees the linen wrappings "rolled up in a place by itself" (v. 6–7). In the second scene, Mary Magdalene first encounters "two angels in white, sitting where the body of Jesus had been lying, one at the head and the other at the feet" (v. 12), and when Jesus arrives, the readers witness Mary's confused body movements as she thinks he is the gardener (vv. 14–16). Also, the last two recognition scenes contain vivid detail (the closed doors, Jesus's hands and side, etc.). Some Johannine scholars take such scenographic detail to be traces of early orally transmitted memories about Jesus.[16] Though this cannot be ruled out as regards John's Gospel in general, the exegetical mainstream emphasizes the symbolic or theological meaning of the details—probably influenced by Clement of Alexandria's momentous interpretation of John's Gospel as the "spiritual Gospel." For example, the darkness in the first scene may serve as backdrop for the "light of the world" that Jesus embodies (8:12; 9:5; 11:9).[17] The race to the tomb may imply that the Evangelist attempts to transfer the traditional high status of Peter to the Beloved Disciple (13:22–25; 21:7, 20).[18] And the garden/gardener motif possibly evokes the garden of paradise in Genesis 2.[19] While such symbolic readings may indeed be adequate in the context of John's Gospel, I propose that an ancient reader aware of rhetorical conventions may as well have taken the details as circumstantial detail in the service of vividness, verisimilitude, and credibility (Dionysius of Halicarnassus, *Lys.* 7; Quintilian, *Inst.* 8.3.70). Even ancient authors would understand detail as *effet de réel* (reality effects), a term coined by the much later literary theorist Roland Barthes.[20] Regardless of their possible historical value, the details in John 20 function as vivid reality effects. This does not mean, however, that such an *ekphrastic* understanding of the Johannine attention to detail needs to clash with the symbolic understanding; rather, as the rhetorical handbooks and the *progymnasmata* often recommended, the details must fit the content of the whole (e.g., Theon, *Prog.* 119.27–120.11; Lucian, *How to Write History* 50).

In John 20 as in John 1, the dramatic present tense is widely used to create a vivid sense of presence (20:1–2, 5–6, 12–19, 22, 26–27, 29). Right before in the concluding part of chapter 19, however, the verbs appear in the past tense and the aorist with the effect that 20:1 becomes a remarkable contrast seldom visible in modern translations. Yet, if we translate the first two verses of John 20 in the following manner, we get a sense of the vividness that John creates in his account of the first Easter morning events:

> Early on the first day of the week, while it is still dark [*skotias eti ousēs*], Mary Magdalene comes [*erchetai*] to the tomb and sees [*blepei*] that the stone has been removed from the tomb. So she runs [*trechei*] and goes [*erchetai*] to Simon Peter and the other disciple, the one whom Jesus loved, and says [*legei*] to them, ... (John 20:1–2)[21]

John 20 is also rich in energetic repetition. The linen wrappings receive mention twice (vv. 5–6), and Mary Magdalene turns in surprise two times (vv. 14, 16). Both the angels and Jesus ask her: "Woman, why are you weeping? (vv. 13, 15), and Jesus greets the disciples twice: "Peace be with you" (vv. 19, 21). A particularly powerful repetition appears in Mary Magdalene's three mournful cries: "We do not know where they have laid him" (v. 2), "I do not know where they have laid him" (v. 13), and "Tell me where you have laid him" (v. 15). The cry becomes a chorus in the first two scenes and grows in intensity: from a general "we" statement, through a personal "I" expression, to an imperative "you" command. When Mary is held in suspense regarding the apparent gardener's true identity, it adds to vividness. Of course, Jesus knows why she is weeping (2:25; 4:17) and could have disclosed his own identity right upon his arrival, but according to Demetrius the vivid narrator must not give the story away "but reveal it only gradually, keeping the reader in suspense and forcing him to share the anguish" (*On Style* 216). In the recognition scenes of chapter 20, recognition does not take place right away but is often delayed so that the readers may share in the characters' distress and joy.

Suspense, visual verbs, dramatic present tense, repetition, and circumstantial detail seem to be the most important elements of vividness in John 20. But some minor features also deserve mention. According to late ancient sources, adverbs of place and pronominal stems have a vivifying effect.[22] By means of such linguistic place markers, the orator or narrator assists the audience in their inner vision of the events. In John 20, Mary Magdalene turns around "behind her [*eis ta opisō*]" (v. 14) and Jesus appears to the disciples standing "in their midst [*eis to meson*]" (vv. 19, 26). The place markers become stage accessories in a virtual scenography.

John also uses mimetic imitation of real discourse to create *ekphrasis* and *enargeia*, just as we saw in 1:21 and 1:51. In the flashbulb moment of recognition, when Jesus identifies Mary Magdalene and calls her by name, thus prompting her recognition of him, they both revert from the Greek to their own original language: "Jesus says to her, 'Mary [*Mariam*]!' She turns and says to him in Hebrew, 'Rabbouni [*rabbouni*]!' (which means Teacher)" (v. 16).[23] Mimesis like this evokes authenticity. The orator and philosopher, Dio Chrysostom, in a speech delivered around the year 100 C.E., praises Homer for using the same effect: "And he also used many barbarian words as well, sparing none that he believed to have in it anything of charm or of vividness [*enargeias*]" (*Disc.* 12.66–67). When the audience hears Jesus speaking in his own language—notice also the myriad of *amēn amēn* ("Very, very truly") sayings in John like the one in 1:51—the language barrier is torn down and Jesus stands before the Gospel audience, apparently unmediated. It is, by the way, an effect that was consequently used in Mel Gibson's movie *The Passion of the Christ* (2004).

THE LIMITS OF RHETORICAL VIVIDNESS
(JOHN 20:29)

Even though, as we now have seen, John places Jesus "before the eyes" by means of *ekphrastic* techniques, he does claim that the abiding presence of Jesus depends on his own rhetorical ability to summon it up vis-à-vis the readers. Rather, in the final chapter John seems to be aware of the fact that the reading experience is coming to an end and that the readers must be transported gently back to their own world, where Jesus is out of eyesight but present in the Spirit and in the message that can be heard: from sight to hearing. Thus, when Thomas ultimately sees Jesus's wounded hands and side, and recognizes his resurrected Lord and God, Jesus responds with the following statement: "Have you believed because you have seen me? Blessed are those who have not seen and yet have come to believe" (v. 29). Whether or not this reply implies a rebuke of Thomas (which I do not think), it certainly serves as an indirect blessing of the readers. In spite of John's *ekphrastic* storytelling, the readers remain readers "who have not seen." This final saying of Jesus in John 20 mirrors his final saying to Nathanael and the readers in chapter 1: "Do you believe because I told you that I saw you under the fig tree? You will see greater things than these" (1:50–51). But whereas in 1:50–51 Jesus promised Nathanael and the readers the opportunity to *see* the upcoming events within the Gospel's story world ("You will see greater things"), in 20:29 he accords special value to the readers' *non-seeing* condition outside the Gospel's story world ("Blessed are those who have not seen," see 16:7).

This Johannine awareness of the limits of rhetorical vividness fits well with the ancient rhetorical mindset. Though the ancients thought highly of vivid language as a physical force that could penetrate the emotions of the audience in the service of persuasion, teachers of *ekphrasis* and *enargeia* would also emphasize what Ruth Webb has called the "as-if"-ness of vividness. The mental images that *ekphrasis* and *enargeia* generate in the audience are always a matter of illusion, whether or not they describe historical "facts."[24] Vivid language neither paints an actual and concrete physical image nor resurrects the dead, but it places "almost" before the eyes (*prope*, Rhet. Her. 4.69; *schedon*, Theon, *Prog.* 119.29). The audience may be "enslaved" by the narrator (*douloutai*; Ps.-Longinus, *On the Sublime* 15.9)—today experimental narratology talks about "narrative transportation"—but when the story ends, it gradually loses its grip on the audience.[25]

In John's Gospel, however, the enduring presence of Jesus not only a rhetorical simulacrum but belongs to the core of the message. As I claimed in the beginning of this chapter, the enduring presence of Jesus is John's "second main question." John's awareness of the limits of rhetorical vividness appears in 20:29 and in the farewell scene in John 13–17, where Jesus's abiding presence does not appear "before the eyes" but in the Spirit-Paraclete. But even in the novelistic scene in John 9 about the healing of the man born blind, John paves the way for the readers' access to Jesus beyond the story world. According to John 9, visual access to Jesus must be understood in a deeper sense. Belief in Jesus is a form of spiritual vision that is not only the privilege of the eyewitnesses, but is even available beyond the boundaries of the Gospel's story world. In the story, the man born blind gains sight on two levels, both physically and spiritually (9:37–38). The Pharisees, however, remain spiritually blind though they do physically see Jesus. He says to them: "I came into this world for judgment so that those who do not see may see, and those who do see may become blind" (9:39). John 9 thus outlines a field of possible modes of visuality depending on physical sight/blindness on the one hand, and spiritual sight/blindness on the other. The following table illustrates the field:

	PHYSICAL SIGHT	PHYSICAL BLINDNESS
SPIRITUAL BLINDNESS	1. The Pharisees (9:40–41; see also 6:36; 15:24)	2. The man born blind before the miracle (9:1, 25)
SPIRITUAL SIGHT	3. The man born blind after the miracle (9:37–38)	[4. "those who have not seen and yet have come to believe"; 20:29]

As the table shows, the Pharisees remain within the first mode of visuality, whereas the man born blind moves from the second to the third mode. The story in John 9 only contains these three modes of visuality (numbers 1–3 in the table) and does not explicitly identify the fourth mode (physical blindness and spiritual sight). That is, however, precisely the mode or attitude that Jesus blesses in 20:29: "Blessed are those who have not seen and yet have come to believe." In spite of John's preference for rhetorical vividness, he concludes his Gospel by reminding the readers that actual physical vision of Jesus is no longer possible. The Gospel of John produces an impression of physical sight by means of rhetorical vividness, but it ultimately aims at inducing the readers to adopt the spiritual sight of belief.

CONCLUSION

When nominating candidates for the hall of fame of rhetorical vividness, ancient rhetoricians and literary theorists consistently elected Greco-Roman authors and orators like Homer, Thucydides, and Cicero due to their mastery of *ekphrasis* and *enargeia*. We shall never know if John ever earned an A+ at his vivid style exams. Some NT scholars would strongly doubt it as they deem John's style to be vague, monotonous, and ethereal.[26] But when we read John's Gospel in light of ancient Greco-Roman handbooks and textbooks that discuss the rhetorical virtues of vividness, the Evangelist appears as a metaphorical painter. In chapters 1 and 20—at the beginning and at the end of his narrative—his use of *ekphrastic* techniques is particularly intense with the consequence that Jesus appears "before the eyes" of the readers. John's *ekphrastic* techniques are multifaceted, as we have seen, but in these two chapters, he favors visual vocabulary, circumstantial detail, repetition, and verbs in the dramatic present tense. John's rhetoric thus supports the Gospel's overall purpose of persuading the readers to embrace belief and eternal life in the presence of Jesus and the Father (20:31; see also 1 John 5:13).

However, as we have also seen, John also displays awareness of the limits of rhetorical vividness. Rhetorical vividness supports John's persuasive aim, but at the end of the day, the readers do not actually see Jesus physically but engage in hearing the Johannine testimony from the alleged eyewitnesses. The perpetual discussion in Johannine scholarship whether John prioritizes visual eye-belief or aural ear-belief, fueled not least by the preference for the latter in Protestant tradition, is maybe not so much a question of theological doctrine as of Johannine rhetoric.[27] When the story opens in chapter 1, *ekphrastic* rhetoric turns the readers into inner-eye spectators with visual eye-belief as described in the Jesus saying in 1:50–51. In the recognition scenes of John 20, this *ekphrastic* sense of presence "before the eyes" continues undiminished, but Jesus's final saying in 20:29 stands as a contrast. It wraps the story up by reminding the readers that even though they have been exposed to a word-picture of Jesus, they are not first-generation eyewitnesses with visual eye-belief. Rather, they belong to the subsequent generations who are blessed if they embrace the aural ear-belief which is based on the Gospel's verbal testimony. In other words, John's Gospel, a very visualizing and *ekphrastic* Gospel, concludes by pointing, not to sight, but to the verbal medium of the gospel message.

But ultimately, in an eschatological perspective, vision may get the last word anyway: In the farewell discourses, Jesus extends a promise to his disciples: "A little while, and you will no longer see me, and again a little while, and you will see me" (16:16). This *au revoir* saying refers to the reunion of Jesus and the disciples in chapter 20 right after the resurrection, but it may also contain an eschatological dimension concerning the disciples' and the readers' ultimate and visual union with Jesus in his Father's abode (see also 14:19; 16:16–19); or as another NT author famously phrased it: "[T]hen we will see face to face" (1 Cor. 13:12).

NOTES

1. Simon Goldhill, "What Is Ekphrasis For?" *CP* 102 (2007): 6. The technical name for rhetorical vividness was not always consistent in ancient rhetoric. Though *ekphrasis* and *energeia* were the most common terms, vividness was also discussed under such headings as, in Latin, *demonstratio, illustratio, imaginatio, perspicuitas, sub oculis subiectio*, and, in Greek, *diatypōsis, enagōnia, hypotypōsis*, and *phantasia*. See Heinrich Lausberg, *Handbook of Literary Rhetoric: A Foundation for Literary Study*, ed. David E. Horton and R. Dean Anderson (Leiden: Brill, 2008), §§ 810–19.

2. For previous studies of *ekphrasis* and *energeia* in John's Gospel dealing with their function in the presentation of Jewish Scripture and of testimony, respectively, see Alicia D. Myers, *Characterizing Jesus: A Rhetorical Analysis on the Fourth Gospel's Use of Scripture in Its Presentation of Jesus*, LNTS 458 (London: Bloomsbury/T&T Clark, 2012), 49–51, 86–93, 182; and Sunny Kwang-Hui Wang, *Sense Perception and Testimony in the Gospel of John*, WUNT 2/435 (Tübingen: Mohr Siebeck, 2017), 87–109. Studies of rhetorical vividness in other NT writings

include Jane M. F. Heath, "Absent Presences of Paul and Christ: *Enargeia* in 1 Thessalonians 1–3," *JSNT* 31 (2009): 3–38; David G. Horrell, Arnold Bradley, and Travis B. Williams, "Visuality, Vivid Description, and the Message of 1 Peter: The Significance of the Roaring Lion (1 Peter 5:8)," *JBL* 132 (2013): 697–716; Nils Neumann, *Hören und Sehen: Die Rhetorik der Anschaulichkeit in den Gottesthron-Szenen der Johannesoffenbarung*, ABG 49 (Leipzig: Evangelische Verlagsanstalt, 2015); Robyn J. Whitaker, "The Poetics of *Ekphrasis*: Vivid Description and Rhetoric in the Apocalypse," in *Poetik und Intertextualität in der Apokalypse*, ed. Stefan Alkier, Thomas Hieke, and Tobias Nicklas, WUNT 346 (Tübingen: Mohr Siebeck, 2015), 227–40; and Sigurvin Lárus Jónsson, "James Among the Classicists: Reading the Letter of James in Light of Ancient Literary Criticism," (PhD diss., Aarhus University, 2019), 126–35.

3. My translation. If not otherwise indicated, Bible translations are from the NRSV.

4. Ruth Webb, "The *Progymnasmata* as Practice," in *Education in the Greek and Roman Antiquity*, ed. Yun Lee Too (Leiden: Brill, 2001), 289–316. The *progymnasmata* are available in translation in George A. Kennedy, *Progymnasmata: Greek Textbooks of Prose Composition and Rhetoric*, WGRW 10 (Atlanta: SBL Press, 2003).

5. Translation is adjusted from Kennedy, *Progymnasmta*.

6. Translations are from LCL volumes unless otherwise noted.

7. The quotation from Quintilian, *Inst.* 9.2.40 is slightly modified. For other examples connecting vividness and visualization, see Aristotle, *Rhet.* 3.10.6; 3.11.1–4 (*energeia*); the anonymous *Rhetorica ad Herennium* 4.68–69; Ps.-Longinus, *On the Sublime* 15.1; 26.2; Dionysius of Halicarnassos, *De Lysia* 7.1–13; Theon, *Prog.* 118.7–8; 119.29; Quintilian, *Inst.* 6.2.29; 9.2.41; Plutarch, *Art.* 8.1.

8. As Ruth Webb has rightly emphasized, the ancients had a much wider definition of *ekphrasis* than the narrow understanding of the concept prevalent in modern literary criticism. *Ekphrasis* included a multitude of rhetorical visualization techniques and was not confined to the detailed descriptions of visual works of art that we encounter in, for instance, the *imagines/eikones* of Philostratus the Elder and Philostratus the Younger and in the examples from Homer and Virgil given above. See Webb's excellent work *Ekphrasis, Imagination and Persuasion in Ancient Rhetorical Theory and Practice* (Surrey: Ashgate, 2009), 1–38.

9. For a similar list of vividness techniques, see Wang, *Sense Perception*, 100–1.

10. The Prologue of 1 John contains a similar formula: "What we have seen with our eyes, what we have looked at . . . and we have seen it and testify to it . . . what we have seen." (1:1–4).

11. My translation.

12. See George Parsenios, "Silent Spaces between Narrative and Drama: *Mimesis* and *Diegesis* in the Fourth Gospel," in *The Gospel of John as Genre Mosaic*, ed. Kasper Bro Larsen, SANt 3 (Göttingen: Vandenhoeck & Ruprecht, 2015), 85–97 and Jo-Ann A. Brant, *Dialogue and Drama: Elements of Greek Tragedy in the Fourth Gospel* (Peabody: Hendrickson, 2004), 3, 74–158.

13. In John's purpose statement in 20:31, the readers are once again addressed, now by the narrator, in the second-person plural ("written so that you all may believe," my translation; see also 19:35).

14. For a study of Johannine recognition scenes in light of ancient generic parallels in biblical narrative and, primarily, Greco-Roman epic, drama, and romance, see my *Recognizing the Stranger: Recognition Scenes in the Gospel of John*, BibS 93 (Leiden: Brill, 2008).

15. See the chart in Wang, *Sense Perception*, 23.

16. Paul N. Anderson, "Why This Study Is Needed, and Why It Is Needed Now," in *John, Jesus, and History, Volume 1: Critical Appraisals of Critical Views*, ed. Paul N. Anderson, Felix Just, and Tom Thatcher, SBLSymS 44 (Atlanta: SBL Press, 2007), 47–54, esp. 53.

17. Craig S. Keener, *The Gospel of John: A Commentary* (Peabody, MA: Hendrickson, 2003), 2:1178–79.

18. C. K. Barrett, *The Gospel According to St John: An Introduction with Commentary and Notes on the Greek Text* (London: SPCK, 1955), 468.

19. R. H. Lightfoot, *St. John's Gospel: A Commentary*, ed. C. F. Evans, rev. ed. (Oxford: Clarendon, 1983), 321–22.

20. Roland Barthes, "L'Effet de réel," *Communications* 11 (1968): 84–89.

21. In v. 2 and also in v. 6, John amplifies the vividness of the dramatic present by means of the Greek *oun* particle that, among other things, signifies vivid transition in the narration ("now," "then," "so," etc.). The particle is highly characteristic of John's style in the Gospel as a whole. In John 20, it also occurs in vv. 3, 8, 10–11, 19–21, 25, 30.

22. See Lausberg, *Handbook of Literary Rhetoric*, § 815.

23. Johannine recognition scenes often have a reciprocal structure illustrating Jesus's good shepherd saying in 10:14: "I know my own and my own know me." See my article "The Recognition Scenes and Epistemological Reciprocity in the Fourth Gospel," in Larsen, *The Gospel of John as Genre Mosaic*, 341–56.

24. On the "as if"-ness of *ekphrasis*, see Webb, *Ekphrasis*, 10–11; see also 103–5.

25. Melanie C. Green and Timothy C. Brock, "The Role of Transportation in the Persuasiveness of Public Narratives," *JPSP* 79 (2000): 701–21.

26. See, for example, the renowned German scholar William Wrede's statement: "In any case, a peculiar unvividness [*Unanschaulichkeit*] remains one of the main characteristics of narration in this gospel." See William Wrede, *Charakter und Tendenz des Johannesevangeliums* (Tübingen: Mohr Siebeck, 1903), 21; see also 5, 11–22 (my translation).

27. See, for example, Rudolf Bultmann's heading "Faith as the Hearing of the Word" in his *Theology of the New Testament* (Waco, TX: Baylor University Press, 2007), 2:70; Bultmann, *The Gospel of John: A Commentary*, trans. G. R. Beasley-Murray (Oxford: Basil Blackwell, 1971), 696; and Craig R. Koester, "Hearing, Seeing, and Believing in the Gospel of John," *Bib* 70 (1989): 327–48. In defense of sight, see, for example, Raymond Brown, *The Gospel according to John*, AB 29–29a (New York: Doubleday, 1966–70), 2:1048–51 and Clemens Hergenröder, *Wir schauten seine Herrlichkeit: Das johanneische Sprechen vom Sehen im Horizont von Selbsterschliessung Jesu und Antwort des Menschen*, FB 80 (Würzburg: Echter Verlag, 1996).

Suggested Readings

The list below offers student-friendly introductions and examples of the four interpretive approaches explored in this collection. This list includes works both that focus on the Gospel of John as well as those which offer more general introductions to the approach or theory.

Bauckham, Richard. "John for Readers of Mark." Pages 147–71 in *The Gospels for All Christians: Rethinking the Gospel Audiences*. Edited by Richard Bauckham. Grand Rapids: Eerdmans, 1998.

———. "The Gospel of John and the Synoptic Problem." Pages 657–88 in *New Studies in the Synoptic Problem: Oxford Conference, April 2008. Essays in Honour of Christopher M. Tuckett*. Edited by Paul Foster, Andrew Gregory, John S. Kloppenborg, and Joseph Verheyden. BETL 239. Leuven: Peeters, 2011.

Brown, Raymond E. *The Gospel According to John*. 2 vols. AB 29-29a Garden City, NY: Doubleday, 1966–1970.

Brown, Sherri and Francis J. Moloney, *Interpreting the Gospel and Letters of John: An Introduction*. Grand Rapids: Eerdmans, 2017.

Carter, Warren. *John and Empire: Initial Explorations*. New York: T&T Clark, 2008.

Culpepper, R. Alan. *Anatomy of the Fourth Gospel: A Study in Literary Design*. Philadelphia: Fortress, 1983.

Dube, Musa and Jeffrey Staley, eds. *John and Postcolonialism: Travel, Space, and Power*. London: Sheffield Academic, 2002.

Estes, Douglas, and Ruth Sheridan, eds. *How John Works: Storytelling in the Fourth Gospel*. RBS 86. Atlanta: SBL Press, 2016.

Gage, John T., ed. *The Promise of Reason: Studies in the New Rhetoric*. Carbondale, IL: Southern Illinois University Press, 2011.

Grant, Jacquelyn. *White Women's Christ, Black Women's Jesus: Feminist Christology and Womanist Response*. Atlanta: Scholars Press, 1989.

Hays, Richard B. *Echoes of Scripture in the Gospels*. Waco, TX: Baylor University Press, 2016.

Hays, Richard B., Stefan Alkier, and Leroy A. Huizenga, eds. *Reading the Bible Intertextually*. Waco, TX: Baylor University Press, 2009.

Junior, Nyasha. *An Introduction to Womanist Biblical Interpretation*. Louisville: Westminster John Knox, 2015.

Koester, Craig R. *Symbolism in the Fourth Gospel: Meaning, Mystery, Community*. 2nd ed. Minneapolis: Fortress, 2003.

Lee, Dorothy A. *Flesh and Glory: Symbol, Gender and Theology in the Gospel of John*. New York: Crossroad, 2002.

Levine, Amy-Jill, and Marianne Blickenstaff, eds. *A Feminist Companion to John*. 2 vols. Feminist Companion to the New Testament and Early Christian Writings 4–5. London: Sheffield Academic, 2003.

Lieu, Judith M. and Martinus C. de Boer, eds. *The Oxford Handbook of Johannine Studies*. Oxford: Oxford University Press, 2018.

Lincoln, Andrew T. *The Gospel According to Saint John*. Peabody, MA: Hendrickson, 2005.

Moyise, Steve. *The Old Testament in the New: An Introduction*. 2nd ed. T&T Clark Approaches to Biblical Studies. London: Bloomsbury/T&T Clark, 2015.

Myers, Alicia D. and Bruce G. Schuchard, eds. *Abiding Words: Perspectives on the Use of Scripture in the Gospel of John*. RBS 81. Atlanta: SBL Press, 2015.

Nässelqvist, Dan. "Stylistic Levels in Hebrews 1.1–4 and John 1.1–18." *JSNT* 35 (2012): 31–53.

Neirynck, Frans. "John and the Synoptics: The Empty Tomb Stories." *NTS* 30 (1984): 161–87.

Parsons, Mikeal C. and Michael Wade Martin. *Ancient Rhetoric and the New Testament*. Waco, TX: Baylor University Press, 2018.

Pernot, Laurent. *Epideictic Rhetoric: Questioning the Stakes of Ancient Praise*. Austin: University of Texas Press, 2015.

Reinhartz, Adele. *Cast Out of the Covenant: Jews and Anti-Judaism in the Gospel of John*. Lanham, MD: Lexington/Fortress Academic, 2018.

Robbins, Vernon K. *The Tapestry of Early Christian Discourse: Rhetoric, Society and Ideology*. London: Routledge, 1996.

Schandorf, Michael. "*A Gesture Theory of Communication*." PhD diss., University of Illinois at Chicago, 2015.

Skinner, Christopher W., ed. *Characters and Characterization in the Gospel of John*. LNTS 461. London: Bloomsbury/T&T Clark, 2013.

Thatcher, Tom, and Stephen D. Moore, eds. *Anatomies of Narrative Criticism: The Past, Present, and Futures of the Fourth Gospel as Literature*. RBS 55. Atlanta: SBL Press, 2008.

Weems, Renita. "Womanist Reflections on Biblical Hermeneutics." Pages 216–24 in *Black Theology: A Documentary History. Volume 2: 1980–1992*. Edited by James H. Cone and Gayraud S. Wilmore. Maryknoll, NY: Orbis Books, 1993.

Bibliography

Aberle, M. von. "Über den Zweck des Johannesevangelium." *TQ* 42 (1861): 37–94.
Abrams, Stacey Y., John Sides, Michael Tesler, Lynn Vavreck, Jennifer A. Richeson, and Francis Fukuyama. "*E Pluribus Unum*? The Fight Over Identity Politics." *Foreign Affairs* 98 (2019): 160–63.
Aichele, George, Fred W. Burnett, Elizabeth A. Castelli, Robert M. Fowler, David Jobling, Stephen D. Moore, Gary A. Phillips, Tina Pippin, Regina M. Schwartz, and Wilhelm Wuellner. *The Postmodern Bible*. New Haven: Yale University Press, 1995.
Alkier, Stefan. "Intertextuality and the Semiotics of Biblical Texts." Pages 3–22 in *Reading the Bible Intertextually*. Edited by Richard B. Hays, Stefan Alkier, Leroy A. Huizenga. Waco, TX: Baylor University Press, 2009.
Allison, Dale C. "The Old Testament in the New Testament." Pages 479–502 in *The New Cambridge History of the Bible: From the Beginnings to 600*. Edited by James Carleton Paget and Joachim Schaper. Cambridge: Cambridge University Press, 2013.
Alter, Robert. *The Art of Biblical Narrative*. New York: Basic Books, 1981.
Anderson, Paul N. "Why This Study Is Needed, and Why It Is Needed Now." Pages 13–70 in *John, Jesus, and History, Volume 1: Critical Appraisals of Critical Views*. Edited by Paul N. Anderson, Felix Just, and Tom Thatcher. SBLSymS 44. Atlanta: SBL Press, 2007.
Argyle, A. W. "Philo and the Fourth Gospel." *ExpTim* 63 (1952): 385–86.
Aristotle. *On Rhetoric: A Theory of Civic Discourse*. Translated by George A. Kennedy. Oxford: Oxford University Press. 1991.
Attridge, Harold W. "The Cubist Principle in Johannine Imagery: John and the Reading of Images in Contemporary Platonism." Pages 47–60 in *Imagery in the Gospel of John: Terms, Forms, Themes, and Theology of Johannine Figurative Language*. Edited by Jörg Frey, Jan G. van der Watt and Ruben Zimmermann. WUNT 200. Tübingen: Mohr Siebeck, 2006.

———. "The Gospel of John and the Dead Sea Scrolls." Pages 107–26 in *Text, Thought, and Practice in Qumran and Early Christianity: Proceedings of the Ninth International Symposium of the Orion Center for the Study of the Dead Sea Scrolls and Associated Literature*. Edited by Ruth Clements and Daniel R. Schwartz. STDJ 84. Leiden: Brill, 2009.

Austin, M. M. "Hellenistic Kings, War, and Economy." *The Classical Quarterly* 36 (1986): 450–66.

Baker-Fletcher, Karen. *Dancing with God: The Trinity from a Womanist Perspective*. St. Louis: Chalice, 2006.

Bakhtin, Mikhail. *Problems of Dostoevsky's Poetics*. Edited and translated by Caryl C. Emerson. Introduction by Wayne C. Booth. THL 8. Minneapolis: University of Minnesota Press, 1984.

Barker, James W. *John's Use of Matthew*. Emerging Scholars. Minnesota: Fortress, 2015.

Barnard, Ian. *Queer Race: Cultural Interventions in the Racial Politics of Queer Theory*. Gender, Sexuality, and Culture. New York: Lang, 2004.

Baron, Lori. "The Shema in John's Gospel and Jewish Restoration Eschatology." Pages 165–73 in *John and Judaism: A Contested Relationship in Context*. Edited by R. Alan Culpepper and Paul N. Anderson. RBS 87. Atlanta: SBL Press, 2017.

Barrett, C. K. *The Gospel According to St. John: An Introduction with Commentary and Notes on the Greek Text*. 2nd ed. Philadelphia: Westminster, 1978.

———. *The New Testament Background: Selected Documents*. New York: Harper & Row, 1961.

———. "The Old Testament in the Fourth Gospel." *JTS* 48 (1947): 155–69.

Barthes, Roland. "L'Effet de réel." *Communications* 11 (1968): 84–89.

———. *The Semiotic Challenge*. Translated by Richard Miller. New York: Hill and Wang, 1988.

———. *S/Z: An Essay*. Translated by Richard Miller. New York: Hill and Wang, 1974.

Barton, Stephen C. "Johannine Dualism and Contemporary Pluralism." Pages 3–19 in *The Gospel of John and Christian Theology*. Edited by Richard Bauckham and Carl Mosser. Grand Rapids: Eerdmans, 2008.

Bauckham, Richard. "The Gospel of John and the Synoptic Problem." Pages 657–88 in *New Studies in the Synoptic Problem: Oxford Conference, April 2008. Essays in Honour of Christopher M. Tuckett*. Edited by Paul Foster, Andrew Gregory, John S. Kloppenborg, and Joseph Verheyden. BETL 239. Leuven: Peeters, 2011.

———. "John for Readers of Mark." Pages 147–71 in *The Gospels for All Christians: Rethinking the Gospel Audiences*. Edited by Richard Bauckham. Grand Rapids: Eerdmans, 1998.

Bauckham, Richard, ed. *The Gospels for All Christians: Rethinking the Gospel Audiences*. Grand Rapids: Eerdmans, 1998.

Beardslee, William A. "Poststructuralist Criticism." Pages 253–67 in *To Each Its Own Meaning: An Introduction to Biblical Criticisms and Their Applications*. Rev. ed. Edited by Steven L. McKenzie and Stephen R. Haynes. Louisville: Westminster John Knox, 1999.

Becker, Eve-Marie, Helen K. Bond, and Catrin H. Williams, eds. *John's Transformation of Mark*. London: Bloomsbury/T&T Clark, 2020.

Beasley-Murray, G. R. *John*. 2d ed. WBC 36. Nashville: Thomas Nelson, 1999.

Beck, David R. "'Whom Jesus Loved': Anonymity and Identity, Belief and Witness in the Fourth Gospel." Pages 221–39 in *Characters and Characterization in the Gospel of John*. Edited by Christopher W. Skinner. LNTS 461. London: Bloomsbury/T & T Clark, 2013.

Bennema, Cornelis. *Encountering Jesus: Character Studies in the Gospel of John*. 2nd ed. Minneapolis: Fortress, 2009.

Beutler, Johannes and Robert Fortna, eds. *The Shepherd Discourse of John 10 and Its Context*. SNTSMS 67. Cambridge: Cambridge University Press, 1991.

Bieringer, Reimund. "Mary of Magdala and Jesus of Nazareth: A Special Relationship in the Light of John 20:17." *PIBA* 30 (2007): 1–14.

Black, C. Clifton and Duane F. Watson, eds. *Words Well Spoken: George Kennedy's Rhetoric of the New Testament*. SRR 8. Waco, TX: Baylor University Press, 2008.

Blass, Friedrich, Albert Debrunner, and Robert W. Funk. *A Greek Grammar of the New Testament and Other Early Christian Literature*. Chicago: University of Chicago Press, 1961.

Boismard, Marie-Emile. *Moïse ou Jésus. Essai de christologie johannique*. BETL 84. Leuven: Leuven University Press/Peeters, 1988.

———. *St. John's Prologue*. Translated by Carisbrooke Dominicans. London: Blackfriars Publications, 1957.

Bond, Helen K. "Gospel of John." Pages 165–85 in *From Paul to Josephus: Literary Receptions of Jesus in the First Century CE*. Edited by Helen K. Bond. Vol. 1 of *The Reception of Jesus in the First Three Centuries*. Edited by Chris Keith, Helen K. Bond, Christine Jacobi, and Jens Schröter. London: Bloomsbury Academic, 2019.

Booth, Wayne. *The Rhetoric of Fiction*. 2nd ed. Chicago: University of Chicago Press, 1983.

Borgen, Peder. *Bread from Heaven: An Exegetical Study of the Concept of Manna in the Gospel of John and the Writings of Philo*. NovTSup 10. Leiden: Brill, 1965.

———. "God's Agent in the Fourth Gospel." Pages 137–48 in *Religions in Antiquity: Essays in Memory of Erwin Ramsdell Goodenough*. Edited by Jacob Neusner. SHR 14. Leiden: Brill, 1968.

———. "Logos Was the True Light: Contributions to the Interpretation of the Prologue of John." *NovT* 14 (1972): 115–30.

———. "Observations on the Targumic Character of the Prologue of John." *NTS* 16 (1970): 288–95.

Bosworth, Brian. "Augustus, *Res Gestae*, and Hellenistic Theories of Apotheosis." *JRS* 89 (1999): 1–18.

Bowen, Clayton R. "Notes on the Fourth Gospel." *JBL* 43 (1924): 22–27.

Bowman, John. *Samaritan Documents Relating to Their History, Religion & Life*. POTTS 2. Pittsburgh, PA: Pickwick, 1977.

Boyarin, Daniel. "The Gospel of the *Memra*: Jewish Binitarianism and the Prologue to John," *HTR* 94 (2001): 243–84.

Brant, Jo-Ann A. *Dialogue and Drama: Elements of Greek Tragedy in the Fourth Gospel*. Peabody, MA: Hendrickson, 2004.

———. "The Fourth Gospel as Narrative and Drama." Pages 186–202 in *The Oxford Handbook of Johannine Studies*. Edited by Judith M. Lieu and Martinus C. de Boer. Oxford: Oxford University Press, 2018.

———. *John*. PCNT. Grand Rapids: Baker Academic, 2011.

Bratcher, Robert G. "What Does 'Glory' Mean in Relation to Jesus? Translating *doxa* and *doxado* in John," *BT* 42 (1991): 401–8.

Brickle, Jeffrey E. "The Memory of the Beloved Disciple: A Poetics of Johannine Memory." Pages 187–208 in *Memory and Identity in Ancient Judaism and Early Christianity: A Conversation with Barry Schwartz*. Edited by Tom Thatcher. SemeiaSt 78. Atlanta: SBL Press, 2014.

Brock, Anne Graham. *Mary Magdalene, the First Apostle: The Struggle for Authority*. HTS 51. Cambridge, MA: Harvard University Press, 2003.

Brown, Raymond E. *The Community of the Beloved Disciple*. New York: Paulist Press, 1979.

———. *The Gospel According to John*. 2 vols. AB 29–29a. Garden City, NY: Doubleday, 1966–70.

———. "The Qumran Scrolls and the Johannine Gospel and Epistles." Pages 183–207 in *The Scrolls and the New Testament*. Edited by Krister Stendahl. New York: Harper & Brothers, 1957.

———. "The Resurrection in John 20: A Series of Diverse Reactions." *Worship* 64 (1990): 194–206.

———. "Roles of Women in the Fourth Gospel." *TS* 36 (1975): 688–99.

Brown, Sherri. *Gift upon Gift: Covenant through Word in the Gospel of John*. PTMS 144. Eugene, OR: Pickwick, 2010.

Brown, Sherri, and Francis J. Moloney. *Interpreting the Gospel and Letters of John: An Introduction*. Grand Rapids: Eerdmans, 2017.

Brown, Sherri, and Christopher W. Skinner, eds. *Johannine Ethics: The Moral World of the Gospel and Epistles of John*. Minneapolis: Fortress, 2017.

Brunson, Andrew C. *Psalm 118 in the Gospel of John: An Intertextual Study on the New Exodus Pattern in the Theology of John*. WUNT 2/158. Tübingen: Mohr Siebeck, 2003.

Bultmann, Rudolf. *The Gospel of John: A Commentary*. Translated by G. R. Beasley-Murray, R. W. N. Hoare, and J. K. Riches. Philadelphia: Westminster Press, 1971. First publication in German, 1941.

———. *Theology of the New Testament*. Translated by Kendrick Grobel. Waco, TX: Baylor University Press, 2007. First published in German in 194–1953.

Burge, Gary M. *The Anointed Community: The Holy Spirit in the Johannine Tradition*. Grand Rapids: Eerdmans, 1987.

Burke, Kenneth. *A Rhetoric of Motives*. Berkeley: University of California Press, 1969.

Burke, Sean. *Queering the Ethiopian Eunuch: Strategies of Ambiguity in Acts 8*. Minneapolis: Augsburg Fortress, 2013.

Burney, C. F. *The Aramaic Origin of the Fourth Gospel*. Oxford: Clarendon, 1922.

Busse, Ulrich. "Open Questions on John 10." Pages 6–17 in *The Shepherd Discourse of John 10 and Its Context: Studies by Members of the Johannine Writings Seminar*. Edited by Johannes Beutler and Robert T. Fortna. SNTSMS 67. Cambridge: Cambridge University Press, 1991.

Butler, Judith. *Bodies that Matter: On the Discursive Limits of "Sex."* New York: Routledge, 1993.

Byers, Andrew J. *Ecclesiology and Theosis in the Gospel of John*. SNTSMS 166. Cambridge: Cambridge University Press, 2017.

Cachia, Nicholas. *The Image of the Good Shepherd as a Source for the Spirituality of the Ministerial Priesthood*. Rome: Editrice Pontifica Universita Gregoriana, 1997.

Cannon, Katie. *Black Womanist Ethics*. Atlanta: Scholars Press, 1988.

———. *Katie's Canon: Womanism and the Soul of the Black Community*. New York: Continuum, 1995.

Carson, D. A. *The Gospel According to John*. PNTC. Grand Rapids: Eerdmans, 1991.

Carter, Warren. "'The Blind, Lame, and Paralyzed' (John 5:3): John's Gospel, Disability Studies, and Postcolonial Perspectives." Pages 128–50 in *Disability Studies and Biblical Literature*. Edited by Candida R. Moss and Jeremy Schipper. New York: Palgrave MacMillan, 2011.

———. "Jesus the Good Shepherd: An Intertextual Approach to Ezekiel 34 and John 10," in *Biblical Interpretations in Early Christian Gospels. Vol. 4: The Gospel of John*. Edited by Thomas R. Hatina. LNTS. New York: Bloomsbury, forthcoming.

———. *John and Empire: Initial Explorations*. New York: T&T Clark, 2008.

———. *John: Storyteller, Interpreter, Evangelist*. Grand Rapids: Baker Academic, 2006.

Casselli, S. J. "Jesus as Eschatological Torah." *TJ* 18 (1997): 15–41.

Castelli, Elizabeth A., et al., eds. *The Postmodern Bible: The Bible and Culture Collective*. New Haven: Yale University Press, 1995.

Charlesworth, James H. *The Beloved Disciple: Whose Witness Validates the Gospel of John?* Valley Forge, PA: Trinity Press International, 1995.

———. "A Critical Comparison of the Dualism in IQS III,13–IV,26 and the 'Dualism' Contained in the Fourth Gospel." *NTS* 15 (1969): 389–418.

———. "A Critical Comparison of the Dualism in 1QS 3:13–4:26 and the 'Dualism' Contained in the Gospel of John." Pages 76–106 in *John and the Dead Sea Scrolls*. Edited by James H. Charlesworth. New York: Crossroad, 1990.

Cheng, Patrick S. "Contributions from Queer Theory." Pages 154–59 in *The Oxford Handbook of Theology, Sexuality, and Gender*. Edited by Adrian Thatcher. Oxford: Oxford University Press, 2015.

Chennattu, Rekha, M. "Scripture." Pages 171–86 in *How John Works: Storytelling in the Fourth Gospel*. Edited by Douglas Estes and Ruth Sheridan. RBS 86. Atlanta: SBL Press, 2016.

Clark-Soles, Jaime. *Engaging the Word: The New Testament and the Christian Believer*. Louisville: Westminster John Knox, 2010.

———. "Mary Magdalene: Beginning at the End." Pages 626–40 in *Character Studies in the Fourth Gospel: Narrative Approaches to Seventy Figures in John*. Edited by Steven A. Hunt, D. Francois Tolmie, and Ruben Zimmermann. Grand Rapids: Eerdmans, 2016.

———. *Scripture Cannot Be Broken: The Social Function of the Use of Scripture in the Fourth Gospel*. Boston/Leiden: Brill, 2003.

Coloe, Mary L. *God Dwells with Us: Temple Symbolism in the Fourth Gospel*. Collegeville, MN: Liturgical Press, 2001.

Comte, Auguste. *System of Positive Polity*. 4 vols. Edited by Edward Spencer Beesly. Translated by John Henry Bridges, Frederic Harrison, Richard Congreve, and Henry Dix Hutton. London: Longmans, Green, and Co., 1875–77.

Condit, Celeste M. "The Functions of Epideictic: The Boston Massacre Orations as Exemplar." *CommQ* 33 (1985): 284–99.

Conway, Colleen. *Behold the Man: Jesus and Greco-Roman Masculinity*. Oxford: Oxford University Press, 2008.

———. *Men and Women in the Fourth Gospel: Gender and Johannine Characterization*. SBLDS 167. Atlanta: SBL Press, 1999.

Culpepper, R. Alan. *Anatomy of the Fourth Gospel: A Study in Literary Design*. Philadelphia: Fortress, 1983.

———. "The Creation Ethics of the Gospel of John." Pages 67–90 in *Johannine Ethics: The Moral World of the Gospel and Epistles of John*. Edited by Sherri Brown and Christopher W. Skinner. Minneapolis: Fortress, 2017.

———. "The Ethics of the Shepherd." Pages 139–62 in *Biblical Ethics and Application: Purview, Validity, and Relevance of Biblical Texts in Ethical Discourse*. Edited by Ruben Zimmermann and Stephan Joubert. WUNT 1/384. Tübingen: Mohr Siebeck, 2017.

———. *The Gospel and the Letters of John*. IBT. Nashville: Abingdon, 1998.

———. "The Pivot of John's Prologue." *NTS* 27 (1980): 1–31.

———. "The Prologue as Theological Prolegomenon to the Gospel of John." Pages 3–26 in *The Prologue of the Gospel of John*. Edited by Jan G. van der Watt, R. Alan Culpepper, and Udo Schnelle. WUNT 359. Tübingen: Mohr Siebeck, 2016.

Culpepper, R. Alan, and Paul N. Anderson, eds. *John and Judaism: A Contested Relationship in Context*. RBS 87. Atlanta: SBL Press, 2017.

Culy, Martin M. *Echoes of Friendship in the Gospel of John*. NTM 30. Sheffield: Sheffield Phoenix, 2010.

Daise, Michael. "Quotations with 'Remembrance' Formulae in the Fourth Gospel." Pages 75–91 in *Abiding Words: The Use of Scripture in the Gospel of John*. Edited by Alicia D. Myers and Bruce G. Schuchard. Atlanta: SBL Press, 2015.

Daly-Denton, Margaret. *David in the Fourth Gospel: The Johannine Reception of the Psalms*. AGJU 47. Leiden: Brill, 2000.

Danker, Frederick W., Walter Bauer, William F. Arndt, and F. Wilbur Gingrich. *Greek-English Lexicon of the New Testament and Other Early Christian Literature*. 3rd ed. Chicago: University of Chicago Press, 2000.

Davies, W. D. *Torah in the Messianic Age and/or the Age to Come*. JBLMS 7. Philadelphia: Society of Biblical Literature, 1952.

De La Torre, Miguel A., ed. *Faith and Resistance in the Age of Trump*. Maryknoll, NY: Orbis Books, 2017.

Deeley, Mary Katherine. "Ezekiel's Shepherd and John's Jesus: A Case Study in the Appropriation of Biblical Texts." Pages 252–64 in *Early Christian Interpretation of the Scriptures of Israel: Investigations and Proposals*. Edited by Craig A. Evans and James A. Sanders. JSNTSup 148. Sheffield: Sheffield Academic, 1997.

Demetrius. *On Style*. Translated by Doreen C. Innes. LCL. Cambridge, MA: Harvard University Press, 1999.

Derrenbacker, Robert A., Jr. "The 'External and Psychological Conditions under which the Synoptic Gospels were Written': Ancient Compositional Practices and the Synoptic Problem." Pages 435–57 in *New Studies in the Synoptic Problem: Oxford Conference, April 2008. Essays in Honour of Christopher M. Tuckett*. Edited by Paul Foster, Andrew Gregory, John S. Kloppenborg, and Joseph Verheyden, BETL 239. Leuven: Peeters, 2011.

Derrida, Jacques. *A Derrida Reader: Between the Blinds*. Edited by Peggy Kamuf. New York: Columbia University Press, 1991.

Dewey, Kim E. "*Paroimiai* in the Gospel of John." *Sem* 17 (1980): 81–99.

Dio Chrysostom. *Discourses 12–30*. Translated by J. W. Cohoon. LCL. Cambridge, MA: Harvard University Press, 1939.

Dodd, Charles H. "The Background of the Fourth Gospel." *BJRL* 19 (1935): 329–43.

———. *The Interpretation of the Fourth Gospel*. Cambridge: Cambridge University Press, 1960.

———. *New Testament Studies*. Manchester: Manchester University Press, 1967.

Downing, F. Gerald. "Writers' Use or Abuse of Written Sources." Pages 523–48 in *New Studies in the Synoptic Problem: Oxford Conference, April 2008. Essays in Honour of Christopher M. Tuckett*. Edited by Paul Foster, Andrew Gregory, John S. Kloppenborg, and Joseph Verheyden. BETL 239. Leuven: Peeters, 2011.

Du Rand, J. A. "A Syntactical and Narratological Reading of John 10 in Coherence with Chapter 9." Pages 94–115 in *The Shepherd Discourse of John 10 and its Context: Studies by Members of the Johannine Writings Seminar*. Edited by Johannes Beutler and Robert T. Fortna. SNTSMS 67. Cambridge: Cambridge University Press, 1991.

Eco, Umberto. *A Theory of Semiotics, Advances in Semiotics*. Bloomington, IN: Indiana University Press, 1979.

Edwards, Ruth B. "ΧΑΡΙΝ ΑΝΤΙ ΧΑΡΙΤΟΣ (John 1.16): Grace and Law in the Johannine Prologue." *JSNT* 10 (1988): 3–15.

Engels, Jeremy. *The Art of Gratitude*. Albany: SUNY Press, 2018.

Enz, Jacob J. "The Book of Exodus as a Literary Type for the Gospel of John." *JBL* 76 (1957): 208–15.

Epp, Eldon Jay. "Wisdom, Torah, Word: The Johannine Prologue and the Purpose of the Fourth Gospel." Pages 128–46 in *Current Issues in Biblical and Patristic Interpretation: Studies in Honor of Merrill C. Tenney Presented by his Former Students*. Edited by Gerald F. Hawthorne. Grand Rapids: Eerdmans, 1975.

Estes, Douglas. "Time." Pages 41–57 in *How John Works: Storytelling in the Fourth Gospel*. Edited by Douglas Estes and Ruth Sheridan. RBS 86. Atlanta, SBL Press, 2016.

Estes, Douglas, and Ruth Sheridan, eds. *How John Works: Storytelling in the Fourth Gospel*. RBS 86. Atlanta: SBL Press, 2016.

Fanon, Frantz. *The Wretched of the Earth*. Translated by Constance Farrington. New York: Grove Press, 1963.

Fish, Stanley E. *Is There a Text in This Class? The Authority of Interpretive Communities*. Cambridge, MA: Harvard University Press, 1980.

Foley, John Miles. *Immanent Art: From Structure to Meaning in Traditional Oral Epic*. Bloomington, IN: Indiana University Press, 1991.

Foucault, Michel. *The Foucault Reader*. Edited by Paul Rabinow. New York: Pantheon Books, 1984.

———. *The History of Sexuality: An Introduction*. Translated by Robert Hurley. New York: Vintage Books, 1978.

Fredrickson, Paula and Adele Reinhartz, eds. *Jesus, Judaism, and Christian Anti-Judaism: Reading the New Testament after the Holocaust*. Louisville: Westminster John Knox, 2002.

Freed, Edwin D. *Old Testament Quotations in the Gospel of John*. NovTSup 11. Leiden: Brill, 1965.

Freeman, Jennifer Awes. "The Good Shepherd and the Enthroned Ruler: A Reconsideration of Imperial Iconography in the Early Church." Pages 159–95 in *The Art of Empire: Christian Art in Its Imperial Context*. Edited by L. M. Jefferson and R. Jensen. Minneapolis: Fortress, 2015.

Frey, Jörg. "Johannine Dualism: Reflections on Its Background and Function." Pages 101–67 in *The Glory of the Crucified One: Christology and Theology in the Gospel of John*. Translated by Wayne Coppins and Christoph Heilig. Baylor-Mohr Siebeck Studies in Early Christianity 6. Waco, TX: Baylor University Press, 2018.

Frier, Bruce. "Roman Demography." Pages 85–109 in *Life, Death, and Entertainment in the Roman Empire*. Edited by David Potter and David Mattingly. Ann Arbor, MI: University of Michigan Press, 1999.

Friesen, Steven J. "Poverty in Pauline Studies: Beyond the So-called New Consensus." *JSNT* 26 (2004): 323–61.

Frye, K. Evangeline. "The Intersectional Significance of Voice and Testimony: Suggestions for a 21st Century Womanist Reclamation of Mary Magdalene." *JITC* 41 (2015): 19–38.

Gage, John T. "Introduction." Pages 1–7 in *The Promise of Reason: Studies in the New Rhetoric*. Edited by John T. Gage. Carbondale, IL: Southern Illinois University Press, 2011.

Garnsey, Peter. *Food and Society in Classical Antiquity*. Cambridge: Cambridge University Press, 1999.

Genette, Gérard. *Narrative Discourse: An Essay in Method*. Translated by Jane E. Lewin. Ithaca, NY: Cornell University Press, 1980.

———. *Paratexts: Thresholds of Interpretation*. Cambridge: Cambridge University Press, 1997.

Giblin, Charles. "Confrontations in John 18, 1–27." *Bib* 65 (1984): 210–31.

———. "Two Complementary Literary Structures in John 1:1–18." *JBL* 104 (1985): 87–103.

Glasson, T. Francis. *Moses in the Fourth Gospel*. Naperville, IL: Allenson, 1963.

Gleason, Maud W. *Making Men: Sophists and Self-Presentation in Ancient Rome*. Princeton: Princeton University Press, 2008.

Glenn, Cheryl. *Rhetoric Retold: Regendering the Tradition from Antiquity through the Renaissance*. Carbondale, IL: Southern Illinois University Press, 1997.

Goldhill, Simon. "What is Ekphrasis for?" *CP* 102 (2007): 1–19.

Good, Deirdre. *Jesus the Meek King*. Harrisburg, PA: Trinity Press International, 1999.

Goodenough, Erwin R. *An Introduction to Philo Judaeus*. 2nd ed. Oxford: Basil Blackwell, 1962.

———. "The Political Philosophy of Hellenistic Kingship." *YCR* 1 (1928): 55–102.

Gooder, Paula. *Searching for Meaning: An Introduction to Interpreting the New Testament*. Louisville: SPCK, 2009.

Gorman, Michael J. *Abide and Go: Missional Theosis in the Gospel of John*. Didsbury Lecture Series. Eugene, OR: Cascade, 2018.

———. *Elements of Biblical Exegesis: A Basic Guide for Students and Ministers*. Revised and expanded. Peabody, MA: Hendrickson, 2009.

Graff, Richard and Wendy Winn. "Kenneth Burke's 'Identification' and Chaïm Perelman and Lucie Olbrechts-Tyteca's 'Communion': A Case of Convergent Evolution?" Pages 103–33 in *The Promise of Reason: Studies in the New Rhetoric*. Edited by John T. Gage. Carbondale, IL: Southern Illinois University Press, 2011.

Grant, Jacquelyn. *White Women's Christ, Black Women's Jesus: Feminist Christology and Womanist Response*. Atlanta: Scholars Press, 1989.

Green, Joel B. "Discourse Analysis and New Testament Interpretation." Pages 218–39 in *Hearing the New Testament: Strategies for Interpretation*. 2nd ed. Grand Rapids: Eerdmans, 2010.

Green, Joel B., ed. *Hearing the New Testament: Strategies for Interpretation*. 2nd ed. Grand Rapids: Eerdmans, 2010.

Green, Melanie C. and Timothy C. Brock, "The Role of Transportation in the Persuasiveness of Public Narratives." *JPSP* 79 (2000): 701–21.

Gunn, David M. "Narrative Criticism." Pages 201–29 in *To Each Its Own Meaning: An Introduction to Biblical Criticisms and Their Applications*. Rev. ed. Edited by Steven L. McKenzie and Stephen R. Haynes. Louisville: Westminster John Knox, 1999.

Gushee, David P. "Why Trump, and What Next? An (Ex-) Evangelical Response." Pages 99–106 in *Faith and Resistance in the Age of Trump*. Edited by Miguel A. De La Torre. Maryknoll, NY: Orbis Books, 2017.

Haenchen, Ernst. *John*. 2 vols. Hermeneia. Philadelphia: Fortress, 1984.

Hagner, Donald A. "The Vision of God in Philo and John: A Comparative Study." *JETS* 14 (1971): 81–93.

Hallerman, Tamar and Greg Bluestein, "Abrams to Deliver Dems' State of the Union Response." *Atlanta Journal-Constitution*. Accessed July 29, 2019. https://www.ajc.com/news/state--regional-govt--politics/abrams-deliver-dems-state-the-union-response/2Oo3TTBaQB8 OMaRNhBoc9L/.

Halperin, David M. "The Normalization of Queer Theory." *Journal of Homosexuality* 45 (2003): 339–43.

Hanson, Ann. "The Roman Family." Pages 19–66 in *Life, Death, and Entertainment in the Roman Empire*. Edited by David Potter and David Mattingly. Ann Arbor, MI: University of Michigan Press, 1999.

Hanson, Anthony. "John I. 14–18 and Exodus XXXIV." *NTS* 23 (1976): 90–101.

Harris, Elizabeth. *Prologue and Gospel: The Theology of the Fourth Gospel*. JSNTSup 107. Sheffield: Sheffield Academic, 1994.

Harris, J. Rendel. *The Origin of the Prologue to St. John's Gospel*. Cambridge: Cambridge University Press, 1917.

———. "The Origin of the Prologue to St. John's Gospel." *The Expositor*. 8th ser. 12 (1916): 147–60, 161–70, 314–20, 388–400, 415–26.

Harrison, Everett F. "A Study of John 1:14." Pages 23–36 in *Unity and Diversity in New Testament Theology: Essays in Honor of George E. Ladd*. Edited by Robert A. Guelich. Grand Rapids: Eerdmans, 1978.

Hartsock, Chad. *Sight and Blindness in Luke-Acts: The Use of Physical Features in Characterization*. BibS 94. Leiden: Brill, 2008.

Hartvigsen, Kirsten Marie. *Prepare the Way of the Lord: Towards a Cognitive Poetic Analysis of Audience Involvement with Characters and Events in the Markan World*. BZNW 180. Berlin: De Gruyter, 2012.

Harvey, W. J. *Character and the Novel*. Ithaca: Cornell University Press, 1965.

Hays, Richard B. *The Conversion of Imagination: Paul as Interpreter of Scripture*. Grand Rapids: Eerdmans, 2005.

———. *Echoes of Scriptures in the Gospels*. Waco, TX: Baylor University Press, 2016.

———. *Echoes of Scripture in the Letters of Paul*. New Haven: Yale University Press, 1989.

———. "Forward to the English Edition." Pages xi–xv in *Reading the Bible Intertextually*. Edited by Richard B. Hays, Stefan Alkier, Leroy A. Huizenga. Waco, TX: Baylor University Press, 2009.

Hearon, Holly E. "The Implications of Orality for Studies of the Biblical Text." Pages 3–20 in *Performing the Gospel: Orality, Memory, and Mark: Essays Dedicated to Werner Kelber*. Edited by Richard A. Horsley, Jonathan A. Draper, John Miles Foley. Minneapolis: Fortress, 2006.

Heath, Jane M. F., "Absent Presences of Paul and Christ: *Enargeia* in 1 Thessalonians 1–3." *JSNT* 32 (2009): 3–38.

Hengel, Martin. *Judaism and Hellenism*. 2 vols. Translated by John Bowden. Philadelphia: Fortress, 1974.

Herford, R. Travers. *Christianity in Talmud and Midrash*. Clifton, NJ: Reference Book Publishers, 1966.

Hergenröder, Clemens. *Wir schauten seine Herrlichkeit: Das johanneische Sprechen vom Sehen im Horizont von Selbsterschliessung Jesu und Antwort des Menschen*. FB80. Würzburg: Echter Verlag, 1996.

Hooker, Morna. *Beginnings: Keys That Open the Gospels*. Harrisburg, PA: Trinity Press International, 1997.

———. "Johannine Prologue and the Messianic Secret." *NTS* 21 (1974): 40–58.

———. "John the Baptist and the Johannine Prologue." *NTS* 16 (1970): 354–58.

Hornsby, Teresa J. and Ken Stone, eds. *Bible Trouble: Queer Reading at the Boundaries of Biblical Scholarship.* Atlanta: SBL Press, 2011.

Horrell, David G., Bradley Arnold, and Travis B. Williams. "Visuality, Vivid Description, and the Message of 1 Peter: The Significance of the Roaring Lion (1 Peter 5:8)." *JBL* 132 (2013): 697–716.

Horsley, Richard A. *Hearing the Whole Story: The Politics of Plot in Mark's Gospel.* Louisville: Westminster John Knox, 2001.

Hoskyns, Edwyn Clement. *The Fourth Gospel.* 2nd rev. ed. Edited by Francis Noel Davey London: Faber & Faber, 1947.

Hull, Gloria, Patricia Bell Scott, and Barbara Smith, eds. *All the Women are White. All the Blacks Are Men, But Some of Us Are Brave.* Old Westbury, NY: Feminist Press, 1982.

Hunt, Steven A., D. Francois Tolmie, and Ruben Zimmermann. "An Introduction to Character and Characterization in John and Related New Testament Literature." Pages 1–33 in *Character Studies in the Fourth Gospel: Narrative Approaches to Seventy Figures in John.* Edited by Steven A. Hunt, D. Francois Tolmie, and Ruben Zimmermann. Grand Rapids: Eerdmans, 2016.

Hylen, Susan E. "The Disciples: The 'Now' and 'Not Yet' of Belief in Jesus." Pages 214–27 in *Character Studies in the Fourth Gospel: Narrative Approaches to Seventy Figures in John.* Edited by Steven A. Hunt, D. Francois Tolmie, and Ruben Zimmermann. Grand Rapids: Eerdmans, 2016.

———. *Imperfect Believers: Ambiguous Characters in the Gospel of John.* Louisville: Westminster John Knox, 2009.

———. "The Shepherd's Risk: Thinking Metaphorically with John's Gospel." *BibInt* 24 (2016): 382–99.

Irigoin, Jean. "La composition rythmique du prologue de Jean (I, 1–18)." *RB* 98 (1991): 5–50.

Isaacs, Marie E. *The Concept of Spirit: A Study of Pneuma in Hellenistic Judaism and its Bearing on the New Testament.* HeyM 1. London: Heythrop College, 1976.

Iser, Wolfgang. *The Act of Reading: A Theory of Aesthetic Response.* Baltimore: John Hopkins University Press, 1978.

———. *The Implied Reader: Patterns of Communication in Prose Fiction from Bunyan to Beckett.* Baltimore: Johns Hopkins University Press, 1978.

Jobling, David and Stephen D. Moore, eds. "Poststructuralism as Exegesis." *Sem* 54 (1991): 1–255.

Jónsson, Sigurvin Lárus. "James among the Classicists: Reading the Letter of James in Light of Ancient Literary Criticism." PhD diss., Aarhus University, 2019.

Junior, Nyasha. *An Introduction to Womanist Biblical Interpretation.* Louisville: Westminster John Knox, 2015.

Käsemann, Ernst. "The Structure and Purpose of the Prologue to John's Gospel." Pages 138–67 in *New Testament Questions of Today.* London: SCM, 1969.

Keener, Craig S. "The Function of Johannine Pneumatology in the Context of Late First-Century Judaism." PhD diss., Duke University, 1991.

———. *The Gospel of John: A Commentary.* 2 vols. Peabody, MA: Hendrickson, 2003.

Keith, Chris. "The Competitive Textualization of the Jesus Tradition in John 20:30–31 and 21:24–25." *CBQ* (2016): 321–37.

Kelber, Werner. "The Birth of a Beginning: John 1:1–18." *Sem* 52 (1990): 121–44.

Kelley, Shawn. *Racializing Jesus: Race, Ideology and the Formation of Modern Biblical Scholarship*. New York: Routledge, 2002.

Kennedy, George A. *Progymnasmata: Greek Textbooks of Prose Composition and Rhetoric*. WGRW 10. Atlanta: Society of Biblical Literature, 2003.

Kermode, Frank. "St John as Poet." *JSNT* 9 (1986): 3–16.

King, Karen. "Canonization and Marginalization of Mary of Magdala." *Concilium* 3 (1998): 29–36.

Kirk-Duggan, Cheryl. *Exorcising Evil: Theodicy and African American Spirituals—A Womanist Perspective*. Maryknoll, NY: Orbis, 1993.

Klink, Edward W. "Audience." Pages 241–57 in *How John Works: Storytelling in the Fourth Gospel*. Edited by Douglas Estes and Ruth Sheridan. RBS 86. Atlanta: SBL Press, 2016.

Koester, Craig R. "Comedy, Humor, and the Gospel of John." Pages 123–41 in *Word, Theology, and Community in John*. Edited by John Painter, R. Alan Culpepper, and Fernando F. Segovia. St. Louis: Chalice, 2002.

———. "Hearing, Seeing, and Believing in the Gospel of John." *Bib* 70 (1989): 327–48.

———. *Symbolism in the Fourth Gospel: Meaning, Mystery, Community*. 2nd ed. Minneapolis: Fortress, 2003.

Kok, Kobus, "As the Father Has Sent Me, I Send You: Towards a Missional-Incarnational Ethos in John 4." Pages 168–93 in *Moral Language in the New Testament: The Interrelatedness of Language and Ethics in Early Christian Writings*. Edited by Ruben Zimmermann, Jan G. van der Watt, with Susanne Luther. WUNT 2/296. Tübingen: Mohr Siebeck, 2010.

Komter, Aafke Elisabeth. "Gratitude and Gift Exchange." Pages 195–212 in *The Psychology of Gratitude*. Edited by Robert A. Emmons and Michael E. McCullough. Oxford: Oxford University Press, 2004.

Konstan, David. "The Emotion in Aristotle *Rhetoric* 2.7: Gratitude, not Kindness." Pages 239–50 in *Influences on Peripatetic Rhetoric: Essays in Honor of William W. Fortenbaugh*. Edited by David C. Mirhady Leiden: Brill, 2007.

Kraemer, Ross Shepard. *Her Share of the Blessings: Women's Religions among Pagans, Jews and Christians in the Greco-Roman World*. Oxford: Oxford University Press, 1992.

Kraske, Steve. "Here's What Hillary Clinton Said Thursday in Kansas City." *Kansas City Star*, September 8, 2016. https://www.kansascity.com/news/local/news-columns-blogs/the-buzz/article100787652.html.

Kristeva, Julia. *Revolution in Poetic Language*. EPS. New York: Columbia University Press, 1984.

———. "Word, Dialogue, and Novel." Pages 34–61 in *The Kristeva Reader*. Edited by Toril Moi. Translated by Léon S. Roudiez and Seán Hand. New York: Columbia University Press, 1986.

Kysar, Robert. "The Contributions of the Prologue of the Gospel of John to New Testament Christology and their Historical Setting," *CurTM* 5 (1978): 348–64.

———. "Johannine Metaphor—Meaning and Function: A Literary Case Study of John 10:1–18." *Sem* 53 (1991): 81–111.

———. *John: The Maverick Gospel*. 3rd ed. Louisville: Westminster John Knox, 2007.

Labahn, Michael. "Simon Peter: An Ambiguous Character and His Narrative Career." Pages 151–67 in *Character Studies in the Fourth Gospel: Narrative Approaches to Seventy Figures in John*. Edited by Steven A. Hunt, D. Francois Tolmie, and Ruben Zimmermann. Grand Rapids: Eerdmans, 2016.

Lamb, Kate. "AirAsia Crash: Crew Lost Control of Plane after Apparent Misunderstanding." *Guardian*, December 1, 2015. https://www.theguardian.com/world/2015/dec/01/airasia-crew-actions-caused-jet-to-lose-control-say-crash-investigators.

Larsen, Kasper Bro. "The Recognition Scenes and Epistemological Reciprocity in the Fourth Gospel." Pages 341–56 in *The Gospel of John as Genre Mosaic*. Edited by Kasper Bro Larsen. SANt 3. Göttingen: Vandenhoeck & Ruprecht, 2015.

———. *Recognizing the Stranger: Recognition Scenes in the Gospel of John*. BibS 93. Leiden: Brill, 2008.

Lausberg, Hans. *Handbook of Literary Rhetoric: A Foundation for Literary Study*. Edited by D. E. Horton and R. D. Anderson. Translated by M. T. Bliss, A. Jansen, and D. E. Horton. Leiden: Brill, 2008.

LeDonne, Anthony. "Memory, Commemoration and History in John 2:19–22." Pages 133–54 in *The Fourth Gospel in First-Century Media Culture*. Edited by Anthony LeDonne and Tom Thatcher. LNTS 426. London: Bloomsbury/T&T Clark, 2011.

Lee, Dorothy A. *Flesh and Glory: Symbol, Gender and Theology in the Gospel of John*. New York: Crossroad, 2002.

———. "Imagery." Pages 151–70 in *How John Works: Storytelling in the Fourth Gospel*. Edited by Douglas Estes and Ruth Sheridan. RBS 86. Atlanta: SBL Press, 2016.

———. *The Symbolic Narratives of the Fourth Gospel: The Relationship of Form and Meaning*. JSNTSup 95. Sheffield: Sheffield Academic, 1994.

———. "Symbolism & 'Signs' in the Fourth Gospel." Pages 259–73 in *The Oxford Handbook of Johannine Studies*. Edited by Judith M. Lieu and Martinus C. de Boer. Oxford: Oxford University Press, 2018.

Lenski, Gerhard. *Power and Privilege: A Theory of Social Stratification*. Chapel Hill, NC: University of North Carolina Press, 1984.

Lewis, Karoline M. *Rereading the "Shepherd Discourse": Restoring the Integrity of John 9:39–10:21*. StBibLit 113. New York: Peter Lang, 2008.

Liddell, Henry George, Robert Scott, and Henry Stuart Jones. *A Greek-English Lexicon*. 9th ed. with revised supplement. Oxford: Clarendon, 1996.

Lightfoot, R. H. *St. John's Gospel: A Commentary*. Edited by C. F. Evans. Rev. ed. Oxford: Clarendon, 1983.

Lincoln, Andrew T. "The Beloved Disciple as Eyewitness and the Fourth Gospel as Witness." *JSNT* 85 (2002): 3–26.

———. *The Gospel according to Saint John*. BNTC 4. London: Continuum, 2005.

———. "John 21." Pages 209–22 in *From Paul to Josephus: Literary Receptions of Jesus in the First Century CE*. Edited by Helen K. Bond. Vol. 1 of *The Reception of*

Jesus in the First Three Centuries. Edited by Chris Keith, Helen K. Bond, Christine Jacobi, and Jens Schröter. London: Bloomsbury Academic, 2019.

Lindars, Barnabas. "The composition of John XX." *NTS* 7 (1960–61): 142–47.

Longenecker, Bruce. *Remember the Poor: Paul, Poverty, and the Greco-Roman World*. Grand Rapids: Eerdmans, 2010.

———. *Rhetoric at the Boundaries: The Art and Theology of New Testament Chain-Link Transitions*. Waco, TX: Baylor University Press, 2005.

Longenecker, Richard N. *The Christology of Early Jewish Christianity*. London: SCM, 1970.

Longinus, *On the Sublime*. Translated by W. H. Fyfe. LCL. Cambridge, MA: Harvard University Press, 1999.

Manning Jr., Gary T. *Echoes of a Prophet: The Use of Ezekiel in the Gospel of John and the Literature of the Second Temple Period*. JSNTSup 270. London: T&T Clark International, 2004.

Martyn, J. Louis. *The History and Theology of the Fourth Gospel*. 3rd ed. NTL. Louisville: Westminster John Knox, 2003.

Maxwell, Kathy Reiko. *Hearing Between the Lines: The Audience as Fellow-Workers in Luke-Acts and Its Literary Milieu*. LNTS 425. London: Bloomsbury/T&T Clark, 2010.

May, Eric. "The Logos in the Old Testament." *CBQ* 8 (1946): 438–47.

McClintock, Anne. *Imperial Leather: Race, Gender and Sexuality in the Colonial Context*. New York: Routledge, 1995.

McKenzie, Steven L., and Stephen R. Haynes, eds. *To Each Its Own Meaning: An Introduction to Biblical Criticisms and Their Applications*. Rev. ed. Louisville: Westminster John Knox, 1999.

McKnight, Edgar V. "Reader-Response Criticism." Pages 230–52 in *To Each Its Own Meaning: An Introduction to Biblical Criticisms and Their Applications*. Rev. ed. Edited by Steven L. McKenzie and Stephen R. Haynes. Louisville: Westminster John Knox, 1999.

McNamara, Martin. "*Logos* of the Fourth Gospel and *Memra* of the Palestinian Targum: Ex 12:42." *ExpTim* 79 (1968): 115–17

Meeks, Wayne A. *The Prophet-King: Moses Traditions and the Johannine Christology*. NovTSup 14. Leiden: Brill, 1967.

Metzger, Bruce M. *The Textual Commentary on the Greek New Testament: A Companion Volume to the United Bible Societies Greek New Testament*. 3rd ed. London: United Bible Society, 1971.

Miller, Ed L. "The Logos of Heraclitus: Updating the Report." *HTR* 74 (1981): 174–76.

Moles, John. "The Date and Purpose of the Fourth Kingship Oration of Dio Chrysostom." *ClAnt* 2 (1983): 251–78.

Moloney, Francis J. *Glory Not Dishonor: Reading John 13–21*. Minneapolis: Fortress, 1998.

———. *The Gospel of John*. SP 4. Collegeville, MN: Liturgical Press, 1998.

———. "John 1:18 'in the Bosom of' or 'Turned Towards' the Father." *ABR* 31 (1983): 63–71.

———. *Love in the Gospel of John: An Exegetical, Theological, and Literary Study*. Grand Rapids: Baker Academic, 2013.

———. "Review Article." *Pacifica* 22 (2009): 90–95.

———. *Signs and Shadows: Reading John 5–12*. Minneapolis: Fortress, 1996.

Moore, Anne. "Longer Ending of Mark." Pages 187–95 in *From Paul to Josephus: Literary Receptions of Jesus in the First Century CE*. Edited by Helen K. Bond. Vol. 1 of *The Reception of Jesus in the First Three Centuries*. Edited by Chris Keith, Helen K. Bond, Christine Jacobi, and Jens Schröter. London: Bloomsbury, 2019.

Moore, Stephen D. "Are There Impurities in the Living Water That the Johannine Jesus Dispenses? Deconstruction, Feminism, and the Samaritan Woman." *BibInt* 1 (1993): 207–27.

———. *Mark and Luke in Poststructuralist Perspectives: Jesus Begins to Write*. New Haven: Yale University Press, 1992.

Mowvley, Henry. "John 1.14–18 in the Light of Exodus 33.7–34.35." *ExpTim* 95 (1984): 135–37.

Muller, V. "The Prehistory of the 'Good Shepherd.'" *JNES* 3 (1944): 87–90.

Murray, Oswyn. "Philosophy and Monarchy in the Hellenistic World." Pages 13–28 in *Jewish Perspectives on Hellenistic Rulers*. Edited by T. Rajak, S. Pearce, J. Aitken, and J. Dines. Berkley: University of California Press, 2007.

———. "Philodemus on the Good King according to Homer." *JRS* 55 (1965): 161–82.

Muzzillo, Jeanne Smith. "Positive Effects of Ambiguity When Created by Rhetorical Devices: To Be or Not to Be." *ETC* 67 (2010): 452–68.

Myers, Alicia D. "Abiding Words: An Introduction to Perspectives on John's Use of Scripture." Pages 1–20 in *Abiding Words: The Use of Scripture in the Gospel of John*. Edited by Alicia D. Myers and Bruce G. Schuchard. RBS 81. Atlanta: SBL Press, 2015.

———. *Characterizing Jesus: A Rhetorical Analysis on the Fourth Gospel's Use of Scripture in its Presentation of Jesus*. LNTS 458. London: Bloomsbury/T&T Clark, 2012.

———. "Rhetoric." Pages 187–202 in *How John Works: Storytelling in the Fourth Gospel*. Edited by Douglas Estes and Ruth Sheridan. RBS 86. Atlanta: SBL Press, 2016.

Myers, Alicia D., and Bruce G. Schuchard, eds. *Abiding Words: The Use of Scripture in the Gospel of John*. RBS 81. Atlanta: SBL Press, 2015.

Nässelqvist, Dan. "Stylistic Levels in Hebrews 1.1–4 and John 1.1–18." *JSNT* 35 (2012): 31–53.

Neirynck, Frans. "John and the Synoptics." Pages 365–400 in *Evangelica: Gospel Studies—Etudes D'Evangile. Collected Essays*. Edited by F. van Segbroeck. BETL 60. Leuven: Leuven University Press, 1982.

———. "John and the Synoptics: The Empty Tomb Stories." *NTS* 30 (1984): 161–87.

———. "The Signs Source in the Fourth Gospel: A Critique of the Hypothesis." Pages 651–78 in *Evangelica II 1982–1991. Collected Essays*. Edited by F. van Segbroeck. BETL 99. Leuven: Leuven University Press, 1991.

Neumann, Nils. *Hören und Sehen: Die Rhetorik der Anschaulichkeit in den Gottesthron-Szenen der Johannesoffenbarung*. ABG 49. Leipzig: Evangelische Verlagsanstalt, 2015.

Neyrey, Jerome H. *The Gospel of John in Cultural and Rhetorical Perspective*. Grand Rapids: Eerdmans, 2009.

———. "The 'Noble Shepherd' in John 10: Cultural and Rhetorical Background." *JBL* 120 (2001): 267–91.

Nienkamp, Jean. "RhETHorICS." Pages 171–82 in *The Promise of Reason: Studies in the New Rhetoric*. Edited by John T. Gage. Carbondale, IL: Southern Illinois University Press, 2011.

Nygren, Anders. *Agape and Eros*. Translated by Philip S. Watson. London: SPCK, 1953.

O'Day, Gail R. "Gospel of John." Pages 517–31 in *Women's Bible Commentary: Twentieth Anniversary Edition*. 3rd ed. Revised and Updated. Edited by Carol A. Newsom, Sharon H. Ringe, and Jacqueline E. Lapsley. Louisville: Westminster John Knox, 2012.

———. "The Gospel of John," in *The New Interpreter's Bible*. Vol 9. Edited by Leander Keck. Nashville: Abingdon, 1995.

Osborn, Andrew. "The Word Became Flesh: An Exposition of John 1:1–18." *Int* 3 (1949): 42–49.

Painter, John. "Tradition, History and Interpretation in John 10." Pages 53–74 in *The Shepherd Discourse of John 10 and its Context: Studies by Members of the Johannine Writings Seminar*. Edited by Johannes Beutler and Robert T. Fortna. SNTSMS 67. Cambridge: Cambridge University Press, 1991.

Pancaro, Severino. *The Law in the Fourth Gospel*. NovTSup 42. Leiden: Brill, 1975.

Parsenios, George L. "Confounding Foes and Counseling Friends: *Parrēsia* in the Fourth Gospel and Greco-Roman Philosophy." Pages 251–72 in *The Prologue of John*. Edited by Jan G. van der Watt, R. Alan Culpepper, and Udo Schnelle. WUNT 1/359. Tübingen: Mohr Siebeck, 2016.

———. "Silent Spaces between Narrative and Drama: *Mimesis* and *Diegesis* in the Fourth Gospel." Pages 85–97 in *The Gospel of John as Genre Mosaic*. Edited by Kasper Bro Larsen. SANt 3. Göttingen: Vandenhoeck & Ruprecht, 2015.

Parsons, Mikeal C. "Reading a Beginning/Beginning a Reading: Tracing Literary Theory on Narrative Openings." *Sem* 52 (1990): 11–31.

Patte, Daniel. *The Religious Dimensions of Biblical Texts: Greimas's Structural Semiotics and Biblical Exegesis*. SemSt 19. Atlanta: Scholars Press, 1990.

Perelman, Chaim, and Lucie Olbrechts-Tyteca. *The New Rhetoric: A Treatise on Argumentation*. Translated by John Wilkinson and Purcell Weaver. South Bend, IN: University of Notre Dame Press, 1971.

Pernot, Laurent. *Epideictic Rhetoric: Questioning the Stakes of Ancient Praise*. Austin: University of Texas Press, 2015.

Peterson, Brian Neil. *John's Use of Ezekiel: Understanding the Unique Perspective of the Fourth Gospel*. Minneapolis: Fortress Press, 2015.

Phelan, James. *Narrative as Rhetoric: Technique, Audiences, Ethics, Ideology*. Columbus, OH: Ohio State University Press, 1996.

Phillips, Gary A., ed. "Poststructural Criticism and the Bible: Text/History/Discourse." *Sem* 51 (1990): 1–240.
Poplutz, Uta. "Paroimia und Parabolē. Gleichniskonzepte bei Johannes und Markus." Pages 103–20 in *Imagery in the Gospel of John: Terms, Forms, Themes, and Theology of Johannine Figurative Language*. Edited by Jörg Frey, Jan G van der Watt, and Ruben Zimmermann, WUNT 200. Tübingen: Mohr Siebeck, 2006.
Popp, Thomas. "Thomas: Question Marks and Exclamation Marks." Pages 504–29 in *Character Studies in the Fourth Gospel: Narrative Approaches to Seventy Figures in John*. Edited by Steven A. Hunt, D. Francois Tolmie, and Ruben Zimmermann. Grand Rapids: Eerdmans, 2016.
Powell, Mark Allan. "Narrative Criticism." Pages 239–55 in *Hearing the New Testament: Strategies for Interpretation*. 2nd ed. Edited by Joel B. Green. Grand Rapids: Eerdmans, 2010.
Pratt, Jonathan. "The Epideictic *Agōn* and Aristotle's Elusive Third Genre." *AJP* 133 (2012): 177–208.
Pryor, John. "Covenant and Community in John's Gospel." *RTR* 47 (1988): 44–51.
Quintilian. *The Orator's Education*. Translated by Donald A. Russell. 5 vols. LCL. Cambridge, MA: Harvard University Press, 2002.
Rabinowitz, Peter J. "Truth in Fiction: A Reexamination of Audiences." *CI* 4 (1977): 121–41.
"'Reclaiming My Time': Rep. Maxine Waters Interrupts Mnuchin's Roundabout Answer." *The Washington Post*. Accessed May 25, 2019. https://www.washingtonpost.com/video/ national/maxine-waters-reclaiming-my-time/2017/08/01/30fae7f4-76d4-11e7-8c17-533c52b2f014_video.html?utm_term=.e3a1233cbf57a.
Reinhartz, Adele. *Befriending the Beloved Disciple: A Jewish Reading of the Gospel of John*. London: Continuum, 2001.
———. *Cast Out of the Covenant: Jews and Anti-Judaism in the Gospel of John*. Lanham, MD: Lexington/Fortress Academic, 2018.
———. "The Jews of the Fourth Gospel." Pages 121–37 in *The Oxford Handbook of Johannine Studies*. Edited by Judith M. Lieu and Martinus C. de Boer. Oxford: Oxford University Press, 2018.
———. "The Lyin' King? Deception and Christology in the Gospel of John." Pages 117–33 in *Johannine Ethics: The Moral World of the Gospel and Epistles of John*. Edited by Sherri Brown and Christopher W. Skinner. Minneapolis: Fortress, 2017.
———. *The Word in the World: The Cosmological Tale in the Fourth Gospel*. SBLMS 45. Atlanta: Scholars Press, 1992.
Resseguie, James L. "The Beloved Disciple: The Ideal Point of View." Pages 537–49 in *Character Studies in the Fourth Gospel: Narrative Approaches to Seventy Figures in John*. Edited by Steven A. Hunt, D. Francois Tolmie, and Ruben Zimmermann. Grand Rapids: Eerdmans, 2016.
———. "A Narrative-Critical Approach to the Fourth Gospel." Pages 3–17 in *Characters and Characterization in the Gospel of John*. Edited by Christopher W. Skinner. LNTS 461. London: Bloomsbury/T&T Clark, 2013.
Rhoads, David M., Joanna Dewey, and Donald Michie. *Mark as Story: An Introduction to the Narrative of a Gospel*. 3rd ed. Minneapolis: Fortress, 2012.

Ricoeur, Paul. *The Rule of Metaphor*. Toronto: University of Toronto Press, 1981.

Ringgren, Helmer. *Word and Wisdom: Studies in the Hypostatization of Divine Qualities and Functions in the Ancient Near East*. Lund: Håkan Ohlssons Boktryckeri, 1947.

Rissi, Mathias. "Jn 1:1–18 (The Eternal Word)." *Int* 31 (1977): 394–401.

Ritivoi, Andreea Deciu. *Paul Ricoeur: Tradition and Innovation in Rhetorical Theory*. Albany, NY: State University of New York Press, 2006.

Robinson, John A. T. "The Relation of the Prologue to the Gospel of John." *NTS* 9 (1963): 120–29.

Scalia, Antonin. *Scalia Speaks: Reflections on Law, Faith, and Life Well Lived*. New York: Crown Forum, 2017.

Schaberg, Jane. *The Resurrection of Mary Magdalene: Legends, Apocrypha, and the Christian Testament*. New York: Continuum, 2002.

Schandorf, Michael. "A Gesture Theory of Communication." PhD diss., University of Illinois at Chicago, 2015.

Schimmel, Solomon. "Gratitude in Judaism." Pages 37–57 in *The Psychology of Gratitude*. Edited by Robert A. Emmons and Michael E. McCullough. Oxford: Oxford University Press, 2004.

Schnackenburg, Rudolf. *The Gospel According to St John*. 3 vols. Translated by Kevin Smyth. London: Burns & Oates, 1980–82.

Schnelle, Udo. *Antidocetic Christology in the Gospel of John: An Investigation of the Place of the Fourth Gospel in the Johannine School*. Translated by Linda M. Maloney. Minneapolis: Fortress, 1992.

Schoneveld, Jacobus. "Torah in the Flesh: A New Reading of the Prologue of the Gospel of John as a Contribution to a Christology without Anti-Judaism." *Immanuel* 24/25 (1990): 77–4.

Schüssler Fiorenza, Elisabeth. *Bread Not Stone: The Challenge of Feminist Biblical Interpretation*. Boston: Beacon, 1984.

Sheridan, Ruth. "Persuasion." Pages 205–23 in *How John Works: Storytelling in the Fourth Gospel*. Edited by Douglas Estes and Ruth Sheridan. RBS 86. Atlanta: SBL Press, 2016.

———. *Retelling Scripture: "The Jews" and the Scriptural Citations in John 1:19–12:15*. BibS 110. Leiden: Brill, 2012.

Skinner, Christopher W. "Characterization." Pages 115–32 in *How John Works: Storytelling in the Fourth Gospel*. Edited by Douglas Estes and Ruth Sheridan. RBS 86. Atlanta: SBL Press, 2016.

———. "'The Good Shepherd Lays down His Life for the Sheep' (John 10:11, 15, 17): Questioning the Limits of a Johannine Metaphor." *CBQ* 80 (2018): 97–113.

———. "Introduction: Characters and Characterization in the Gospel of John: Reflections on the *Status Quaestionis*." Pages xvii–xxxii in *Characters and Characterization in the Gospel of John*. Edited by Christopher W. Skinner. LNTS 461. London: Bloomsbury/T & T Clark, 2013.

———. "John's Gospel and the Roman Imperial Context." Pages 116–29 in *Jesus is Lord Caesar is Not: Evaluating Empire in New Testament Studies*. Scot McKnight and Joseph B. Modica. Downers Grove, IL: IVP, 2013.

Skinner, Christopher W., ed. *Characters and Characterization in the Gospel of John.* LNTS 461. London: Bloomsbury/T&T Clark, 2013.

Slabodsky, Santiago. "Jewish Resistances: Trumpism, Holocaustic Memories, and the Paradoxes of New Whiteness." Pages 27–36 in *Faith and Resistance in the Age of Trump*. Edited by Miguel De La Torre. Maryknoll, NY: Orbis Books, 2017.

Smith, D. Moody. *John Among the Gospels: The Relationship in Twentieth Century Research*. Minneapolis: Fortress, 1992.

Smith, R. R. R. "The Imperial Reliefs from the Sebasteion at Aphrodisias." *JRS* 77 (1987): 88–138.

―――. "*Sacra Gentium*: The *Ethne* from the Sebasteion at Aphrodisias." *JRS* 78 (1988): 50–77.

Soga, Aki. "Bernie Sanders Faces Progressive Backlash over State of the Union Response." *USA Today*. Accessed May 25, 2019. https://www.usatoday.com/story/news/politics/2019/ 02/06/bernie-sanders-backlash-state-union-response/2790717002/.

Staley, Jeffrey. "The Structure of John's Prologue: Its Implications for the Gospel's Narrative Structure." *CBQ* 48 (1986): 241–63.

Stibbe, Mark W. G. *John*. Sheffield: Sheffield Academic, 1993.

―――. *John as Storyteller: Narrative Criticism and the Fourth Gospel*. SNTSMS 73. Cambridge: Cambridge University Press, 1992.

Stolbeg, Sheryl Gay and Nicholas Fandos, "Brett Kavanaugh and Christine Blasey Ford Duel with Tears and Fury." *The New York Times*. Accessed July 29, 2019. https://www.nytimes.com/2018/09/27/us/politics/brett-kavanaugh-confirmation-hearings.html.

Stuart, Moses. "Exegetical and Theological Examination of John 1:1–18." *BSac* 7 (1850): 13–54, 281–327.

Suggit, John. "John XVII.17: O LOGOS O SOS ALHQEIA ESTIN." *JTS* 35 (1984): 104–17.

Talbert, Charles H. *Reading Luke-Acts in Its Mediterranean Milieu*. NovTSup 107. Leiden: Brill, 2003.

Talmon, Shemaryahu. "The 'Comparative Method' in Biblical Interpretation—Principles and Problems." Pages 320–56 in *Congress Volume: Göttingen, 1977*. VTSup 29. Leiden: Brill, 1978.

Teeple, Howard M. *The Mosaic Eschatological Prophet*. SBLMS 10. Philadelphia: Society of Biblical Literature, 1957.

Thatcher, Tom. "Jesus, Judas, and Peter: Character by Contrast in the Fourth Gospel." *BSac* 153 (1996): 435–48.

―――. *The Riddles of Jesus in John: A Study in Tradition and Folklore*. SBLMS 53. Atlanta: SBL Press, 2000.

―――. "The Signs Gospel in Context." Pages 191–97 in *Jesus in Johannine Tradition*. Edited by Robert T. Fortna and Tom Thatcher. Louisville: Westminster John Knox, 2001.

Thielman, Frank. "The Style of the Fourth Gospel and Ancient Literary Critical Concepts of Religious Discourse." Pages 169–83 in *Persuasive Artistry: Studies in New*

Testament Rhetoric in Honor of George A. Kennedy. Edited by Duane F. Watson. JSNTSup 50. Sheffield: JOST Press, 1991.

Thompson, Marianne Meye. *John: A Commentary*. NTL. Louisville: Westminster John Knox, 2015.

Tobin, Thomas. "The Prologue of John and Hellenistic Jewish Speculation." *CBQ* 52 (1990): 252–69.

Toner, Jerry. *Popular Culture in Ancient Rome*. Cambridge: Polity Press, 2009.

Tong, Rosemarie and Tina Fernandes Botts. *Feminist Thought: A More Comprehensive Introduction*. New York: Routledge Taylor & Francis Group, 2018.

Tovey, Derek. "Narrative Strategies in the Prologue and the Metaphor of ὁ λόγος in John's Gospel." *Pacifica* 15 (2002): 138–53.

Townes, Emilie Maureen. *A Troubling in My Soul: Womanist Perspectives on Evil and Suffering*. Maryknoll, NY: Orbis, 1993.

———. *Womanist Justice, Womanist Hope*. Atlanta: Scholars Press, 1993.

TripAdvisor. "Imagine the Best—and then be Surprised at Even Better." March 12, 2011. https://www.tripadvisor.com/ShowUserReviews-g303492-d1201905-r99930836-Cachoeira_Inn-Armacao_dos_Buzios_State_of_Rio_de_Janeiro.html.

———. "Imagine the Best of Pompeii, But in More Detail." January 23, 2013. https://www.tripadvisor.com/ShowUserReviews-g670330-d195507-r150433924-Ruins_of_Herculaneum-Ercolano_Province_of_Naples_Campania.html

Trozzo, Lindsey M. *Exploring Johannine Ethics: A Rhetorical Approach to Moral Efficacy in the Fourth Gospel Narrative*. WUNT 2/449. Tübingen: Mohr Siebeck, 2017.

Turner, John D. "The History of Religions Background of John 10." Pages 33–52 in *The Shepherd Discourse of John 10 and Its Context*. SNTSMS 67. Edited by Johannes Beutler and Robert Fortna. Cambridge: Cambridge University Press, 1991.

Urbach, Ephraim E. *The Sages: Their Concepts and Beliefs*. 2nd ed. 2 vols. Translated by Israel Abrahams. Jerusalem: Magnes, 1979.

Vancil, Jack. "The Symbolism of the Shepherd in Biblical, Intertestamental, and New Testament Material." PhD diss., Dropsie University, 1975.

van der Watt, Jan G. *Family of the King: Dynamics of Metaphor in the Gospel according to John*. BibS 47. Leiden: Brill, 2000.

van der Watt, Jan G., and Ruben Zimmerman, eds. *Rethinking the Ethics of John: "Implicit Ethics" in the Johannine Writings*. WUNT 291. Contexts and Norms of New Testament Ethics 3. Tübingen: Mohr Siebeck, 2012.

von Wahlde, Urban C. *The Gospel and Letters of John. Vol. 2: Commentary on the Gospel of John*. ECC. Grand Rapids: Eerdmans, 2010.

Vos, Geerhardus. "The Range of the Logos-Title in the Prologue of the Fourth Gospel." *PTR* 11 (1913): 365–419, 557–602.

Walbank, F. W. "Monarchy and Monarchic Ideas." Pages 62–100 in *The Cambridge Ancient History, Second Edition*, Vol VII, Part 1, *The Hellenistic World*. Edited by F. W. Walbank, A. E. Astin, M. W. Frederiksen, and R. M. Ogilvie. Cambridge: Cambridge University Press, 1984.

Walker, Jeffrey. *Rhetoric and Poetics in Antiquity*. Oxford: Oxford University Press, 2000.

Wallis, Jim. "White Christian Complicity in Trump's Victory and Responsibility Now for Faith, Resistance, and Healing." Pages 156–64 in *Faith and Resistance in the Age of Trump*. Edited by Miguel De La Torre. Maryknoll, NY: Orbis Books, 2017.

Wang, Sunny Kwang-Hui. *Sense Perception and Testimony in the Gospel of John*. WUNT 2/435. Tübingen: Mohr Siebeck, 2017.

The Washington Post. "'Reclaiming My Time': Rep. Maxine Waters Interrupts Mnuchin's Roundabout Answer." Accessed May 25, 2019. https://www.washingtonpost.com/video/national/maxine-waters-reclaiming-my-time/2017/08/01/30fae7f4-76d4-11e7-8c17-533c52b2f014_video.html?utm_term=.e3a1233cbf57a.

Webb, Ruth. *Ekphrasis, Imagination and Persuasion in Ancient Rhetorical Theory and Practice*. Surrey: Ashgate, 2009.

———. "The *Progymnasmata* as Practice." Pages 289–316 in *Education in the Greek and Roman Antiquity*. Edited by Yun Lee Too. Leiden: Brill, 2001.

Weems, Renita. "Womanist Reflections on Biblical Hermeneutics." Pages 216–24 in *Black Theology: A Documentary History. Volume 2: 1980–1992*. Edited by James H. Cone and Gayraud S. Wilmore. Maryknoll, NY: Orbis Books, 1993.

Whitacre, Rodney A. *Johannine Polemic: The Role of Tradition and Theology*. SBLDS 67. Chico, CA: Scholars Press, 1982.

Whitaker, Robyn J. "The Poetics of Ekphrasis: Vivid Description and Rhetoric in the Apocalypse." Pages 227–40 in *Poetik und Intertextualität in der Apokalypse*. Edited by Stefan Alkier, Thomas Hieke, and Tobias Nicklas. WUNT 346. Tübingen: Mohr Siebeck, 2015.

Whitenton, Michael R. *Configuring Nicodemus: An Interdisciplinary Approach to Complex Characterization*. LNTS 549. London: Bloomsbury/T&T Clark, 2019.

———. *Hearing Kyriotic Sonship: A Cognitive and Rhetorical Approach to the Characterization of Mark's Jesus*. BibS 148. Leiden: Brill, 2017.

Williams, Catrin H. "Composite Citations in the Gospel of John." Pages 94–127 in *New Testament Uses*. Vol. 2 of *Composite Citations in Antiquity*. Edited by Sean A. Adams and Seth M. Ehorn, LNTS 593. London: Bloomsbury/T&T Clark, 2018.

———. "How Scripture 'Speaks': Insights from the Study of Ancient Media Culture." Pages 53–69 in *Methodology in the Use of the Old Testament in the New: Context and Criteria*. Edited by David Allen and Steve Smith. LNTS 579. London: Bloomsbury/T&T Clark, 2019.

———. "Isaiah in John's Gospel." Pages 101–16 in *Isaiah in the New Testament*. Edited by Steve Moyise and Maarten J. J. Menken. London: T&T Clark, 2005.

Wilson, Brittany E. *Unmanly Men: Refigurations of Masculinity in Luke-Acts*. Oxford: Oxford University Press, 2015.

Witherington, Ben, III. *Jesus the Sage: The Pilgrimage of Wisdom*. Minneapolis: Fortress, 1994.

Wohl, Victoria. "Rhetoric of the Athenian Citizen." Pages 162–77 in *The Cambridge Companion to Ancient Rhetoric*. Edited by Erik Gunderson. Cambridge: Cambridge University Press, 2009.

Wolfson, Harry Austryn. *Philo: Foundations of Religious Philosophy in Judaism, Christianity, and Islam*. 4th rev. ed. 2 vols. Cambridge, MA: Harvard University Press, 1968.

Wrede, William. *Charakter und Tendenz des Johannesevangeliums*. Sammlung gemeinverständlicher Vorträge und Schriften aus dem Gebiet der Theologie und Religionsgeschichte 37. Tübingen: Mohr Siebeck, 1903.

———. *The Origin of the New Testament*. Translated James S. Hill. New York: Harper & Brothers, 1909.

Zarefsky, David. *President Johnson's War on Poverty: Rhetoric and History*. Tuscaloosa, AL: University of Alabama Press, 1986.

Zauzmer, Julie. "The Alleged Synagogue Shooter was a Churchgoer who Talked Christian Theology, Raising Tough Questions for Evangelical Pastors." *The Washington Post*. Accessed May 26, 2019. https://www.washingtonpost.com/religion/2019/05/01/alleged-synagogue-shooter-was-churchgoer-who-articulated-christian-theology-prompting-tough-questions-evangelical-pastors/?utm_term=.a08a6944e58b.

Zimmermann, Ruben. "Jesus im Bild Gottes: Anspielungen auf das Alte Testament im Johannesevangelium am Beispiel der Hirtenbildfelder in Joh 10." Pages 81–116 in *Kontexte des Johannesevangeliums: Das vierte Evangelium in religions- und traditionsgeschichtlicher Perspektive*. Edited by Jörg Frey and Udo Schnelle. WUNT 1/175. Tübingen: Mohr Siebeck, 2004.

———. *Puzzling the Parables of Jesus: Methods and Interpretation*. Minneapolis: Fortress, 2015.

Zumstein, Jean. *L'Évangile selon Saint Jean (1–12)*. CNT IVa. Genève: Labor et Fides, 2014.

Index

Abraham, 60, 71, 92
actual reader, 8–9, 141–43
allusion, 68–71, 76–82, 121–24, 131, 182
ambiguity, 19, 52n17, 65–66, 69–70, 75, 84
ancient biography (*bios*), 126. *See also* genre
Aristotle, 66–67, 69, 73–74, 123n20, 177, 187, 190, 198n7

Baruch, 54, 55, 63n34
Beloved Disciple, 142–46, 160–63, 174–76, 188, 192
Ben Sira, 54, 56, 58
binary, 11–13, 44–46, 49, 50n2, 52n18

characterization, 15, 52n17, 70, 81, 92–93, 94n5, 112–13, 135, 143, 145, 147, 153n4, 165
charis (gift or grace), 35–36, 59, 73–74
chiasm, 31–33, 68
chreia, 69–70
Christ. *See* Messiah
Cicero, 68, 70–71, 74, 186–87, 190, 196
Colossians, 57
creation, 33, 35–36, 39n12, 49, 54–57, 66–69, 74, 172, 180

David, 100–101, 108n15, 115–17, 119–20, 123n28, 128
Dedication, Feast of (*Hanukkah*), 82–83, 89, 91, 99, 137n17
Demetrius, 113, 115, 128–29, 186, 189–90, 192–93
Dio Chrysostom, 103, 106, 109n27, 194
drama, ancient Greek, 29–31, 190, 199n14
dramatic present, 189, 191, 193–94, 196, 199n21
dualism, 12–13, 43, 45–47, 49–50, 50n2, 51n17, 84

ekphrasis and *enargeia*, 20, 186–88, 191, 194–96, 196nn1–2, 198n8
1 Enoch, 54, 56, 64n50, 97
Ephesus, 101, 108n12, 161, 167n20
evangelist, Fourth Evangelist and John the Evangelist, 4, 29–31, 33–37, 40n19, 190–92, 196
Exodus, 2, 16, 35, 58–61, 108n15, 115, 177, 184n21
the exodus, 54, 82, 184n21
extratextuality, 14–15
Ezekiel, 16, 55, 97–101, 107, 108n15, 116–19, 123n26, 180, 184n21

225

feminist criticism, 6, 10–11, 23n27
figurative language. *See* figure of speech
figure of speech, 19, 65, 71, 83, 115–17, 122n18, 125–29, 132–35, 137n21

gender, 10–12, 23n17, 25n60, 44–45, 47, 49, 52n17, 52n18, 157–60, 166
Genesis, 32–37, 39n15, 55–56, 68–69, 108n15, 123n22, 172, 180, 192
genre, 83, 108n12, 187
gift or grace. *See charis*
glory, 15–16, 35, 38, 55, 57–61, 64n36, 64n40, 67, 102, 131, 134, 163, 168n33, 179, 188

Hanukkah. *See* Dedication, Feast of (*Hanukkah*)
Hebrew Bible, 3–4, 15–16, 54, 56, 58–59, 74, 84, 91, 94n15, 95n22, 97, 100, 106, 111–12, 114, 116, 118–20, 171–72, 181, 184n21
hermeneutics: definition of, 6; hermeneutical approaches, 5–7, 11, 20, 156–57, 163, 165
heteronormativity, 11, 44
historical criticism, 65, 168n33
hoi Ioudaioi. *See* "the Jews" in John
Homer, 38n4, 101–3, 109n27, 122n20, 180, 187, 194, 196, 198n8

ideological criticism, 9–10, 159
imagery, 16, 20, 54, 58, 65, 81–82, 84–89, 93, 94n3, 111–12, 114–19, 121, 123n27, 125, 135, 137n13
imperial criticism, 12–13, 99–101, 106–7
implied audience, 7, 22, 89, 94n4
implied author, 7, 22
implied reader, 7, 9, 22, 81, 94n4, 141–42, 144–45, 148, 151
incarnation, 8, 13, 31, 34–36, 46, 48, 54, 56, 68, 74, 172
intersectionality, 11, 169n41
intertextual approach, 4–5, 13–17, 53, 97, 100–101, 107, 112–13, 117;

intertextuality, definition of, 8, 14–15, 18, 24n42, 171
intratextuality, 3, 14–15
irony, 7, 56, 81, 94n5, 113
Isaiah, 15, 55, 58–59, 63n25, 64n36, 108n15, 116, 171, 178, 184nn18, 21

Jeremiah, 55, 59, 108n15, 116, 179, 184n21
Jewish Scriptures. *See* Hebrew Bible
"the Jews" in John (*hoi Ioudaioi*), 7, 37–38, 76n17, 84, 94n14, 98, 107, 119, 126, 130, 133–35, 137n19, 149, 159, 163, 168n35, 169n36, 179. *See also* Pharisees
John the Baptist, 3, 31, 33, 37, 40n18, 69–70, 92, 188–90
Josephus, 99, 105

Lamb of God. *See* paschal lamb
Law. *See* Torah (Law)
Lazarus, 82, 86, 93, 144–46, 151–52, 176, 183n13
LGBTQIA, 12, 23n36, 44, 168n34. *See also* queer biblical interpretation, queer theory
liberation criticism, 11–12
literary criticism, 7–8, 10, 14, 22n13, 81, 89, 93, 175, 186–87, 189, 193, 196, 198n8
logos, Logos (word), 15, 33–35, 39n16, 40n22, 53–58, 61, 61n2, 66–70, 73, 85, 127, 172
Lucian, 181, 187, 193
Luke, Gospel of, 16, 68, 112, 126, 150, 160, 172–77, 179–82, 183nn9–10, 184n20. *See also* Synoptic Gospels

1–4 Maccabees, 55, 64n36, 91, 110n39, 177, 181
Mark, Gospel of, 16, 112–13, 160, 172–74, 177, 179, 181–82, 182n2, 183n8. *See also* Synoptic Gospels
Mary Magdalene, 13, 16, 135, 142–50, 153n5, 155–56, 159–66, 167n18,

169nn40–41, 174–80, 191–94. *See also* women
Matthew, Gospel of, 16, 160, 172–74, 178–82, 183n6, 184n15. *See also* Synoptic Gospels
Messiah, 37, 49, 57, 59–60, 66, 108n15, 119–120, 124n32, 152, 185, 190
metaphor, 2, 7, 14, 19, 45, 48, 67–68, 71–72, 81, 83, 85, 87, 111–13, 116, 118, 128, 137nn13, 21, 178, 196
Moses, 35–36, 41n34, 54, 57–61, 69, 95n22, 101, 108n15, 111, 115
mujerista readings, 11–12

narrative: approach, 4, 7–9, 29–31, 34, 38n3, 81–89, 91–93, 94n4, 94n7, 95n33, 101, 141, 146, 148, 150–52, 153n3, 173, 185–86; narrative criticism, 6–7, 141–42. *See also* prose
narrator, 7, 29, 31, 36, 38n3, 67, 70, 142, 146, 195
Nathanael, 189–91, 195
national consciousness, 13, 155–60, 165–66

Old Testament. *See* Hebrew Bible

parable, 82–85, 87–90, 113; definition of, 83
paroimia. *See* figure of speech
parrēsia, 19, 119, 126–31, 134–35
paschal lamb, 82, 178; and Lamb of God, 150, 190
Passover, Feast of, 82, 130–31
Paul, 57, 73–74, 163, 165, 183n8
persuasion. *See* rhetoric
Peter, 142–46, 149, 153n9, 160–63, 165, 168n24, 173–76, 183n8, 192–93
Pharisees, 3, 7, 19–20, 70, 98–99, 107, 117, 126, 129, 132–35, 195–96
Philo, 54, 56, 103, 105, 109n25, 115, 123n20
Plato, 67, 102, 123n20, 185, 192

plot, 7, 81–82, 108n12, 123n26, 142–43, 145, 148–50, 177
poetry, 38n4, 39n18, 67–68, 187
point of view, 7, 81, 183n12
postcolonial criticism, 6, 8, 10–13, 156–58
poststructural criticism, 7–8, 10–11, 14
progymnasmata, 66, 69–70, 73, 187–88, 193, 195, 198nn4, 7
prose, 5, 30, 38n4, 39n18, 68, 73, 187. *See also* narrative
Psalms, 91, 97, 116, 121, 180

queer biblical interpretation, 11–12, 49–50
queer theory, 11–13, 23n36, 43–50, 51nn5–6, 14, 52nn18, 24
Quintilian, 25n60, 51n8, 68–70, 113, 126, 128–29, 186–87, 189–90, 192–93, 198n7

reader-response criticism, 167n17
recognition (*anagnorisis*), 142, 145–49, 166, 177–80, 184n16, 191–94, 197, 199nn14, 23
redaction criticism, 6
rhetoric: classical, 17–19, 24n49, 70, 126; epideictic, 18, 25n52, 66, 68, 71; New Rhetoric, 17–20; spiritual or religious, 100
rhetorical approach, 4, 8, 16–20; rhetorical criticism, 17, 65, 75
Rome, 99–101, 103, 105, 107, 110n35, 137n19

Sabbath, 82, 90–91, 130–31, 143, 159, 183n8
Seneca, 126–27
setting, 7, 30, 83, 113–14, 117, 130, 137n17, 142–44, 149, 151, 156, 174
shepherd, 8, 16, 83–89, 97, 111–12, 114–17, 132–35; good shepherd, 13, 16, 87, 93, 97–100, 104–7, 118–21, 125, 134, 148, 169n40, 178, 199n23; as a metaphor for rulers/kings,

100–104, 108n15, 109nn16–17, 27, 116, 122nn15, 20, 123n28; noble shepherd, 100, 106, 110n39, 125, 133; simile, 14, 188, 190. *See also* figure of speech, metaphor
Sinai, 34–36, 53, 55–56, 58–59, 73
social science criticism, 6
sociocultural: analysis, 8; approach, 3–5, 9–13, 43
sociopolitical criticism, 3, 11–12, 97, 99
Socrates, 67, 192
Song of Solomon, 178
spirit, 3, 47, 149–50, 173, 176, 180, 182, 186, 190, 194–95
standpoint criticism, 6, 9–10. *See also* ideological criticism
structure, 29, 31–32, 38, 46, 81–83, 112, 172, 174
Suetonius, 103, 110n35, 181
symbolism, 7, 33, 81, 86–88, 94n3, 122n19, 174
Synoptic Gospels, 16, 83, 128, 150, 172, 174, 181–82, 182nn2–3, 182n5. *See also* Luke, Gospel of; Mark, Gospel of; Matthew, Gospel of

Tabernacles, Feast of (*Sukkot*), 2, 125

Theon, Aelius, 66, 69–70, 73, 187, 193, 195, 198n7
Thomas, 142–43, 148–49, 151–52, 154n16, 174, 180–81, 191–92, 194–95
Torah (Law), 15, 33, 35–36, 40, 53–61, 131

vivid description. *See ekphrasis* and *enargeia*

wisdom, 15, 35, 53–58, 61
Wisdom of Solomon, 54
womanist readings, 11–13, 155–71
women, 10, 13, 51n17, 136n10, 155–57, 159–65, 166n2, 167n9, 168nn22, 24, 169n43, 173–75, 181–82, 183n8, 184n15
word. *See logos*, Logos (word)
world, 34–35, 43, 45–49, 56, 59–61, 69–70, 74, 88, 106, 132, 134–35, 150, 152, 190–92, 195

Xenophon, 64n49, 101

Zechariah, 97, 108, 116, 184n21

About the Contributors

Helen K. Bond is Professor of Christian Origins and Head of the School of Divinity, University of Edinburgh, Edinburgh, Scotland. She has written books on the life and times of the historical Jesus, biblical characters, and Mark's Gospel. She is co-editor (with Eve-Marie Becker and Catrin H. Williams) of *John's Transformation of Mark* (Bloomsbury/T&T Clark, 2020).

Jo-Ann A. Brant is Emeritus Professor of Bible, Religion, and Philosophy, Goshen College, Goshen, Indiana. In addition to leading the Johannine Literature Section of the SBL from 2012 to 2017, she is author of *Dialogue and Drama: Elements of Greek Tragedy in the Fourth Gospel* (Hendrickson) and *John* in the Paideia Commentaries on the New Testament series (Baker Academic).

Sherri Brown is Associate Professor of New Testament, Department of Theology, Creighton University, Omaha, Nebraska. She teaches in all areas in biblical literature and has authored, co-authored, and co-edited several books on both the Johannine literature and the New Testament generally. In addition, she has authored more than a dozen scholarly and popular articles on the texts of the New Testament and is co-editor of the Interpreting Johannine Literature series (Lexington/Fortress Academic).

Warren Carter is LaDonna Kramer Meinders Professor of New Testament, Phillips Theological Seminary, Tulsa, Oklahoma. He is particularly interested in the ways in which the early Jesus movement negotiated Roman power. His books on John's Gospel include *John: Storyteller, Interpreter, Evangelist* (Hendrickson/Baker) and *John and Empire: Initial Explorations* (T&T Clark).

Lindsey S. Jodrey is Associate Director of Digital Learning, Princeton Theological Seminary, Princeton, New Jersey. She oversees the Office of Digital learning, which works to enrich learning for students, enhance teaching for faculty, support campus departments, and engage the broader community in learning through digital means. Lindsey also teaches courses in the Bible department and, in both research and teaching, explores how diverse groups of people find and make meaning as they encounter biblical texts. She has served as co-editor of the Interpreting Johannine Literature series.

Craig S. Keener is F. M. and Ada Thompson Professor of Biblical Studies, Asbury Theological Seminary, Wilmore, Kentucky. Craig's academic focus in most of his commentaries, including his two-volume commentary on John's Gospel (2003), is the ancient Jewish and wider Greco-Roman context of early Christian works.

Craig R. Koester is Asher O. and Carrie Nasby Professor of New Testament, Luther Seminary, St. Paul, Minnesota. His research focuses on the imagery, cultural context, and theology of John's Gospel. Among his publications are *Symbolism in the Fourth Gospel: Meaning Mystery and Community* (Fortress), *Word of Life: A Theology of John's Gospel* (Eerdmans), and commentaries on Revelation and Hebrews for the Anchor Yale Bible series.

Kasper Bro Larsen is Associate Professor of Biblical Studies, School of Culture and Society, University of Aarhus, Aarhus, Denmark. His studies on John include *Recognizing the Stranger: Recognition Scenes in the Gospel of John* (Brill) as well as an edited collection titled *The Gospel of John as Genre Mosaic* (Vandenhoeck & Ruprecht).

Dorothy A. Lee is Stewart Research Professor of New Testament, Trinity College, University of Divinity, Melbourne, Australia. She has published widely in the area of New Testament theology, including gender studies and spirituality. Some of her publications on John include *Flesh and Glory: Symbol, Gender, and Theology in the Gospel of John* (Crossroad) and *Hallowed in Truth and Love: Spirituality in the Johannine Literature* (Wipf & Stock).

Alicia D. Myers is Associate Professor of New Testament and Greek, Campbell University Divinity School, Buies Creek, North Carolina. Her studies focus on the rhetoric of intertextuality as well as gender performance, particularly as they relate to character formation. Some of her publications on John include *Reading John and 1, 2, 3 John* (Smyth & Helwys) and *Characterizing Jesus* (Bloomsbury/T&T Clark).

About the Contributors

Angela N. Parker is Assistant Professor of New Testament and Greek at James and Carolyn McAfee School of Theology, Mercer University, Atlanta, Georgia. Her teaching, research, and writing revolve around New Testament texts studied through the lens of womanist and postcolonial thought. She sees this work as particularly important for contemporary Christian communities seeking to wrestle with Scripture in light of violence and injustice.

Catrin H. Williams is Reader in New Testament Studies, University of Wales Trinity Saint David, Lampeter, Wales; Research Fellow in the Department of Old and New Testament Studies, University of the Free State, Bloemfontein. She has published widely on the Gospel of John, especially its reception of the Jewish Scriptures.

www.ingramcontent.com/pod-product-compliance
Lightning Source LLC
Chambersburg PA
CBHW021848300426
44115CB00005B/62